POSTCARDS FROM THE NET

Jon Casimir

ALLEN & UNWIN
http://www.allen-unwin.com.au

Copyright © Jon Casimir 1996

All rights reserved. No part of this book may be reproduced or transmitted in any form or by any means, electronic or mechanical, including photocopying, recording or by any information storage and retrieval system, without prior permission in writing from the publisher.

First published in 1996 by
Allen & Unwin Pty Ltd
9 Atchison Street, St Leonards, NSW 2065 Australia
Phone: (61 2) 9901 4088
Fax: (61 2) 9906 2218
E-mail: 100252.103@compuserve.com
URL: http://www.allen-unwin.com.au

National Library of Australia
Cataloguing-in-Publication entry:

Casimir, Jon, 1964– .
Postcards from the net.

Includes index.
ISBN 1 86448 280 X.

1. Internet (Computer network). I. Title.

004.67

Designed by Nada Backovic
Set in 11/13.5 pt Cochin by DOCUPRO, Sydney
Printed by McPherson's Printing Group, Australia

10 9 8 7 6 5 4 3 2 1

CONTENTS

A short glossary of terms — viii
Introduction — xii

OPENING SALVOS

How to Behave Online — 3
A Day in the Life of Cyberspace — 8
Can You Trust What You Find? — 13
The Nasty Bits—Hate on the Net — 17
The Naughty Bits—Pornography — 24
Cyber Rights and Censorship — 30

THE LIGHTER SIDE

Cameras Attached to the Web — 43
Cyber Soap Operas — 49
Why Dumb Ideas Are Often the Best Ideas — 57
Distractions, Games and Web Tricks — 63
Haiku Fans Online — 71

FAME

Sites About Celebrities — 79
Gossip, Scuttlebutt and Rumour — 84
Famous People Who Hang Out Online — 88
Elvis Presley Is Alive and Well in Cyberspace — 95
The Net Court Room—Did Kurt Cobain Kill Himself? — 101
Nostalgia for the 1980s — 108

AUSTRALIA

What Does the Rest of the World See of Australia? — 115
Aboriginal Sites — 121

Politics and the 1996 Net Election	127
Queer Resources	133
Sport	138

THE DIGITAL HUMAN

Finding Community in Cyberspace	147
geekgirl and Women Online	152
Body Modification	159
Death—No More Taboos	163
Bad Hair Days	170

BELIEFS

Alternative Alternative Religions	177
Astrology	184
Conspiracy Theories	191
UFOs and Aliens	199
Urban Legends	205

MEDIA

Abundance vs Scarcity	211
The New Distribution Network	217
The Newspaper in a Wired World	222
Keeping Up With the News	229
Wired, HotWired and the Digital Backlash	236

WORLD WIRED WEIRD

A Case for Bad Taste	245
Pets on the Net	250
Weird Science	256
Beer Lovers	263
Virtual Vampires	267
Yes, There Is a Hell	274

RESOURCE FILES

Finding Your Way Around	281
Film	287
TV	298
Music	311
Books and Literature	321
Cartoons and Comics	331
Zines	342
The Overflow	353

APPENDICES

A Declaration of the Independence of Cyberspace	365
Books That Might Be Helpful	369
Acknowledgements	371

A Short Glossary of Terms

bandwidth

What do we want? Bandwidth. When do we want it? Now. Bandwidth is the carrying capacity of Net technology. In the simplest terms, the more bandwidth, the more traffic is possible, the bigger and more sophisticated the things being sent back and forth down the pipes can be.

browser

The software car you use to drive around the Internet. Netscape Navigator has corralled more than 90 per cent of the market, but that doesn't mean there aren't others out there.

cyberspace

Where you are when you're on the phone. Where all the constituent parts of the Internet would be, if you imagined them as 3D spaces instead of bits of computer data. The word comes from William Gibson's sci-fi novel, *Neuromancer*, which, curiously enough, he wrote on a typewriter, not a computer. In his hands, it meant a virtual, three-dimensional environment whose elements were made up of electronic data that could be seen, heard and touched. It translates to the Internet with ease.

e-mail

The most popular part of the Internet. As its name suggests, a system of sending electronic letters back and forth, almost instantly, around the world. For those who use it to keep in touch with friends in far-flung places, it soon becomes hard to imagine how they ever survived without it.

flame

The art (or usually, the lack of it) of electronic disagreement. If you post something even mildly contentious to many newsgroups, you can be certain of being flamed by spleen-venters from around the world. There are actually places for them to go (newsgroups such as **aus.flame**) which let the non-flamers among us go about our business with a little more peace.

IRC

Internet Relay Chat (not the Industrial Relations Commission). It's one of the parallel Internet structures, along with the Web and newsgroups. IRC allows people to get together and 'chat', in real time, in any one of thousands of 'rooms' or channels. You just type in your addition to the conversation and it appears on the computer of everyone in the conversation within a second or two. It's like a worldwide party line, and lets people play all kinds of games. Most people use it anonymously, pretending to be someone else, trying on personalities for size.

Java

It's described on Sun Systems' home page as 'a simple, object-oriented, distributed, interpreted, robust, secure, architecture neutral, portable, high-performance, multi-threaded, and dynamic language'. Translate that and what you're left with is a programming tool which has allowed the Internet to beef up its attack by making it much easier to animate parts of Websites.

hypertext

A kind of document, or more to the point, a method of making documents which allows the grouping and organisation of text, graphics, sound and video and allows the elements to point to one another.

HTML

HyperText Markup Language. The computer formatting language the World Wide Web uses to display its information.

http
   The little bit at the front of the Web address stands for HyperText Transport Protocol. It's the protocol for moving hypertext files about the Web. Basically, as long as you can remember to type it, you don't need to know anything more about it.

link
   A hypertext point on a site that lets you click on it and gain access to another, usually related site, or another part of the same one.

newsgroup
   The old, text-based part of the Net (also known as Usenet). Newsgroups are essentially discussion forums, in which you write your thoughts on a topic down, ask a question, or respond to someone else's ideas, and then 'post' them on the Net equivalent of a bulletin board. Other users can read all posts in order. They are stored in each newsgroup chronologically and automatically cross-indexed.

search engines
   Web sites that have sprung up offering indexes for the millions and millions of sites on the Web. Most work on a simple search field, which allows you to type in key words. It runs a search program and returns with a list of options to your request. The results are often amazing, and often bizarre.

spam
   A luncheon meat. An obsession of many Netheads, mostly due to its Monty Python derivation. It's also a verb in cyberspace. To spam is to insensitively post unwanted messages (such as ads) across a range of newsgroups, or into people's e-mail boxes. It is frowned upon.

URL
   A Web address, otherwise known as a Uniform Resource

GLOSSARY

Locator. It's that line of gobbledegook at the top of the screen: *http://something.com.au/somethingelse.html*. A URL can actually tell you quite a lot about a site if you learn how to read it. The first bit, *http://*, is the transport protocol. The second and most crucial part, *something.com.au*, tells you the name of the company hosting the Website (Something), as well as the fact that it is a company (*com*), rather than a government institution (*gov*), a university (*edu*), a military outpost (*mil*), or one of many other options. The *au* part signifies that the site is Australian. Other countries have their own abbreviations, except for America, which leaves them off, regarding itself as the centre of the Universe. The rest of the address can vary greatly in size and content, and is usually in-house administration for the site creator, a codeword to help identify which area of his or her site it is.

Introduction

Blah blah blah *information superhighway* blah blah blah *brave new world* blah blah blah *democracy and freedom for all* blah blah blah *the end of the world as we know it* blah blah blah ... oh forget it, you know the rest of the hype.

You've been hearing the sales pitch for a couple of years now. The Net will change your life. The Net will pay your bills. The Net will get rid of acne and wrinkles. The Net will make you attractive to the opposite sex. It won't. Well, it hasn't done for me anyway. But you might be luckier...

What is this Net thing? A friend of mine once said that cyberspace is impossible to describe to someone who hasn't been there. But, once you actually go there, it makes sense immediately. The tumblers just lock into place. The Internet is basically very simple. It's just a lot of computers linked up by phone lines. Millions of them. These computers live in places like government offices, universities and homes. The Internet is what happens when you connect the computers, and the material on them, to each other.

Though we talk about it as a place, there really isn't a 'there'. It doesn't exist somewhere specifically. Every computer attached is part of the Net. There is no centre. You can't go visit it like a TV station. It doesn't have an owner (though many have tried, and will continue to try).

The Internet has been around since the '50s. It was designed in America as a decentralised communications medium. It works by sending little packets of information from one place to another, along a variety of routes. If one is blocked or shut down, the packets route around it, reassembling at the destination. Developed by the US military, it found its real home among the academic community, many of whom have been using it to keep in touch and share information for decades.

INTRODUCTION

The World Wide Web is the most popular and widely used part of the Internet, and the part this book is mostly concerned with. Until 1993, people communicating via the Internet could only do so by words, by plain old text. The Web is simply a means by which text, graphics, and sound can be combined to present information in a multimedia fashion. It is also extremely easy to use. If you can 'point and click' using a mouse, then you can use the Web.

The first time I saw the Net was in 1994, when a friend showed me one of the Star Trek newsgroups—billboard discussion areas where people post their own comments and read those of others. I got to see a technology that linked hundreds of people from around the world, offering them the chance to get together and swap information so arcane and obscure as to be meaningless to anyone but the deepest Trek addict.

By the time I saw the Web a few months later, I had come to realise, like so many others, that this is not just another medium in a long line of broadcasting media. It's a revolution, with political, social and cultural ramifications, as well as technological ones. The information placed on the Net can be seen by anyone, from anywhere in the country or world. You have as much access to it as Rupert Murdoch, both as consumer and publisher. Anyone can do the Net thing.

There are currently millions of Internet users worldwide. How many is actually anybody's guess. Surveys disagree radically. The absolute agreed minimum is 10 million. The maximum is around 40 million. Most of them live in the US, but that is changing fast.

There were an estimated one million users in 1993. By 1994, this number increased to almost 4 million. Massachusetts Institute of Technology new media guru Nicholas Negroponte estimates there will be one billion by the year 2000. I wouldn't like to have $100 on his prediction, but it's an interesting possibility.

The most recent estimate was that one million Australians are now using it, at least for email. A mid-1996 survey found that one in five Australians has had first-hand experience of the Net. Of those who hadn't, the same figure expected to do so before the middle of 1997. Younger people made up the bulk of the casual users, but in the heavy user category, the numbers were pretty evenly spread all the way from 18 to 54. Squashing one of the Net's main myths, women were two-thirds more likely to spend a lot of time (more than 11 hours a week) hooked up to the Net than men.

Meanwhile, with no-one in control and people across the world scurrying to get involved, the Net continues to grow like The Blob. Through the second half of 1995 and into 1996, the Web was doubling in size every 50 days. In the middle of 1995, there were 3 million pages of information out there. In the middle of 1996, the figure was more like 40 million.

To gauge the growth another way, in 1993 the *Sydney Morning Herald* carried 12 stories which made reference to the Internet. In 1994, that figure was 255. In 1995, 1216. Things slowed down a little in the first six months of 1996 — only 800 stories mentioned the Net — but the trajectory is still impressive.

This new technology is coming fast. At the moment, we're all using phone lines and standard modems to connect. The big telephony companies have promised cable modems in 1997, using the optic fibre technology that they're laying in our streets. This could make the Net anything up to 100 times faster than it is now.

Around the same time, three major computer companies expect to have Net capable computers on the market for as little as $700. Things will not stop there. Within a couple of decades,

INTRODUCTION

the Net is the medium that will bring you television, radio, film and phone.

But enough of the stats. This is a travel book. The interesting thing about the Net is not so much what it is, but what it can do, where it can take you. For all the importance of the Net as a new distribution medium, what makes it fun is the content, the people you meet, and their odd ideas. Cyberspace really is a parallel universe. And this book is a kind of *Lost in Space* journey to just a few of its planets.

Most books about computers are written for propeller heads. This one, I hope, is not. It is written both for the Net surfer and the armchair traveller, the person who is simply curious, intrigued by this thing they've been reading or hearing about. I've tried to keep the jargon to the absolute minimum, partly because I can't spell all those computer words, and partly because I can't tell a silicon from salt 'n' vinegar in the chip stakes. I also avoid delving into questions of online commerce. There are thousands of books that will tell you how to make your first million from the Net. I'm really not interested. To me, the beauties of the Net are social rather than commercial. And to put it as politely as possible, corporate sites pretty much all suck.

Oh, one other thing. Some of the Web addresses in this book (the URLs) will be out of date by the time it's made its way into your hands. Things move around a lot on the Net, appearing and disappearing with a rapidity that is hard to keep up with. Frustrating as that is, it's just part of the joy of Net cruising (and writing about it). Net years make dog years look eternal. All I can say is that, as I send these pages off on their journey to the printer, all the addresses are right.

Bon voyage, and don't forget to write! My email address is: *casimir@smh.com.au*

JON CASIMIR
August 1996

OPENING SALVOS

How to Behave Online

THIS bit is for the people who have just got wired. It's for the people who tore off the coloured wrapping at Christmas or their birthday and discovered an Internet connection. It's for the people who just got an account—a licence to go out and waste their cash searching for information about obscure pet diseases or alien character motivations on *The X-Files*. It's for Net newcomers.

It can be intimidating being a newbie. Everybody else, if you want to believe them, has been on the Internet since, oh, the early 1970s. Many were no doubt there when it was invented, passing the scones to the guy soldering the last wire and saying, 'No, you're not doing that right.' They act like they own it, and they want to tell you what to do in *their* domain. People who have been connected for all of six weeks pride themselves on their veteran status and get eerily overprotective about the whole place.

You, of course, feel like you're naked and in the middle of a packed stadium, with thousands watching your every move. You feel like everyone is lurking, ready to catch you committing some minor faux pas and then flame you into oblivion. 'OK, I admit it, I asked a question that was asked last week. Just hand me my leper card and never speak to me again.'

And it seems like there's so much to learn, particularly if you're going to move in the text-heavy worlds of the news and chat groups. Not just how to behave, but how to talk, how to write, how to decipher all those self-consciously wacky acronyms and abbreviations (such as LOL for 'laugh out loud' and IYKWIMAITYD for 'If You Know What I Mean And I Think You Do').

Don't panic. I have one piece of advice. Stuff them. Stuff the lot of them. Flip the binary bird. Raise the digital, er, digit.

STUFF 'EM IF THEY CAN'T TAKE A JOKE

Just get out there and have a good time. Remember this acronym: FYRIDWIWYSF ('File Your Rules, I'll Do What I Want, You Unfriendly Person').

Sure, feel free to read up on Netiquette. Find out about the social systems and codes that have sprouted and flourished in the Net's petri dish. Get to know what the social historians are on about—if nothing else, it's fascinating sociology.

Check out Arlene Rinaldi's sterling work at **The Net: User Guidelines and Netiquette.** Her sane and sage advice is available not only in English, but in German, French, Spanish and Italian, should you be bored with the mother tongue.

Though Rinaldi claims her home page does not make her the Miss Manners of the Internet, there aren't a lot of other nominations in that category. The agony-aunt offerings of **Dear Emily Postnews**, a handbook of contemporary cyber-mores, turn out to be written by a man, Brad Templeton, so he's out, even though his satirical suggestions contain wit and insight. And Virginia Shea might be another Miss Manners contender, but her book, **Netiquette**, is only available in excerpt form. The information you get at these sites is simple and well written, but ultimately, no matter how much of it you read, it's hard to escape a basic, simple truth.

For all the worlds within worlds of cyberspace, for all the possibilities of bogging yourself down in arcane laws, rituals and red tape, the rules of behaviour are pretty much the same online as they are off it. Be yourself. Do unto others. Be polite. Lurk before you leap. Don't lie, cheat or steal. Keep your inferiority/superiority complex to yourself. Stand up for what you believe in. Don't spill my pint.

Or to put it another way, as Virginia Shea does: 'Remember the human.'

Common (or perhaps that should be 'uncommon' these days) decency will get you by. Please and thank you both work,

OPENING SALVOS

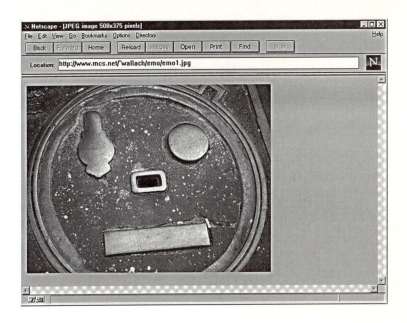

amazingly well. Beyond the simple convivialities, your behaviour is up to you. There's only one rule I try to live by, a personal and probably completely irrational one. It is this: I have vowed never, in the course of my digital life, in e-mail or in public discussion forums, to use an emoticon.

You know what I'm talking about, the stupid smiley things, the little symbols that people use to add inflection to their messages or posts. For some reason, they always remind me of those 1970s greeting cards with the two fat cherubs standing hand in hand above the slogan 'Love is . . .'

If you're still drawing a blank, **The Unofficial Smiley Dictionary** will fill you in on hundreds of them. Some, it has to be said, are creative and funny. (The most appealing, by the way, are Harlan Wallach's **Smileys in Real Life**.) I can appreciate them, I just don't want to use them. Because I can't bring myself to believe that the English language doesn't have the bandwidth for online communication.

Likewise, I'm not much chop on **abbreviations and acronyms**, but if you feel that way inclined, you'll find a handy library of terms in the addresses section below.

Really, the bottom line is that you should trust yourself. Remember that cyberspace belongs to all of us. And if it doesn't (thank you, Chairman Gates *et al.*), let's ignore that fact and act as if it does for as long as we can. Do whatever the hell you want. Have fun. Make up your own rules. And then, if you do anything, break them. :-)

Addresses

The Net: User Guidelines and Netiquette
http://www.fau.edu/rinaldi/net/index.htm

Dear Emily Postnews
http://www.clari.net/brad/emily.html

Netiquette
http://www.bookfair.com/Publishers/1887164/samNetiquette/0963702513p35.html

The Unofficial Smiley Dictionary
http://www.queensu.ca/eegtti/eeg_286.html

Smileys in Real Life
http://www.mcs.net/~wallach/emo/emo.html

Acronyms and Abbreviations
http://umiacs.umd.edu/staff/amato/AC/main.html

OPENING SALVOS

See also...

Internet Timeline
http://www.amdahl.com/internet/events/timeline.html

A succinct history of the medium. It starts in 1957, when the USSR launched *Sputnik*, the first artificial earth satellite, and the US, in response, formed the Advanced Research Projects Agency (which soon after began to develop the Net). Follows the process through to 1994, the year the World Wide Web exploded.

The Websurfer's Handbook
http://asylum.cid.com/handbook/handbook.html

A growing dictionary of facetious Web terminology, e.g. 'arachnerd, n. Someone who spends way too much time weaving and climbing around in the web. (If you've found this page, you probably are an arachnerd) . . . cyberlinguidiot n. A marketing executive that adds techie prefixes (like cyber) to words to make them sound hi-tech.'

The Cyber Dorktionary
http://www.latech.edu/~jlk/jwz/dorktionary/index.shtml

Another dictionary of jargon for the Online world: 'FAQ (fak) n: An extremely long list of answers someone has put together for no reason other than to respond to nonexistent questions ... Female (fēmāl) n. soft warm things capable of bearing children. The number of sightings in computer labs is roughly equal to the number of Bigfoot sightings in North America. Verifying sightings is almost as difficult.'

A Day in the Life of Cyberspace

ON 8 February 1996, more than 1000 professional and amateur photographers, journalists and net surfers from around the globe contributed to *A Day in the Life of Cyberspace*, an American project to capture and preserve a slice of the Internet as it was on that day.

Six weeks later, on 18 March, the site began to display its public face. The collection is broken down into six galleries, dealing with: the nurturing of community spirit online; the impact of the Net on commerce; its role in the study of our planet; its effects on religion and culture; its ability to connect people—doctors with patients and loved ones with each other; and a catch-all category (Sex, Lies and Websites), which deals with whatever is left over—everything from crime and censorship to online sex. It brags:

> There are hundreds of photographs on this website selected from the more than 200 000 shot on February 8. But even 200 000 images barely hint at the infinite moments that passed through the hills and homes and hearts of humanity on that day ... For decades to come, our children and our children's children will look with wonder at this photographic record of an ordinary day when millions of people around the planet took the time to paint their own names on the walls of the digital cave.

Or maybe our children's children will just take the night off and go bowling. As always with these Day in the Life projects, the result is huge and impressive in its scope and reach, but it's somehow hard to suppress the feeling that the whole thing is just a little stage-managed, a little contrived. The producers always seem to go for the romantic, memorable image, for the tug at the heartstrings or the wow! factor. They describe

OPENING SALVOS

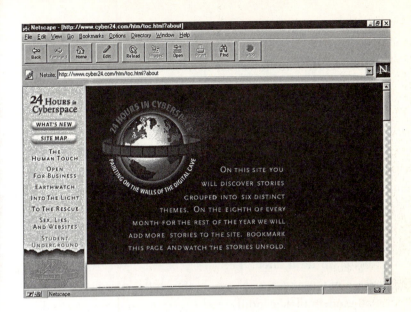

life in the way real estate agents describe houses. They're like TV current affairs: all front end with little or no follow-through.

I'm not saying the project shouldn't have happened. The site is cute. It's fun, it's worth dropping in to and it has a bunch of high points. But basically, it misses the point for the vast majority of Net users. For millions and millions of us, most cyberdays are remarkably uneventful. It's been, oh, weeks since I have used the Net to save somebody's life or make myself another million bucks. This is what a day on the Net is like for me:

10 a.m.: Wake up late, having stayed up past midnight waiting for Net traffic to thin out enough to make surfing worth bothering with.

10.30 a.m.: Make cup of tea, connect to Net. Wade through e-mail from companies trying to sell their half-baked, double-priced gadgets. Write to new pen pal in US — discover I have nothing to say.

11 a.m.: Decide to download new version of Netscape, as old one is about to expire. Program is about a billion megabytes. Computer behaves like it's trying to suck a brick through a straw. Wait.

11.15 a.m.: Do washing up from night before. Look in fridge for snack. Find none. Wait.

11.30 a.m.: Still downloading. Read little sign on screen telling me that at this rate of download, I should have the entire program by, oh, next Tuesday. Go into insecurity and self-doubt mode. Should I be doing this now? Wouldn't it be better to do it later? Fret.

11.45 a.m.: Make cup of tea, watch little 'receive data' light on modem flicker indifferently every minute or so as packets of information arrive. Stare out window. Wish I had a dog to play with.

Midday: Three-quarters of the way there, the line drops out. The transfer is abandoned. Pace around flat trying not to get angry. Kick imaginary dog.

12.15 p.m.: After a few deep breaths and a cup of tea, check out favourite newsgroups. Realise the brilliant, eloquent, insightful posts I made last night before were actually poorly expressed and badly written. Take small comfort in discovering responses to them are worse. Find post about downloading in **alt.bitterness** from person who has had a worse time of it than me. Cheer up instantly.

1 p.m.: Give up surfing for a few hours owing to bottleneck. Net slows down as public servants, uni students and business geeks spend their lunchtimes punishing their free accounts. Decide to take sandwich break.

1.30 p.m.: Make cup of tea. Go for walk to the shops. Spend fortune on loads of splashy, groovy Internet magazines. Add them to unread pile at home.

2.30 p.m.: Think about reconnecting. Decide traffic will still be too heavy. Think about reading magazines, but don't. Separate growing pile of washing into whites and colours so it will look like there's less of it. Take garbage out. Twiddle thumbs.

3 p.m.: Try to get back on Net. Line is busy. Read last Friday's newspaper. Find out which rock bands and great pieces of theatre I missed on the weekend because I was chained to the computer.

3.30 p.m.: Phone line connects, but no carrier. God laughs at me. Make cup of tea. Phone friend, whose line is engaged— obviously his modem is connected. Bastard.

3.45 p.m.: Line busy.

4 p.m.: Get through. Log on to chat group. Meet 14-year-old boy pretending to be overendowed love goddess. Feel bored enough to attempt conversation anyway. Fail. Skulk away, feeling strangely unfulfilled by the encounter.

4.30 p.m.: Make cup of tea. Find out what the weather is like in Bogotá. Wonder why the Net makes me want to find out things I never wanted to know before. Like what the weather is like in Bogotá.

5 p.m.: Visit a few old favourites. Check out new sites. Add them to Bookmark file, never to be accessed again. Decide that the Net is a great place, no matter what anybody says about it, after an hour without major technological incident.

7 p.m.: Realise that I have spent more than 30 minutes pretending to be a loud-mouthed, wisecracking medieval wizard on the wrong MUD. Locals just thought I was some kind of kink. On the Internet, no-one knows you're embarrassed. Sign off for dinner.

8 p.m.: Listen to well-founded accusations of neglect from 'woman of my dreams' (her description), who now also calls herself 'the cyber widow'.

8.30 p.m.: Begin daily hunt for pornographic and violent material. Immediately find loads of things that could corrupt and warp the minds of Australia's kiddies.

8.35 p.m.: Turn television off and go back to computer.

9 p.m.: Make cup of tea. Write letter while waiting for ridiculously over-graphic, Bayeux Tapestry–like home page to download.

9.15 p.m.: Write brilliant, eloquent, insightful posts for a couple of favourite newsgroups.

9.30 p.m.: Give up trying to get onto new site as surfers return in droves after dinner (and on Wednesday in particular, after *The X-Files* — the Net jams at exactly 9.30). Decide to wait until after 11 p.m. to try again.

10.45 p.m.: Fall asleep in front of television.

Address

A Day in the Life of Cyberspace
http://www.cyber24.com/

Can You Trust What You Find?

THE ease with which the Net moves information is one of its main selling points. Net advocates lure us towards cyberspace with promises that it will foster political and personal freedoms. We are drawn by the theory that information should be shared, that connecting minds and ideas instantly, independent of time, place, age, sex and social class, can create something wondrous and new.

Capturing the idea, Stewart Brand, author and co-founder of the influential WELL electronic conferencing system and, before that, the *Whole Earth Catalog*, coined the digital age's most frequently bandied aphorism. 'Information,' he waxed romantically, 'wants to be free.' Controlling the flow of information, which governments and businesses of all kinds have long done to help maintain their power and profits, is becoming increasingly difficult. Once information is freed, the argument goes, we can all use it, for both our own and the greater good.

It's a charming, optimistic notion and, to an extent, I subscribe to it. But information is not, and probably never will be, free. Things are just not that simple, not that binary, that either/or. If information is free at one end, chains will appear at the other. Nobel Prize–winning economist Herbert Simon, writing in the September 1995 issue of *Scientific American*, argued that the freedom that information has on the Net can also be a handicap: 'What information consumes is rather obvious: it consumes the attention of its recipients. Hence a wealth of information creates a poverty of attention.'

Freedom has a tendency to bring about a form of paralysis, an inability to choose. Paradoxically, one of the Internet's biggest strengths creates one of its biggest problems.

The other problem, and one that runs much deeper, is that with information, quantity is no guarantee of quality. A lot of the information you find on the Net is like a letter arriving on your desk with no signature, no recognisable handwriting and no return address. It consists of clusters of words or pictures with no context, no identifiable author, no pre-understood frame of reference. Disinformation, unfortunately, looks the same as information. So does propaganda.

If you're coming to the Net for research instead of entertainment, you may have a tough time. Unless you are visiting sites of companies, universities or entities you know and believe in (almost always from the off-line world), what you hit very quickly with the Net is a question of trust. How can you trust what is mostly disembodied information?

Chuck Farnham's Weird World has a bloody, deeply unattractive photo it claims shows Nirvana's Kurt Cobain in an ambulance after he died. Shotgun wounds, of course, would have left Kurt unrecognisable, so how can we know if it's a photo of him or not? I suspect it isn't—the subject appears to be hooked up to life-support equipment, yet when Cobain was found he had been dead for some time. Also at Chuck's site (does 'Chuck' exist?) is Cobain's death certificate, as well as 'transcripts' of Nicole Brown Simpson's emergency telephone calls and the cabin conversation from the final seconds of the exploded space shuttle *Challenger*, supposedly taken from the black box tape. Both are fascinating reads. You want to believe them? That's your choice. I'd like to, but it's hard.

A few technical limitations aside, any website is as easy to get to as any other. There is no hierarchy on the Net—any piece of information is presented as just as valid as any other. The medium has not yet developed to the point where good information rises and bad information sinks. It will, though. It has to. It might be just a question of time. We might have to allow the Net to throw up its own trustworthy institutions and learn to take everything else with the requisite grain of salt.

OPENING SALVOS

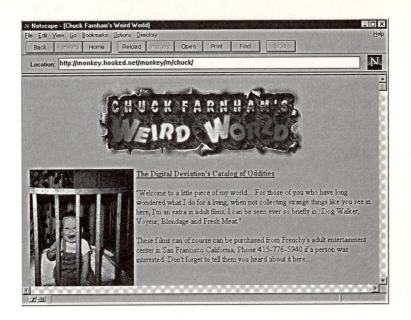

The situation does appear to be changing as more and more major off-line information providers crop up in the digital world. Though their sites are often less attractive, creative and brash than those of their cowboy cousins, they provide anchors, islands of surety. We'll have to wait and see what long-term drawbacks may arise from the corporatisation of some of the Net's information flow. But there are as many reasons for optimism as pessimism.

Until it becomes easier to trust, the Net will remain a wonderful informational tool with serious limitations. But even when those are overcome, one problem will linger. Commentators like Clifford Stoll, author of *The Cuckoo's Egg* and the overreaching *Silicon Snake Oil*, say the breast-beating about information freedom is mostly misguided. 'The information highway is being sold to us as delivering information,' Stoll says, 'but what it's really delivering is data.' We like to imagine that all those facts and factoids we scoop up from the Net will help us by enhancing our knowledge. Maybe we should think again. Data is as far from information as information is from knowledge. Access to numbers does not make someone a mathematician. Access to paint does not make an artist. Access to a library does not make you smart.

Address

Chuck Farnham's Weird World
http://monkey.hooked.net/monkey/m/chuck

The Nasty Bits—Hate on the Net

CLICK. The screen goes blank for a few seconds, and then it comes up: **The World Wide Web National Socialism Primer**. 'Why do you give the Hitler salute?' it asks, before answering itself: 'The Aryan salute today symbolises peace, respect and goodwill towards comrades or friendly strangers to whom it is extended . . .'

'Why do you worship Hitler?' it continues. 'National Socialists do not "worship" Adolf Hitler. National Socialists do offer Hitler deserving veneration for his role in bringing our race a message of hope . . .'

It goes on. And on. The questions and answers are written by Milton J. Kleim, one of America's most outspoken neo-Nazis—thousands of words of white supremacist canon dressed up as calm, rational discussion. Like so many other facets of real life, hate has jumped through the screen into cyberspace. It's on the Web in showy, well-designed sites crammed with ugly spiels. And it's on Usenet, in the discussion forums where people air their views.

And since the people in cyberspace are the same people as those in the real world, it isn't surprising to find all the usual extremists: neo-Nazis, skinheads, Holocaust deniers, anti-Semites, Asian bashers, the Ku Klux Klan, the Nation of Islam . . . the entire hate parade.

Click. Here's the **Resistance Records** site, where you can read about and order CDs by proud white-power rock acts such as Bound For Glory, Nordic Thunder and RAHOWA ('Racial Holy War').

Click. Here's the **Stormfront** site, run by the former leader of a Klan group, Don Black. It offers acres of information, the usual conspiracy theories (Waco, Oklahoma), and links to the sites of many other white supremacists, such as Ernst **Zundel**, a Canadian Nazi who was taken to court for his anti-Holocaust statements in the 1980s and has become something of a martyr for the deniers. Black's site also has downloadable graphics and cartoons, as well as news and letters pages.

Click. Here's the **Aryan Crusader** page. It's run by Reuben Logsdon, a skinhead and senior in the University of Texas physics department. It's a library and launchpad to a lot of other pages Logsdon thinks like-minded people would be interested in.

The page is also connected to Usenet. Logsdon's favourite newsgroups, he says, are **alt.politics.white-power** ('the newsgroup I call home'), **alt.skinheads** and **alt.politics.nationalism.**

Click. No-one doubts that the Internet has extraordinary potential as a propaganda tool. For a few hundred dollars, you can establish a website and preach your message to tens of millions of Net surfers, to those who happen across your page or go looking for it. For the cost of a modem and computer, you can log on to Usenet and leave your messages, or posts, for anyone passing by.

The good news for Net Nazis is that freedom of speech is part of the fabric of cyberspace. It's practically uncensorable. The Internet, as it now exists, is an electronic speaker's corner. You have the right to express your opinions. The question is how many people you can get to listen to them.

'USENET offers enormous opportunity for the Aryan resistance to disseminate our message to the unaware and the ignorant,' Milton J. Kleim writes in an online essay, 'On Tactics and Strategy for USENET'. 'It is the only relatively uncensored [so far] mass medium which we have available . . . NOW is the time to grasp the WEAPON which is the INTERNET and wield it skilfully and wisely.'

Click. But while governments establish committees and think-tanks to deal with the problems associated with the lack

OPENING SALVOS

of restrictions on the Internet, the Net community establishes its own equilibrium. Like water, it finds a level. In January 1991, a Canadian service station manager, Ken McVay, stumbled across hatred online. He found articles on Usenet claiming the Holocaust had not happened.

McVay decided that the most appropriate method of defence was attack. Know thine enemy, he says. He has since made it his job to keep tabs on the hate mongers, to follow their movements and refute the claims they make. Over the past four years, he has painstakingly collected more than 3000 documents disproving the claims of the Aryan supremacists about the Holocaust, and he's made them all available on the Net.

McVay, who was awarded the Order of British Columbia in June 1995 for this work, is writing a book on denying the deniers and now devotes himself full time to the Net. 'It's a rather abrupt change for me,' he says, 'although I now realise that this is what I want to do. Racism and hatred must be confronted, or we all lose.' McVay says that although the hard-core hate mongers only number 'a few dozen' of the millions on line, and that although they are really only fooling 'folks with low self-esteem', it is important that they be brought into the open.

Others agree. McGill University in Montreal established the **Hate on the Net** Web page, which links together all of the racists, their Websites, their news groups, their mailing lists and their private bulletin boards. Then, underneath the jump-off points to this material, it offers links to those people crusading against the racists, including McVay, with his enormous project, the **Nizkor** site.

Click. **Greg Raven**'s home page. Raven is the president of The Institute for Historical Review, for 20 years the most prominent Holocaust-denying organisation in the world. His site contains the usual links and items such as '66 Questions and Answers about the Holocaust'.

> 1. What proof exists that the Nazis killed six million Jews?
> None. All we have is postwar testimony, mostly of individual 'survivors.' This testimony is contradictory, and very few claim to have actually witnessed any 'gassing'. There are no contemporaneous documents or hard evidence: no mounds of ashes, no crematories capable of disposing of millions of corpses, no 'human soap', no lamp shades made of human skin, and no credible demographic statistics.

Click. Jamie McCarthy, a computer programmer based in Kalamazoo, Michigan, is another of the loose band of Net surfers who have taken it upon themselves to balance the hate, and who post replies to the screeds wherever they find them. How smart are the racists' techniques?

'They're not real smart,' McCarthy says, 'but they're getting smarter. There are maybe two or three people who seem to be using the Web effectively. But for each of them, there are a dozen who just don't understand how they could use the technology.

And Usenet? 'There's no effective way for them to use Usenet. There are too many gifted amateurs like Danny Keren, Mike Stein, Barry Shein and Ken for anyone to get away with anything.'

McCarthy says that all the prominent revisionists have stopped visiting the discussion-based groups on Usenet over the past few years, owing to the concerted refutation of their claims. Mostly, they have moved to the Web, which is closer to the broadcast model and doesn't include debate. But they still monitor newsgroups, looking for potential converts, who will be contacted privately by e-mail.

McCarthy believes that confronting and exposing haters is the only way to deal with them on the Net. Many people, he says, argue that extremists should be ignored, that paying attention gives them publicity. He disagrees, although he thinks academics and professionals should not waste their time:

> For professional historians to debate the Holocaust deniers, or even discuss the Holocaust with them, would be like the astronomer Carl Sagan debating whether the Earth is flat. It would be undignified at best, and would lend the wackos credibility at worst. But on the Net, we're exclusively amateurs. We have no dignity and no credibility to lend. When the deniers get their asses kicked by a bunch of computer programmers and a service station manager, it doesn't do much for their cause.

Click. Jeremy Jones, the executive vice-president of the Executive of Australian Jewry, says he believes people like Ken McVay and Jamie McCarthy are doing an important job, but that it would be naive to think they can decisively trounce the deniers. 'They may win the debate,' he says. 'They may win the argument in front of the audience reading it in that context.

But to the person who receives e-mail without a response from a Ken McVay, or to someone who receives a print-out of some of the material not accompanied by the information which is historically true, it becomes another problem altogether.'

The problem is by no means exclusively American. Australian bulletin boards such as the Sydney Bible Believers Bulletin Board and newsgroups like **aus.religion** have hosted inflammatory racist and anti-Semitic material. Last year I downloaded a handful of files from the Bible Believers which were clearly anti-Semitic and anti-Catholic and included accusations of conspiracies by both religions to create an anti-Christian New World Order.

The Net fighters may be waging an uphill battle, but at least they have made a good start. And for all those concerned about the power of new technologies to spread the word of evil, there was an exquisite moment last year in **alt. politics.white-power**. It came in a post by the Aryan Crusader Reuben Logsdon. After writing of the white state he believes should be created, which would not include Jews, blacks, Asians or other non-Aryans, he offered a thought. 'The main problem with racial separation,' he wrote, 'is that with all this damn communications technology, Jewish media can still be broadcast into the country to corrupt Whites, and Whites can still meet marriage partners over the net from outside Greater White Amerikkka.'

Those who live by the sword . . .

Addresses

Resistance Records
http://www.resistance.com

Stormfront
http://204.181.176.4/stormfront/

Aryan Crusader's Library
http://www.io.com/~wlp/aryan-page/index.html

The Zundelsite
http://www.webcom.com/~ezundel/english/welcome.html

Hate on the Net
http://www.vir.com/shalom/hatred.html

Nizkor
http://nizkor.almanac.bc.ca

Greg Raven's Home Page
http://www.kaiwan.com/~ihrgreg/

NB: At the time of writing, the National Socialism Primer had been taken down. Logsdon's site, which had been down, had just resurfaced elsewhere. Kleim, too, will undoubtedly reappear.

The Naughty Bits—Pornography

SURE, there's porn on the Internet. There's porn in the local newsagency too, and I don't see moral crusaders outside hitting shoppers with placards. As I write, I have Netscape running in another window, checking up on what Tracy has been doing lately. Tracy is a young lass who likes to lie around, in and out of her underwear, while people take photos of her. Sometimes she has partners in these photos. And sometimes they are doing things that most people believe little kiddies shouldn't see, consenting-adult kind of things. Nothing worse or more graphic than you'd find in a sex shop, but definitely Adults Only.

Tracy likes to take these photos and make them available on the Web to anyone who, for whatever obscure reason, would want to have a look at them. She puts up three new ones every Monday and Thursday. How do I feel about it? Mostly just embarrassed on her behalf. I'd give you the address for her site, but there's no way it'll stay up for the time it takes to get this book through the presses. Odds are the site won't be there next week.

This is one of the two truths of porn online. You might find something naughty. You might even like it. But don't bother bookmarking it. It won't be there the next time you get back. In fact, don't even go to the kitchen for coffee. Porn sites go walkies all the time. They're a constantly moving needle in the Net haystack.

Let me explain why. By and large, porn sites are not taken down from the Web because the service provider discovered what was on them and rang the site author to say 'Shame on you for peddling such indecent rubbish.' Porn sites are more likely to die because, if they're any good, they attract so much traffic that the server just falls over and dies. Long before

BREASTS! THERE, I SAID IT.

OPENING SALVOS

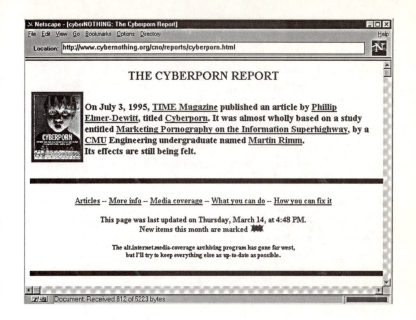

anyone has a chance to be outraged, the public has voted, and its vote is so overwhelming that it smothers the site.

The second truth is that most pornographic sites on the Net wised up very quickly to the idea that there's a buck to be made. You don't get past the front door without coughing up your credit card number.

The third truth, and I swear I'll learn how to count one day, is that there are probably fewer sites of the hard-core kind out there than you think. In late 1995, the NSW Office of Film and Literature Classification's informal search of the Net — 27 hours of porn hunting — yielded the discovery that 'restricted and refused classification material was difficult to find, at times difficult to download and was more prevalent on Usenet newsgroup files than on the World Wide Web.'

The porn on the Web is generally harder to get to, and of lower quality, than its counterpart in your newsagency. The newsgroups are a different thing. There is, in some of them (not many), a traffic of undesirable photographs. Kids do not stumble on these things, as parents often worry they will—they have to go looking for them.

So, yes, there is porn on the Net. But the Internet porn scare is still exactly what it sounds like: a scare. Most people, including our politicians and our media commentators, don't know what's out there, so it's very easy for them to get scared.

And public perceptions are hard to shake. In July 1995, *Time* magazine released an issue with a screaming headline. 'Cyberporn', it shrieked, above an artist's impression of a wide-eyed child about to be led astray by the evils of computer technology. Though the study the article was based on was quickly discredited (it turned out to be an exercise in cataloguing the types of explicit images listed on porn bulletin boards, part of a marketing report on selling porn on the infobahn), the story was more significant for its language, visual and written. It contained subheadings like 'There's an awful lot of porn on-line' and an illustration of a man having sex, or something similar, with a computer screen. It managed to reflect both of the equal and opposite responses that the Net has so far inspired in the mainstream media: extreme hype and excessive paranoia.

The former can be pretty tiresome and offputting, but the latter, with its twin obsessions with pornography and paedophilia, is even more troublesome. Millions of Australians who haven't yet had the chance to find out what the Internet is about have been confronted by nightmare visions of the Net as a drop-in centre for raincoat-wearing sickos waiting to prey on their children.

Few people would argue that the possibility of children being stalked via e-mail and live chat is not a worrying one. Few would say that the transmission of the vilest types of pornography is a good thing. But what has happened to our sense of perspective? The Internet has a worldwide community of tens of millions of people. So far, there have been only a couple of stalking cases worldwide. If Australia, with half of cyberspace's population, had the same sex crime rate, we'd be declaring a national holiday.

The sense of the other that has attached itself to the Net is distorted. By and large, the people in cyberspace are just like the people working and living beside you. They're good and bad, smart and dumb, funny and dull. Why, then, would what is available in cyberspace be different from what is available in the real world? Who decided the Internet was some utopian dream? There are perverts in our suburbs and there are perverts in cyberspace. And just as children have to be taught how to deal with strangers in real life, they must also be taught how to do so online.

By concentrating on the negatives, the news media are demonising the Net, inadvertently encouraging the growing gulf between the people who understand the new technology and those who don't. An artificial generation gap is being created in which a lot of people under 25 are not scared of the Net, and a lot of people over 25 are being encouraged to see it as a corrupting force. We're back in the 1950s, and the Net is being treated just like rock and roll.

Censorship of the Net is a thorny issue, fraught with structural, cultural and geographical problems (more of those next). Calling for bans and going into denial are neither useful nor viable. The trick with considering what can be done about online pornography, if it offends you, is to look through the other end of the telescope.

If we want to combat the porn problem, we should start at the reception point instead of the transmission one. First and foremost, parents and kids need more education, more information and more rational discussion of what's on the Net. And parents, in particular, need to accept responsibility for monitoring their children's Internet usage. If you can't be there while they're surfing, lock up the computer. It's not so hard.

And it is important that we continue to encourage the development and spread of software which allows parents to limit the access of their children to areas of the Net. There are already software packages out there, such as Net Nanny and Surf Watch, which go a long way to preventing kids hitting the easy-to-find sites.

Basically, the more people talk, and the calmer the discussion is, the more solutions will arise. But we won't get anywhere until we start to break down the fear barrier.

Addresses

Uncle Bob's Kids Page
http://miso.wwa.com/~boba/kids.html

Has links for concerned parents to the various downloadable software programs designed to filter Net Nasties.

Cyberporn Fear Storm
http://www.virtualschool.edu/mon/CyberPorn/index.html

Excellent site that catalogues debate during and after the *Time* debacle. Sees the funny side of it, and has links to some of the kinds of material online that are supposedly causing such a fuss. Is this what all the fuss is about?, the site justifiably asks.

The Cyberporn Report
http://www.cybernothing.org/cno/reports/cyberporn.html

An enormous collection of links to the debate surrounding the *Time* cover story and its analysis and debunking.

Project 2000: The Cyberporn Debate
http://www2000.ogsm.vanderbilt.edu/cyberporn.debate.cgi

Another source of links on both sides of the issue.

Smut 'n' Stuff
http://sunsite.unc.edu/smut.html

Smaller site, but broader perspective than the two above. Also covers the landmark Communications Decency Act legislation.

Net Nymph
http://www.fadetoblack.com/netnymph.htm

'Introducing "Net Nymph", the only software on the Internet that lets you view *only* pornography, without the annoyance and nuisance of all other useless information. Using a unique program code, "Net Nymph" will screen all the pages you try to access to predetermine if there is anything of a pornographic nature to be found. If "Net Nymph" determines that the information on the page is not related to pornography, it blocks it out, not allowing you to have access.' Sadly, it's a joke.

Cyber Rights and Censorship

IN JANUARY 1996, a teenager in Perth blew himself up with a home-made pipe bomb. The police said he learned how to make the bomb from the Internet. Six months later, in early August, Sydney police attributed an apparent rise in local pipe bombings to the same cause.

When I was a kid, people I knew made pipe bombs too. Who knows where they got the information on how to build them, but they got it. Kids do that sort of thing. And kids then get it wrong. They blow themselves up.

They also, the boys at least, have a thing for pornography. There was a thriving black market for nudie mags at my high school. You could buy used (and I mean well-thumbed) mags for about $1 each. The more cash you had, the more hard-core your options were. I had seen plenty of X-rated porn by the time I turned eighteen, and if I'm strange and perverted, I can assure you that is not the reason for it. Again, who knows where kids got the porn, but they got it.

The big difference between then and now is that we now know where kids are going to get these kinds of information and pictures. Or at least some of them. They're going to get them from the Internet.

That frightens the trousers off a lot of people. It has helped to create the excess of fear about the Net that is abroad in our community. As usual, it boils down to being a fear of what we don't understand. The problem is that this fear, this ignorance, is fuelling media and government concern about this new medium. **John Perry Barlow**, founder of the **Electronic Frontiers Foundation**, a cyberspace civil rights watchdog, puts it succinctly: 'Our leaders feel the impulse to regulate the unknown. We have government by the clueless, over a place they've never been, using means they don't possess.'

OPENING SALVOS

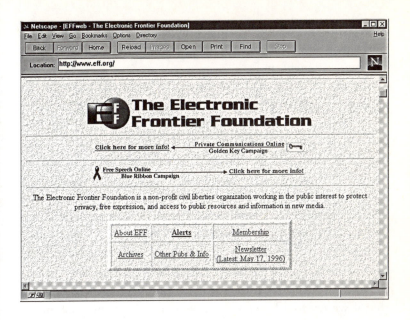

No-one is saying that some of the material available on the Net is not cause for concern. But there are other sides to the story. On the last page of *The Virtual Community*, his landmark 1994 book envisioning some of the ways the Internet could change our lives for the better, American author and Net activist **Howard Rheingold** predicted that the late '90s would be seen in retrospect as 'a narrow window of historical opportunity'. He argued that during this window, very important technology battles would be won and lost. People would either act, or fail to act effectively, to ensure that the potential of the Net for open communication was protected. This would ensure that the millions who used the Net to share and discover knowledge were not just ploughed into infobahn speed humps by governments and corporations looking for another way to sell us stuff we don't know we want yet. 'I think we're in the window,' he said to me last year. 'This is it. It's a train, it's a juggernaut and it's leaving the station. You can still run alongside it and jump on board, but pretty soon it's going to have this huge momentum.'

At the moment, the Internet is a new technology with amazing potential. If you stop and think about it, it's easy to see why. To date, all communications media have been built on a one-to-many broadcast idea, in which the audience was a passive consumer. A TV station or newspaper pumps an endless feed to a willing, but basically inert audience. Our biggest power leap came with the invention of the remote control. The Net is not this. It's a two-way deal, many-to-many communication. The user has power here. People are connecting, swapping and sharing information. Some of it is good and some of it is not so good. The thing to remember is that the Internet has extraordinary potential for both. And we have to be careful that if we try to affect the bad, we don't affect the good more. Or, as an American judge put it this year, we have to make sure we don't burn the village to roast the pig.

There are ways to 'regulate' the Net, but most of them don't suit the legislate first, ask questions later atmosphere. Most of them are simple software solutions. Most are good ideas that just need a little prodding along. The Internet is a strangely self-regulating world already. Jackboots and major clampdowns are not going to be needed. For a start, there are software programs on the market that will filter out pornographic Net sites. And there are many other ways to stop inquisitive kids from tracking the material down, ranging from simple computer key locks to intricate password systems. A little parental responsibility goes a long way.

What is more important as this debate continues to rage, Rheingold's window slowly closes, is calmness and a willingness to understand this new medium. Because every time a politician or talk radio host looking for an easy target (and aren't they always?) mentions banning or censoring the Net, the Net-heads laugh. They laugh because Net mythology has many of them believing that they are the last boundary riders of the twentieth century, a bunch of frontier-busting cowboys that no pencil-pushing public servant could stop. But they also laugh because they know it's not that simple. The old methods won't work. The Internet does not conform to the traditional broadcast model of communications. There is no backbone to it. There is no central radio or TV transmitter that you can monitor or simply turn off. There are no presses you can stop rolling. There is no plug to pull, unless you want to take out all the phone lines in the world. The Net was designed, three decades ago, as a decentralised communications structure. You can cut off limbs, but the body won't die. It grows almost organically. And part of its nature is to find ways around roadblocks.

Then there is the problem of collapsing geography. It's one thing to prosecute someone putting offensive material onto the Net in Kingaroy or Kalgoorlie. But how could you legislate against material from, say, Korea, which can be accessed directly or via an American relaying computer? Or a British one? Or a Finnish one? You could pass as many laws as you want stopping Australians from pulling unwanted material onto the Net, but you couldn't stop Australians logging on and getting it from elsewhere. The Net doesn't recognise place. Geography is all the same.

Even beyond that, how could you legislate against fragments? I could seek a bomb recipe or pornographic picture which could arrive as two or more packets of information, two or more streams of bits, from different places. Those bits would be meaningless until my computer reassembled them.

'This decentralisation of control means that the delivery system for salacious materials is the same worldwide network that delivers economic opportunity, educational resources, civic forums, and health advice,' Rheingold wrote in 1994. 'This technological shock to our moral codes means that in the future, we are going to have to teach our children well. The only protection that has a chance of working is to give our sons and daughters moral grounding and some common sense.'

In America, the first major battles for control in cyberspace have been fought in and around Congress with the Communications Decency Act (CDA), a clean-up-the-Net initiative which, was signed into law on 8 February 1996, to take advantage of the free publicity offered by the *Day in the Life of Cyberspace* project. The Act ostensibly extended legislation against telephone harassment to cyberspace, but was worded in such a broad way that consenting adults exchanging rude words in private could be liable for a $100 000 fine and two years in prison.

There was widespread protest on the day, as large numbers of site operators turned their pages black in dismay. John Perry Barlow penned an angry Cyberspace Declaration of Independence (see Appendix 1). Soon after, the EFF launched its Blue Ribbon campaign, with the support of other civil liberties groups including the **American Civil Liberties Union**, the **Center for Democracy & Technology**, the **Electronic Privacy Information Center** and **Voters' Telecom Watch**. The groups asked site operators to display blue ribbon graphics 'to show support for the essential human right of free speech'.

Two weeks later, the **Citizens Internet Empowerment Coalition** (CIEC) filed a lawsuit seeking to overturn the Act on the grounds that it violated First Amendment rights of Internet users. Tens of thousands of people signed on to the lawsuit. Rheingold says:

> Censorship is really just a smokescreen issue for control. It always comes in the guise of decency and always ends up as tyranny, with some people wanting to control what other people say.

> Everybody who is online now needs to go and talk to people who are not, and convince them that even though they may not be enthusiastic about technology or care about technology, the decisions made about the technology are going to have an impact on their liberty. The biggest problem, of course, is that the bottom line here is convincing people to fight for rights that they don't actually know they have.
>
> Any number of different esoteric technology issues are going to affect the kind of democracy we might have in five, ten or twenty years. The laws will be in place and the rights will be eroded before people understand what's at stake with technology. The decisions are going to be made now, when there are tens of millions of people online in the world, that [will] affect the kind of world we're in when there are hundreds of millions of people online.

In Australia, the battles have not been quite as noisy as those surrounding the CDA, but in their own way they have been just as ugly. There have been two government-sponsored investigations into the regulation of the Net. The first, the inquiry of the Senate Select Committee on Community Standards Relevant to the Supply of Services Utilising Electronic Technologies (who comes up with these catchy titles?), tabled its report in November 1995. (The second, the **Australian Broadcasting Association**'s Online Services Investigation, delivered its findings in June 1996—we'll get to those a little further down.)

The Select Committee's report was marked by what a spokesman described as a 'fairly benign' set of recommendations. It suggested, essentially, a system of Internet self-regulation through codes of practice. Access/service providers would be largely relieved of liability for material which passes through their networks, subject to their acceptance of certain responsibilities, such as the verification of the age of their clients (in reality, a very tough thing to do).

The responsibility would be sheeted home at an individual

level. The report argued that it should be an offence to 'transmit, obtain possession of, demonstrate, advertise or request the transmission of material equivalent to RC (refused category—the really ugly stuff), R or X categories'.

This seems ridiculously over-eager. On the one hand, it would mean that bogeys like child porn and bestiality could be policed more effectively. On the other, it would mean that X- and R-rated erotica, the kind of thing that (certainly in the case of the latter) you can get at the local newsagent, would be banned. It would mean that the online world would be restricted by tighter standards than the off-line world. Offensiveness is not a concrete idea. It is related to community standards. And there's no doubt that the standards of the Net community are looser than those of the wider community.

A few months later, at the start of April (no, it wasn't a joke), NSW Attorney General Jeff Shaw raised the stakes considerably by announcing the Carr government's intention to pass laws that would make it a criminal offence for a person to transmit, advertise, allow access to or retrieval of 'objectionable material' through online services. The proposed laws, which were marketed as a model for all Australian states, would have banned the extreme types of material that are normally refused classification. Nobody wants to see violent or child pornography made freely available, but our existing laws cover the distribution and possession of this material more than adequately. More worryingly, they went past the banning of R- and X-rated material, all the way to banning anything MA, unsuitable for those under 15.

The local Net industry mobilised, roundly criticising the proposals. The dissent culminated in a rally in Sydney, organised by the local arm of **Electronic Frontiers Australia**, whose Stop! Campaign was hastily set up to draw attention to the inadequacy and inappropriateness of the government response. The proposed laws were set to be discussed in July at a meeting of state and federal attorneys-general. It looked like they might be adopted countrywide. By May, things were looking bleak for Net advocates on both sides of the Pacific Ocean. But in June, everything turned around. The first positive sign was that a panel of three judges in a Philadelphia District Court overturned the CDA. The case against it had been built on its contravention of the First Amendment of the Bill of Rights. At the time of writing, the Supreme Court is still to have its say, but the District Court verdict was so resounding that, for the first time, the anti-CDA push appears to have gained the upper hand.

For cyber-rights advocates, the court's finding was the best news in ages. And not just because of the decision itself, but because of the way it was put. The comments of the three judges in the 175-page decision (which can be found in its entirety online at a number of sites) border on the amazing. Judge Stewart Dalzell wrote in the decision:

> The Internet deserves the broadest possible protection from government-imposed, content-based regulation. Some of the dialogue on the Internet surely tests the limits of conventional discourse. Speech on the Internet can be unfiltered, unpolished, and unconventional, even emotionally charged, sexually explicit, and vulgar—in a word, 'indecent' in many communities.
>
> But we should expect such speech to occur in a medium in which citizens from all walks of life have a voice. We should also protect the autonomy that such a medium confers to ordinary people as well as media magnates.

Those who claim that the Net fosters democracy, often scoffed at by critics, are not exaggerating, according to Dalzell:

> Individual citizens of limited means can speak to a worldwide audience on issues of concern to them. Federalists and Anti-Federalists may debate

the structure of their government nightly, but these debates occur in newsgroups or chat rooms rather than in pamphlets. Modern-day Luthers still post their theses, but to electronic bulletin boards rather than the door of the Wittenberg Schlosskirche. More mundane (but from a constitutional perspective, equally important) dialogue occurs between aspiring artists, or French cooks, or dog lovers or fly fishermen.

Though our legal system differs significantly from the American one, local Net users took comfort from the Findings of Fact at the beginning of the decision. It comprises the first legal and philosophical definition of what the Internet actually is, how it works, who uses it and why. And because of its origin, that definition carries with it a stamp of legitimacy. It may well provide an appropriate framework to debate many of the issues we are all trying to come to terms with, from the value of anonymity to the suitability of blocking software. It recognises many things that Net advocates have held to be truths: that the Net is not a broadcast medium, like television or radio; that its uses are not an 'audience', but a community; that communications do not 'invade' an individual's home or appear on one's computer screen unbidden; and much more. If nothing else, it gives us a reasoned, lengthy, independent opinion, an outside judgment, a context in which to have our own discussions and debates.

A fortnight after the verdict, the ABA tabled its long-awaited **Report** which, like the Senate Select Committee before it, refused to go as far as the NSW government, recommending a self-regulation regime based on Codes of Conduct, which would be developed in consultation with the industry. With the pendulum clearly swinging the other way, the attorneys-general, in their July meeting, put aside the NSW legislation, agreeing to forge ahead with the ABA's suggested Codes of Conduct scheme. An EFA spokesman later said:

> This is a great day for Internet democracy in Australia. The voice of reason finally appears to be winning against the voice of ignorance. It is clear that the widespread opposition to the NSW proposals reached the Commonwealth Minister for Communications and the Arts, Senator Alston, who played a key role in convincing the Censorship Ministers to abandon state-based legislation in favour of the ABA approach.
>
> Although EFA has some reservations about the ABA report, in particular where it leaves individual Net users and private content creators, we are hopeful that the Authority will carry through its brief of wide consultation and take account of these concerns.
>
> However, there is still a long road ahead.

And as we have already seen, those pendulums just keep swinging.

Addresses

John Perry Barlow Home Page
http://www.eff.org/~barlow

Electronic Frontiers Foundation
http://www.eff.org

Howard Rheingold
http://www.well.com/user/hlr/index.html

Blue Ribbon Campaign
http://www.eff.org/blueribbon.html

American Civil Liberties Union
http://www.aclu.org/

Center for Democracy & Technology
http://www.cdt.org/

Electronic Privacy Information Center
http://www.epic.org/

Voters' Telecom Watch
http://www.vtw.org/

Citizens Internet Empowerment Coalition
http://www.cdt.org/ciec/

Australian Broadcasting Association
http://www.dca.gov.au/aba/hpcov.htm

Electronic Frontiers Australia
http://www.efa.org.au

ABA Report
http://www.dca.gov.au/aba/olsrprt.htm

See also...

Censor-U Movement (CUM)
http://www.cum.net/main.html

A parody of the right wing, with its own pro-censorship red ribbon.

THE LIGHTER SIDE

Cameras Attached to the Web

THE MACHINE has not yet been invented that human beings haven't found a dumb use for. Put a photocopier in an office and, sooner or later, some dolt will make copies of his bum and fax them to Uruguay. Future mental illness historians will no doubt refer to this as multimedia syndrome, the compulsion to let technologies do whatever they *can* do rather than use them to do the things we *need* to do — the preference for gimmick potential over practical value. You see it on every CD-ROM on the market: 'Hey, if you click here, it will do this faaaaabulous trick.' Fine, but does it *mean* anything?

The online manifestation of this syndrome is the exponentially increasing number of cameras connected to the Net, bringing us live, real-time pictures from around the world. Though there are pictures, such as those of the 1995 volcano eruption in New Zealand, that make some sense to broadcast in this way, most Net cameras are pointed willy-nilly at any old box of fluff. Why? Because they can.

We've had reality TV. Now we have reality Web. And the reality, of course, is that reality, unedited, is boring. Almost all the live-picture sites are more interesting in theory than practice. It takes much longer to get to the images than anyone would stick around to look at them for. There's something Sisyphean about it all: lots of effortful journey, no arrival.

Anyway, for those who want to check them out, **Yahoo** has a long list. Likewise, the **Peeping Tom Homepage** has a choice of outdoor scenes, offices and labs, animals, oddities and interactive vistas which allow you to move the camera. I spent a morning tooling about a few of the sites in an attempt to make sense of the phenomenon.

Santa Monica Beachcam: A view of this Los Angeles beach, updated every ten minutes. Thanks to time-zone differences, we see it mostly in the middle of the night. *What I Found Out*: There's a beach at Santa Monica.

A Street in Boulder, Colorado: A shot of a house on a corner, with a street crossing and lots of trees. It's updated every five minutes and can be viewed as a time-lapse movie of the last 24 hours. *WIFO*: It's windy there.

Sydney: Two views from the apartment of Matthew Perkins. One shows the city skyline, the other, the harbour. *WIFO*: What the weather was like, but I could have looked out my window with a lot less effort.

Hoga, the Golden Gate Bridge of Sweden: Engineering fetishists will come over all gooey at the regularly updated pix of the construction of one of the world's largest suspension bridges. *WIFO*: Hypertext is easy to understand in Swedish. 'Klicka Har,' it said, so I did.

HomeCom, Atlanta: See the site of the 1996 Olympics. This company has two cameras, one looking out its window at the city (oddly dark at night) and one in the office, mounted 'on a state of the art oscillating tripod' which turns out to be a fan. *WIFO*: It's a myth that computer geeks don't go home in the evenings. At 6 p.m. Atlanta time, there's not a keyboard puncher in sight.

Indiana Center for Innovative Computer Applications: The visitor can spy on a couple of workers, such as research director Dennis Gannon. 'It should be noted that Dennis is somewhat shy these days,' the site warns, 'and usually points his camera towards his door . . . Occasionally, you can see his shadow on the wall in the hallway if the sun is shining, and if you're lucky, you may see him entering or leaving his office.' Right. The definition of luck is apparently catching a glimpse of some portly, bearded computer guy. And I thought it was winning the lottery. *WIFO*: Nothing, it was

THE LIGHTER SIDE

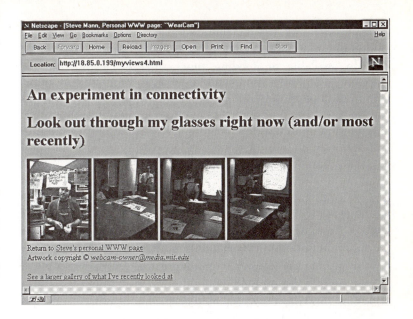

turned off. Strange how a large number of these sites use expensive technology so that someone sitting in front of a computer can find out what someone sitting in front of a computer looks like.

Steve's Wearable Wireless Webcam: See the world from his perspective. Steve has mounted a camera on his head. *WIFO*: Steve knows some guy with glasses who appears to be telling him about a fish that got away. He also needs, seriously, to get some kind of life going.

Miles' Television, Berkeley, California: Whatever is on-screen—football when I drop by. *WIFO*: the potential for finding out what's happening on Melrose Place, one frame at a time, without sound, is low.

Interactive Model Railroad: You drive the train, racing against another drop-in. A lot of technology and effort, little return. *WIFO*: Model trains are just as dull in cyberspace.

Almost Amazing Turtle Cam: Very groovy aquarium full of frolicking shell carriers. Picture taken every 60 seconds. Info available on feeding times. *WIFO*: Despite the old hare-and-tortoise reputation, turtles are frisky little critters.

The Trojan Room Coffee Machine: Still the original and best. Trained on a coffee pot, showing how full it is. The experiment began in 1991, predating the Web. It came about because a bunch of Cambridge academics were sick of traipsing up flights of stairs to get to the coffee machine, only to find out it was empty. *WIFO*: Stay where you are, it's running low.

Steve's Ant Farm: This one has appeal, too. 'See the live ants dig tunnels, build bridges, move mountains.' *WIFO*: The best part is *Ant The Movie*, 'a time-lapse tour de force that will make your skin crawl'.

Random Internet Cam: Saves you all this trouble in the first place, by simply selecting one of the cameras and sending you in that direction. No need to make up your mind or click through the Web to find things. *WIFO:* You always find the easiest solution last.

Addresses

Yahoo—Devices Attached to the Web
http://www.yahoo.com/Computers_and_Internet/Internet/Entertainment/Interesting_Devices_Connected_to_the_Net/

The Peeping Tom Homepage
http://www.ts.umu.se/~spaceman/camera.html

Santa Monica Beachcam
http://www.fountainhead.com/livecam.html

THE LIGHTER SIDE

A Street in Boulder, Colorado
http://www.gwha.com/cgi-bin/bouldercam

Sydney
http://spectrum.com.au/citcyam.html

Hoga, The Golden Gate Bridge of Sweden
http://www.connection.se/hoga-kusten/uk/livedok

HomeCom, Atlanta
http://vista.homecom.com/webcam/cam2.html

Indiana Center for Innovative Computer Applications
http://www.extreme.indiana.edu/spy/

Steve's Wearable Wireless Webcam
http://wearcam.org/

Miles' Television, Berkeley, California
http://www.csua.berkeley.edu:8000/~milesm/ontv.html

Interactive Model Railroad
http://rr-vs.informatik.uni-ulm.de/rrbin/ui/RRPage.html

Almost Amazing Turtle Cam
http://www.campusware.com/turtles/

The Trojan Room Coffee Machine
http://www.cl.cam.ac.uk/coffee/coffee.html

Steve's Ant Farm
http://sec.dgsys.com/AntFarm.html

Random Internet Cam
http://www.xmission.com/~bill/randcamera.html

See also . . .

Yahoo's Collection of Webcam Site Indexes
http://www.yahoo.com/Computers_and_Internet/Internet/Entertainment/Interesting_Devices_Connected_to_the_Net/Spy_Cameras/Indices/

Cyber Soap Operas

IN 1995, **The Spot** waltzed away with the hotly contested Coolest Site of the Year gong at the 'Webbies', the Los Angeles Internet awards ceremony organised by InfiNet's Cool Site of the Day service.

The Spot is a cyber-soap. Or, as InfiNet put it, 'the world's first episodic Web site, where you can interact with the characters and affect their lives in a virtual hangout that exists somewhere between fantasy and reality'. At first glance, The Spot looks like *Melrose Place*. At second glance, it looks like *Beverly Hills, 90210* as well. Tens of thousands of years of human evolution and what have we got? Aaron Spelling in cyberspace.

The 'Spot' of the title is an old wooden house in a groovy part of Los Angeles shared by a bunch of spunky twenty-somethings and their dog, a blue-eyed 'cyberian husky' called Spotnik.

The story began in June 1995, with 23-year-old Tara Hartwick, a graduate student in film, explaining that her housemates at The Spot had all agreed to take part in an online journal experiment. We were introduced to Carrie Seaver, brainy gal from back east; Lon Oliver, narcissist and actor; Michelle Foster, the designated sex goddess; and Jeff Benton, the brooding, James Dean one.

Every day, two or three of these characters file photo-boosted journal entries about the kind of things going on in their lives: parties, love problems, drunk-driving charges, ghosts and infatuations with local dogs (Spotnik). Visitors to the site can move forward or backwards through each journal, or take a calendar overview and click on the entries day by day. You can also check out the video and audio grabs of the characters, browse the snapshots from various parties and social outings, or work through a compilation of various letters to the Spottites.

Really, it's pretty hokey. The storylines are obvious and the characterisations are thinner than the walls in a $20-a-night hotel. But that's not important. It may not be the smartest thing you've ever read, but The Spot was an important step forward for the Net, an artistic work which utilises the medium for what it is rather than trying to impose on it what it isn't.

The Spot is not a book. It's not television. It's not, as so many other sites are, a newsletter or a magazine reproduced online. The Spot could only exist on the Internet. It is interactive, insofar as all the participants can be e-mailed (suggestions from site visitors about how to solve their problems often turn up in later journal entries). And it is immediate. An event that happens in the world today can be incorporated into The Spot today.

Within twelve hours of the Coolest Site awards being announced, journal entries from Tara and Carrie had news of the victory and photographs from the celebrations. Not willing to break the illusion, the actors hired to be the housemates in the photos and videos had gone to the awards ceremony.

The Spot is an experiment in narrative. By allowing the user to go both ways through individual journals or hover above them all at once, it successfully abandons linear storytelling. It is evolutionary, in that it grows and changes with each new chunk of information added to its archive. Presented with a number (now in the thousands) of pieces of narrative, the user can shape his own version of the story.

The creator of this particular cyber-soap was not Tara Hartwick, of course, but a Californian advertising agency, Fattal & Collins. There was much speculation about how the agency, which had clearly ploughed a fortune into this good-looking site, could justify the expense. Then it announced it

THE LIGHTER SIDE

would carry ads on its pages and incorporate promotions into the stories ('For dinner he took me to a restaurant in LA called Roscoe's House of Chicken and Waffles'). And suddenly it all made sense—bring a site to critical mass on the Web (The Spot gets half a million hits a day) and it will create its own ways of making money.

In keeping with Net tradition, The Spot already has a parody, **The Squat**, featuring a bunch of no-hopers sharing a mobile home in nowhere, Missouri. An excerpt from the diary of Woody, the central character:

> Earl still ain't around, but me and Cleitus and Val and Bettyjo and Larlene even—we all went down to the Silver Bullet to have a few beers. Bein' Sunday and all, there weren't no one ridin' the Mechanical Bull. We talked Cleitus into ridin' 'im, and that Cleitus, he's a talented man. He can ride that bull with the best of them and still get up in the morning and pump some gas at the Sinclair station. I guess we all got our talents.

Net equilibrium — something to be thankful for.

The Spot was not the first cyber-soap. That honour belongs to Parallel Lives, a set of three weekly episodic stories which began in March 1995, on @times, The New York Times Company's news and information service on America Online. Readers could suggest plot twists via e-mail.

But it was The Spot which really captured the Internet community's imagination. It produced copycats small and large, from the bare-bones simple to the extravagantly ambitious. At the former end of the scale is **Barnaby Woods**, by Julia Slavin, a Washington, DC writer, which is no more than a few hundreds words a week of a serial. Others, like **Techno3**, are writ on a larger scale:

> This is the story of 3 lovely ladies who carry a personal hidden secret. By day, Jillian works as a lawyer, Helen works as a media relations director in an entertainment company and Marie, a former beauty queen from Puerto Rico, works as an A & R person for Sony Latino. By night, these roles change as each is controlled by a diabolical cyber terrorist who fulfills their every desire and for whom each would give their lives.

Yep, its a high-tech Charlie's Angels. Each episode is littered with photos and hyperlinks, which turn out to be sound files, recordings of the dialogue and the in-head secret thoughts of the characters.

Ferndale is even more technologically competitive. Its home page offers a promotional video and a theme song, and as you work your way through you'll find photos, sound files and all sorts of mocked-up props, from newspaper stories to hospital documents. The story takes place in a mountain retreat in California. The residents of this facility share their problems over the Internet, using what head medico Dr Randolph Mix calls 'Net therapy'. This means personal journals of the type employed by The Spot's characters.

THE LIGHTER SIDE

The biggest, splashiest cyber-soap to date has been **The East Village**, a kind of *Central Park West* to The Spot's *Melrose Place*, though it would, understandably, hate the comparison. The East Village debuted on the Web in March 1996, a couple of months later than it promised in various high-profile press articles, but still packing enough punch for people to forgive it. Set in and around Manhattan's lower east side, it follows the usual tangle of fashionable lives.

One character is marrying another because she has amnesia. A third character has just come out of a coma with an entirely different personality and can't remember the guy she's meant to be head over heels about. Eve, the main character, is sleeping with her best friend (it'll end in tears). And her boss reckons he's now telepathic as the result of his abduction by experimenting aliens. Just the usual soap stuff.

'Tonight is the eighth anniversary of my first infidelity,' Eve began. As opening lines go, it wasn't bad. The East Village, the brainchild of New York Multimedia company Marinex, started off running and continues that way. It tries to dazzle its audience with up to 40 photos per episode, audio narration, background music, and video clips. Another bunch of spunky twentysomethings has been hired to look cute for the pics.

So is the computer the place for a soap? As more than one writer has pointed out, cyber-soaps require some level of interactivity, while TV soap operas are a purely passive form of entertainment. You just sit on your couch with a box of Dairy Milk chocolates and shout at the screen occasionally: 'Heather, don't do it, she's blackmailing you!', 'Who is dressing you, babe?'

What a cyber-soap gives us that its TV counterpart can't is the illusion of intimacy. It lets us read the characters' diaries and hear their private thoughts as well as their dialogue. And as the interactive aspects make users participants in the proceedings, it offers an experience that is both shared and individual. Let's see television do that.

Addresses

The Spot
http://www.thespot.com

The Squat
http://www.thesquat.com/welcome.html

Barnaby Woods
http://www.wald.com/living/cybersoap.html

Techno3
http://www.bluepearl.com/entertainment/soap/techno3text.html

Ferndale
http://www.ferndale.com/

The East Village
http://www.theeastvillage.com

See also...

Friday's Beach
http://www.msn.com.au/fridaysbeach

Australia's first big budget soapie, launched in late August, features video and sound files along with the usual text, photos and graphics. Written by soap veteran Helen Townsend, it's filmed in Sydney at Tamarama Beach and Birchgrove Oval, and chronicles the lives, loves and links of, sigh, five spunky teenagers.

THE LIGHTER SIDE

Above the Unicorn
http://www.chiweb.com/entertainment/unicorn/

'You are the team leaders of the groups that make up this organisation. Our goal is to use genetic engineering, technology and any resource at our disposal, to create the perfect employee.' A daily drama that looks at what it would be like to plan the replacement of corporate employees and, by implication, what it would be like to redesign the human race.

Affairs of the Net
http://www.chiweb.com/entertainment/affairs/

From the same stable as Above the Unicorn, this is a romance by e-mail. 'I just "happen" to have access to the e-mail messages of a couple who are just beginning to develop their relationship via the Internet. Every week I'll collect their messages and you can see them—uncut, uncensored, unedited. Together we can find out what love on the net is all about.'

Diary of a Madwoman in the Attic
http://www.chiweb.com/entertainment/madwoman/

'It's an allusion to the book titled *The Madwoman in the Attic*. I don't remember the authors—though I know I should—but I'll look it up and put it in another entry ... Well, Diary, this is going to be my attempt to get inside my own head and see if I can figure out who I am and what this life of mine is all about. I don't know what I'll talk about; I don't know how often I'll write in this thing.'

Lake Shore Drive
http://www.chiweb.com/chicago/lsd/

Thirteen people (small photos). Every day, a file of their e-mail to each other is presented on the Web. The best thing about it is that you can create your own character and become a bit player.

As the Web Turns
http://www.metzger.com/soap/

Soap in the *Dallas* tradition: 'Rosalia sat behind the wheel of her red BMW 320i in the parking lot of the Denver Center for the Performing Arts. Bizet's *Carmen* was as stirring as ever, Preston thought as he sat beside her. At a time, it probably made as much commotion as Rosalia did tonight in her daring red velvet evening dress. She was fiery, alright. She wore red and only red. But even the passion she wore it with every day could never exhaust the fire that burned inside her.'

Cracks in the Web
http://www.directnet.com/~gmorris/title.html

A weekly espionage thriller. One of the earliest of episodic Web sites, this is a sure-footed crime drama. If guns and police departments and investigations are your bag, try also:

Scrolling Mystery Theatre
http://www.fiction.com/

This brings us 'groundbreaking detective fiction and thrillers' in three-month story arcs. 'We were still shaken by the discovery of the body, in fact the police had returned in the morning and were still downstairs gathering whatever clues there were to be gathered, when Jennie's boyfriend Peter arrived. It was obvious that he had seen the police presence downstairs and had bounded up the stairs to see what was going on; now he stood in the doorway, a little out of breath, a little astonished. "Martin downstairs is dead," Alyssa told him, saying "downstairs" as if it were his last name.'

Melrose East
http://www.inx.net/~mvo/MelrosEast.html

The lowdown from creator Jade Austen: 'OK . . . you might not find Billy or Alison or the gay guy here. But the friends I'm writing about are equally screwed up. That's why they're interesting. Who cares about normal, well-adjusted people? As if you could even find any . . . Melrose East is about the adventures of young neighbours living in Gramercy Park. Their "pool" complex is just a cement courtyard. But there's lots of scandal just the same.'

Why Dumb Ideas Are Often the Best Ideas

WE ALL have our dumb days. Sometimes you double-click on Netscape, the software most people use to navigate the Net, for no other reason than that there's nothing worth watching on TV. Sometimes you have absolutely no idea where you want to go. Your favourite newsgroups have stalled and you've clocked in at all your bookmarked sites.

These are the days you want to step off the safely defined paths of the Net and enter the electronic jungle, armed only with your info-machete and a packet of Iced VoVos (you never know when you're going to get lost).

I have those days all the time. They're fun. You just think of the dumbest thing that comes into your head and go searching for it. Dumbest? Hmmm. I typed 'John Howard' into the Lycos Web searcher just to see what its warped little workings would come up with.

It gave me a whole lot of stuff about the American restaurant chain Howard Johnson's, a biography of **John Howard Falloon**, the New Zealand Minister of Agriculture, Minister of Forestry and Minister for Racing, and **John Howard's Home Page**—this JH lives in Birmingham, England, and wants us to look at photos of his motorbike holiday in Spain.

Then, hey presto! **The Johnny Howard Comedy Store Page**, a site run by Steve McDonald, creator of the now-defunct Paul Keating Fun Page, which used to feature a splendid hybrid of PJK's head on the body of a naked woman. It still being fairly early days, the Comedy Store has been light on for material, but as the Howard government moves into its second and third years you can be sure it will provide ample cause for mirth. The official **Prime Minister's Home Page** is much less interesting.

STUPID IS AS STUPID DOUBLE CLICKS

One of the things I love about the Internet is that it not only encourages but actually rewards stupidity. You don't have to be silly to use the Net, but it really does help. Back at the Infoseek search engine, I typed in 'leprous pig'. The first suggestion that came up was **Trip to India**, which unsurprisingly turned out to be an enormously long description of one man's subcontinental journey. I'm not sure whether the search mechanism found a reference to pigs or leprosy in it—it got dull and I bolted.

The **Guinea Pig FAQ** turned out to be a font of information for non-guinea pig owners such as myself. If one of the little critters ever comes to stay, I'll know how to trim its toenails, what position to take in the breeding versus desexing debate, and why I should leave alfalfa off the menu—it gives them bladder stones.

Of genuine interest was the **Pig Decoy Carving** site. This turned out to be the electronic home of the National Pig Carvers Association of America, dedicated to the preservation and advancement of pig decoy carving skills. Apparently, wild-pig hunters used to use the decoys to attract their prey, but the carvers became so proficient at their art that the pig population plummeted and the decoys were banned. The skills have survived, though, thanks to these good people. And if you believe that . . .

Men Are Pigs!, from those friendly folk at the She Women Man Haters Society, in theory allows women to download their anger at those of us who are oestrogen-challenged. In practice, everyone seems to be fairly kind and understanding: 'They're pigs but we love 'em'.

Other sites I turned up included the home page of a Hong Kong student called **Pig Pig**, the **Pig Gene Mapping Project** and the **Fabulous Miss Piggy Page**, a cyber altar to the most famous Muppet. Oh, and the home page for **Babe**.

THE LIGHTER SIDE

Looking around my desk, I spotted a packet of Smarties. That word took me to an adults-only site (which unfortunately I needed a credit card to get into) before finding **Mr Smarty Pants Knows**, a Website of the *Austin Chronicle* newspaper, full of important information: did you know that in 1990 there were 75 000 accordionists in the United States?

That site linked to **Global Cheese Online**, which itself links **CheeseNet** (write your own cheese poetry, Ask Dr Cheese and more) and **The Cheese Page** ('Better computing through fermented curd products' is its unforgettable motto).

Picking a word at random from the dictionary, I typed 'ermine', which is a weasel that turns white in winter. That took me to the **Ferret Photo Gallery**, where I saw lots of pics of baby ferrets doing cute things. That killed thirty seconds of my life that might have been wasted watching a shampoo ad.

The word 'thumb' found a site devoted to **Korean Traditional Archery** and another to **String Figures From Around the World** before alighting on **Mr Menace: The Film Reviewer,** a man who guarantees he has not seen any of the films he reviews. Some samples: *Showgirls:* 'Hooterfest.' *Waterworld*: 'In his newest film, *Waterworld*, Mr Costner has grown a set of gills, apparently so he can suck even harder.'

Addresses

John Howard Falloon
http://www.parliament.govt.nz/exec/bio/falloon.htm

John Howard's Home Page
http://ourworld.compuserve.com/homepages/John_Howard/

Johnny Howard Comedy Store
http://www.pcug.org.au/~stmcdona/howard.html

Prime Minister's Home Page
http://www.nla.gov.au/pmc/howard.html

Trip To India
http://hubcap.clemson.edu/~nsankar/india/trip.to.india.html

Guinea Pig FAQ
http://www.princeton.edu/~ecrocke/html/gpfaq.html

Pig Decoy Carving
http://www.tfb.com/~rharper/npca.html

Men Are Pigs!
http://www.rtis.com/nat/ent/pigs/

THE LIGHTER SIDE

Pig Pig
http://www.cs.cuhk.hk/~kfyip

Pig Gene Mapping Project
http://www.public.iastate.edu/~pigmap/pigmap.html

Fabulous Miss Piggy Page
http://www-leland.stanford.edu/~rosesage/Piggy.html

Babe
http://www.mca.com/universal_pictures/babe/

Mr Smarty Pants Knows
http://www.auschron.com/mrpants

Global Cheese Online
http://ccwf.cc.utexas.edu/~hope/global.html

CheeseNet
http://www.wgx.com/cheesenet/

The Cheese Page
http://www.zennet.com/cheese

Ferret Photo Gallery
http://www.optics.rochester.edu:8080/users/pgreene/gallery/

Korean Traditional Archery
http://www.dongguk.ac.kr/duvernay/korarch.html

String Figures From Around the World
http://www.ece.ucdavis.edu/~darsie/string.html

POSTCARDS FROM THE NET

Mr Menace: The Film Reviewer
http://www.seeokc.com/movies/menace/menace.html

Distractions, Games and Web Tricks

LET'S FACE it, the Net is a procrastinator's medium. And not just because sites take so long to download that you can wander off to read the paper or make a fresh pot of coffee while you're waiting.

No, the Net is made for procrastinators because … hang on, I've got a game of Hangman going here at **NetNoose**, I'll just be a moment …

OK, back with you. Now I know I was meant to be explaining something, but I can't quite recall what it was … hey, here's good old **Blue Dog**, one of the earliest and cutest sites on the web. Give him two numbers to add up and he'll bark the reply. What a smart pooch! His cousin, **Blue Pig**, is as stupid as a sock—ask him to add up by oinking and you could wait all day…

Sorry, what I was trying to say is that the Net has this terrible habit of distracting you from the task at hand. You know you should be researching seventeenth century philosophers or the habits of the boll weevil, but somehow you just can't keep your attention away from the cute (and usually pointless) diversions on offer.

Who could resist **Ferret Frenzy**, the Web's first interactive ferret racing game? This playful British site gives you £50 and your choice of furry steed from a line-up sporting names like Gnasher and Trouser King. You make your bet, head down to the track and watch your play money get frittered away.

Who would not be lured by **Web-A-Sketch**, a site which invites you to twiddle with your keyboard and make drawings on-screen? Log in and see a daily updated site, featuring efforts along the lines of 'Naked Crazy Guy Taking Shower'. There are monthly awards and a hall of fame. And at least if you shake your computer, that silver powdery stuff doesn't come out at the knobs and get all over your fingers.

Another childhood favourite revamped for the Web is **Battleship**. Deploy your fleet of five on the grid, then battle against the machine. It's slow, but oddly transfixing. The same site offers **Noughts and Crosses**. Another Web golden oldie, the **Mr Edible Starchy Tuber Head Page** (those toy companies always want to sue) allows you to dress a Mr Potato Head lookalike in all sorts of funky clobber.

If it's games you're looking for, try **The Case**, a weekly mini-mystery. If you sign up to the service, you get a new case mailed to you once a week. Additional clues are available on the Website (they have to keep up the hit rates or they'll never get advertisers), and they post the solution 36 hours later. I reckon the Webmaster did it.

In **The Peg Game**, you try to outwit the computer opponent by moving pieces off a board in a certain order. It looks easy, but like all bad things in life, it takes skill and careful thought, and can really put a dent in your afternoon if you're not careful. Similarly, **The Web Puzzler** randomly rearranges pictures of people and cartoon characters. It is your job to put them back together, but you can only swap pieces adjacent to each other.

Another game in which you try to outwit the machine is **Guess the Evil Dictator and/or Television Sitcom Character**. Who would have thought that Roseanne and Genghis Khan had more in common than just family likeness? Think of a television icon and then let the computer guess your target by asking you questions like: 'Do you have hair of gold like your mother's?' It's not for fans of Australian sitcoms, which are not included, but it's fun seeing how many moves it takes to get to the end.

Some of these little Web distractions are really rather lovely. **The Electric Postcard** is one of the sweetest and simplest sites

THE LIGHTER SIDE

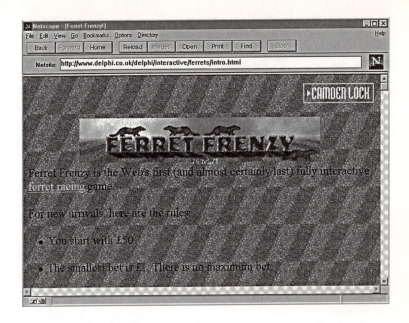

yet invented. It allows you to choose an image from the virtual Postcard Rack, compose and address a message to a friend and click the Mail button. That person will then be e-mailed with a note that includes a claim number and instructions on how to retrieve the card at the Electric Postcard Pick-up Window. Images include works by da Vinci, Vermeer, Gauguin, Van Gogh, Monet, Kandinsky, Magritte, Hopper and many others.

The Interactive Ego Booster is a site which behaves like an obsequious boot-licker, worshipping at the user's altar. Basically, I love it because it loves me like a shameless, pathetic puppy, updating its sycophancy a few times a minute: 'No-one is quite like you,' 'You are the nicest person I know,' 'When they made you, they broke the mould.' Some days, you just need unquestioning adoration.

Other days, of course, you're more likely to find solace in **The Surrealism Compliment Generator**: 'Your teeth are as soft as liquid stones poured from an aquamarine vase of solidifying flesh.' Stop. Reload. 'ENGINEER YOUR AUNT! Do it! You will be grateful for having done so. Yolutsky promises to cease his diddling with your ears.' Stop. Reload. 'Certainly your trout are more prosperous to vacuum than the flying coachmen of Czar Nicholai!'

If neither of these sites manages to brighten your morning, you obviously need help. **Bad Answer Man** is the Net oracle. Ask him a question and get an answer you don't want. **World Wide Web Ouija** is just as much use. Ask it a question and click on the mouse. Wow, nothing happens. Just like a real ouija board.

If you're looking for exercise, work out with **Let's Play Darts**, the geek version of a couple of laps of the pool. Shut your eyes, move the mouse and see if you can hit the target by instinct.

On the literary side of things, **Wacky Web Tales** is one of a number of stupid story generators. The idea is that you come up with a few words and it fills in the blanks, providing you with a story on a theme of your choice.

I know what you're saying. All this technological progress, all these billions of dollars of research and development, and the most the Net can come up with is cheap thrills. Well, the budget doesn't go much lower than **Kevin's Fridge Magnets**, a site that invites you to type in a line which will be rearranged on Kev's cyber-fridge door. **The Foam Bath Fish Time Page** is similar: ask it the time and it will rearrange foam fish on the screen to tell you. Who said everything has already been invented?

One of my favourite sites on the whole Web is **Buttons Galore**. Though the accompanying guff is kind of dorky, this is the place to go when all the blood has drained from your head and you're gripped in a mouse-clicking frenzy. It lets you click on hundreds of buttons that don't do anything. Mmmm, sweet relief.

The Virtual Keyboard is another spectacularly useless but enjoyable site: 'Click on the piano keys below to hear the notes they represent. It's just like a real piano, except that it's slower, smaller, sillier, and doesn't sound nearly as good.' And if you've got nothing better to do for 30 seconds after that, you could do worse than try the **Random Number Generator**, a site which . . . gives you random numbers.

It takes a special kind of boredness, though, to find excitement in the **Pig Latin** page. Type in any URL and this site will automatically convert it for you. When you start finding this fascinating, head to the **Confession Booth**, where you can bury your head in your hands, weep to the virtual cleric about your badness and receive a penance. I told it that my sin was misplaced priorities—I waste lots of time on stupid Web tricks when I should be working. 'This is a very serious matter,' it replied. 'If you are truly repentant, you must prove your remorse with the following act of contrition: Eat a bug and put up a picture of Barney (TV's hideous purple kiddy dinosaur) as your background window image.'

It's a good thing I don't know what 'repentant' means.

And if you must go back for one more time waster, I heartily recommend **This Is Where You Screwed Up**.

Addresses

NetNoose
http://home.netscape.com/people/nathan/netnoose/index.html

Blue Dog Can Count
http://kao.ini.cmu.edu:5550/bdf.html

Blue Pig Don't Oink
http://www.pigweb.com/bluepig.html

Ferret Frenzy
http://www.delphi.co.uk/delphi/interactive/ferrets/intro.html

Web-A-Sketch
http://www.digitalstuff.com/web-a-sketch/

Battleship
http://csugrad.cs.vt.edu/htbin/battleship?

Noughts and Crosses
http://csugrad.cs.vt.edu/~jfink/ttt.html

The Mr Edible Starchy Tuber Head Page
http://winnie.acsu.buffalo.edu/potatoe/

The Case
http://www.thecase.com/

The Peg Game
http://www.bu.edu/htbin/pegs

The Web Puzzler
http://imagiware.com/puzzle.cgi

Guess the Evil Dictator and/or Television Sitcom Character
http://sp1.berkeley.edu/dict.html

The Electronic Postcard
http://postcards.www.media.mit.edu/Postcards/

THE LIGHTER SIDE

The Interactive Ego Booster
http://web.syr.edu/~ablampac/ego/ego3.html

The Surrealism Compliment Generator
http://pharmdec.wustl.edu/cgi-bin/jardin_scripts/SCG

Bad Answer Man
http://www.tiac.net/users/lou35

World Wide Web Ouija
http://www.math.unh.edu/~black/cgi-bin/ouija.cgi

Let's Play Darts
http://weber.u.washington.edu/~kbroder/target.html

Wacky Web Tales
http://www.hmco.com:80/hmco/school/tales/

Kevin's Fridge Magnets
http://www.northcoast.com/cgi-bin/fridge

The Foam Bath Fish Time Page
http://redwood.northcoast.com/cgi-bin/fishtime

Buttons Galore
http://www.sas.upenn.edu/~pitharat/buttons.html

The WWW Virtual Keyboard
http://www.xmission.com/~mgm/misc/keyboard.html

Random Number Generator
http://www.ee.ethz.ch/~saibrahi/randnum.html

Pig Latin Converter
http://voyager.cns.ohiou.edu/~jrantane/menu/pig.html

Confession Booth
http://anther.learning.cs.cmu.edu/priest.html

This Is Where You Screwed Up
http://www.leonardo.net/a8/AHOME.html

Zarf's List of Interactive Games on the Web
http://www.leftfoot.com/realgames.html

Haiku Fans Online

SOMETIME in the late 1970s, punk poet John Cooper Clarke, known to his fans as The Bard of Salford, created what many scholars (not really, but it sounds more impressive) consider to be the finest haiku of the English language:

> *Writing a poem*
> *In seventeen syllables*
> *Is very diffic*

Of course, Shiki Masaoka, one of the greatest Japanese haiku poets, might have thought otherwise. Born in Matsuyama in 1867, he taught haiku and insisted that the short form must have three lines, of five, seven and five syllables, and include 'a special word which evokes the season'. 'The poet must be concise because of the brevity,' Shiki wrote, 'while concentrating deep spiritual understanding into the poem. The best haiku is clearly written, without metaphor, personification and other literary devices.'

The **Shiki Internet Haiku Salon** is a Web project intended to introduce the joy and wonder of dwarf poetry to the world in the hope that, with proper education and understanding, we will become appropriately familiar with and respectful of it.

The site is maintained by staff at Matsuyama University and includes a mailing list, where poems by contributors (yours are welcome) are criticised by serious haiku poets. It's a nice site but, really, haiku needs no introduction. The form is spreading like lantana through cyberspace, popping up where you'd least expect it.

Perhaps it's because at seventeen syllables, it matches the attention span of the average Net cruiser. Or maybe it's just that haiku is an intellectually egalitarian school of poetry, easy for beginners to get a grasp of, but also impossible to perfect. It's kind of like a literary *Tetris* — as you get better, the damn thing just gets harder.

Dhugal J. Lindsay's **Haiku Universe** is a good place to start if you wish to take up the hobby. A solid resource for haiku-related material, it has links to other pages, online essays, zines and complex (some would say obsessive) discourse on the various schools of haiku.

Haiku appears to be a global phenomenon. Most Net lovers rave about the way the medium collapses borders, even though what that means most of the time is that we have all moved even closer to America. As you wander about the haiku sites it becomes obvious that Net haiku fans may like the form, but they're really not that fussed with the old rules. Mostly, the cyber-poets manage to keep their efforts in three lines, but syllabically, well, near enough is often seen as good enough. And as for the idea of having a special word that evokes the season, well, that one gets left in the dictionary most of the time.

This is not the case at **Halloween Haikus**, a site which compiles kids' attempts at the form, a sort of naive literary art.

> On Halloween night
> With the full moon shining bright
> Death in the graveyard.

Mmm, very cheery. Despite the way our friends at the Shiki Internet Salon would have us behave, most Net users are incapable of taking things seriously, particularly when, as in this case, writing these poems feels more like doing a puzzle, a short brain-teaser.

It was obviously in this spirit that some Net jockey arrived at the (inevitable, really) idea of **SciFaiku**, 'a distinctive and powerful new form of expression for science fiction. It packs

THE LIGHTER SIDE

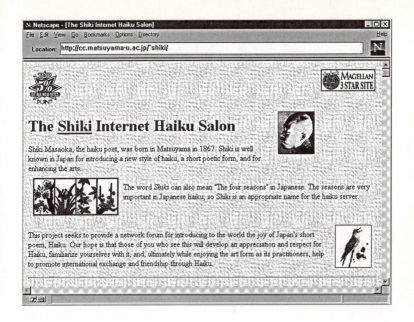

all the human insight, technology and vision of the future into a few poignant lines.' Like this:

> *Asteroids collide*
> *Without a sound*
> *We manoeuvre between fragments*

Très poignant. Almost as poignant as the entries in **The Bill Bixby Memorial Haiku Bakeoff**, a site dedicated to the star of TV programs such as *The Hulk*, *The Courtship of Eddie's Father* and *My Favorite Martian*. The haiku range from the merely nostalgic:

> *Silver things come up . . .*
> *Whoops! Here comes next door neighbour!*
> *Hide them with a hat!*

. . . to the incredibly moving:

73

> *Bill Bixby is dead.*
> *Dead, dead, dead, dead, dead, dead, dead*
> *Dead, dead, dead, dead, dead.*

Random Word Haiku 'borrows the verse form of haiku, but uses words chosen at random to fit the syllable structure. Of course, any meaning in such verse is accidental, yet it can be surprising how often it can seem to be more meaningful, whether profound, humorous or just delightfully bizarre, than chance would allow.'

> *Silicic enamel,*
> *listing atypical rectum,*
> *Pyrrha ovaritis.*

If you can handle the bastardisation of the haiku idea, the biggest and most interesting site is the **Spam Haiku Archive**. It has thousands of tributes to luncheon meat, archived by number or indexed by subject: addiction, art, cannibalism, childhood trauma, cinema, ingredients, jazz, literature, love, news, poverty, puns, recipes, religion, science, sex and versatility.

> *Old man seeks doctor.*
> *'I eat SPAM daily,' he says.*
> *Angioplasty.*

The archive is curated by John Cho, a globetrotter currently residing in Puerto Rico, who has also launched **The Editorial Haiku Page**, a site which publishes current affairs-oriented verse.

> *Farrakhan orates.*
> *Where was Leni Riefenstahl*
> *When he needed her?*

THE LIGHTER SIDE

Addresses

Shiki Internet Haiku Salon
http://mikan.cc.matsuyama-u.ac.jp:80/~shiki

Haiku Universe
http://www.ori.u-tokyo.ac.jp/~dhugal/haikuhome.html

Halloween Haikus
http://longwood.cs.ucf.edu/~MidLink/haikus.html

SciFaiku
http://www.crew.umich.edu/~brinck/poetry/manifesto.html

The Bill Bixby Memorial Haiku Bakeoff
http://www.mcs.net/~jorn/html/bixby.html

Random Word Haiku
http://www.cs.indiana.edu:800/cgi-bin/haiku

Spam Haiku Archive
http://www.naic.edu/~jcho/spam/archive.html

Editorial Haiku Page
http://www.naic.edu/~jcho/editorial/ehp.html

FAME

Sites About Celebrities

IN THE early days, one of the appeals of the Internet was that it was a celebrity-free zone, a place where ordinary people came to chat and share information and experiences. The World Wide Web, of course, changed all that by bringing multimedia potential, photographs, sound files, all manner of colour and movement.

There is now a site for virtually every famous person you can think of. Not only that, but the Web has developed into an alternative chat-show circuit—everyone from *HotWired* to Compuserve to the *Sydney Morning Herald* to the funky New York site **Sonic Net** has been setting up chat rooms and using celebs to attract punters to them.

The Net is a fan's medium. It allows anyone to publish his own demented ravings about stars, to build a cyber-chapel where others can come and pay tribute to Miss Next Big Thing or Mr I've Been Around. **Yahoo** has lists of sites devoted to various kinds of celebrities. Its alphabetical **Film Star** list has 200 links under 'A', 'B' and 'C' alone. Sandra Bullock has more than 30 sites in her honour. **Celebrity Addresses** is a list of sites dedicated to various actors, singers, comedians, models, politicians, athletes and authors. There are even sections for the deceased and the inhuman. Anything that links you to the fan tribute site for porn stalwart Ron Jeremy and breast film pioneer Russ Meyer can't be ignored. **Celebrities On-line** does a similar job, with a focus on TV and movie stars.

The Celebrity Chronicle looks at things from the fan's point of view. It's an online storage house for stories of close brushes with famous people. It also tells fans the three best ways to meet their idols: use public toilets, hang out near limos and eat out.

Many of the celeb sites on the Web are commercially

'(INSERT NAME HERE) IS A GOD/GODDESS!'

motivated. **Lifestyles International Astrological Foundation Famous Celebrities** offers 'astrological and psychological profiles for over 30 000 celebrities'. They'll cost you $US25 each. For another $20 you can find out if you and your celebrity obsession are sexually compatible.

Celebrity Lookalikes doesn't have much to offer yet, but there is a guy here who looks eerily like Jack Nicholson. **Doubletake Celebrity Doubles** is a much bigger service, with more than 300 lookalikes (unfortunately, there are only pictures of a few of them). Managed by Bruce Springsteen impersonator Arlen Pantel, the company offers lookalikes for hire, and covers everyone from Jim Carrey to Pope John Paul II—'Forgiveness of sins *not* guaranteed!'

If it's supermodels you're into, **Digital Catwalk** is the best directory of modelling resources on the Net, with directions to fashion houses, agencies, supermodels and specialist newsgroups. It has a huge collection of links and will take you to more photos of beautiful women than you could possibly want to see.

I'd rather get my jollies from a photo-free site, **Speaking Words of Wisdom: Bon Mots of the Supermodels**. Linda 'I don't wake up for less than $10,000 a day' Evangelista features prominently. My fave is one of Claudia Schiffer's contributions: 'I've looked in the mirror every day for 20 years—it's the same face.' Who was she expecting?

Dead Celebrities is a sprawling collection of pics of those who have gone to the Great Chat Show in the Sky (with links).

Some celebrities are famous just for being famous. **Angelyne** is blonde. She lives in Los Angeles. She has ambition. But more to the point, she has enormous breasts, the number of a good plastic surgeon and a husband who can afford to have billboards in LA, New York and Paris adorned with her image. 'These promotional advertisements, in effect, are her "agent",'

FAME

her site explains. 'Angelyne receives calls from all over the world through her billboards for magazine interviews, photo layouts, television and talk show appearances, personal appearances, and feature film roles.' (No, I've never seen them either.) 'Angelyne is a true star of Hollywood. Not content to be labelled a singer, actress, dancer, or performer of any kind, her image and persona capture the glamour and magic of stardom in its purest form.'

Addresses

Sonic Net
http://www.sonicnet.com/sonicore

Yahoo
http://www.yahoo.com

Yahoo Film Stars
http://www.yahoo.com/Entertainment/Movies_and_Films/Actors_and_Actresses/

Celebrity Addresses
http://www2.islandnet.com/~luree/fanmail.html

Celebrities On-line
http://www.mgal.com/links/celeb.html

The Celebrity Chronicle
http://www.polaris.net/~merlin/fame.html

Lifestyles International Astrological Foundation Famous Celebrities
http://www.lifeintl.com/celeb.html

Celebrity Lookalikes
http://www.netgrafx.com/lookalikes/

Doubletake Celebrity Doubles
http://nwwnet.com/ww/dbltake.htm

Celebrity Heads
http://www.aseere-systems.com/stars/welcome.html

Digital Catwalk
http://www.bloodshot.com/Digital_Catwalk/

Speaking Words of Wisdom: Bon Mots of the Supermodels
http://www.sils.umich.edu/~sooty/thoughts.html

Dead Celebrities
http://www.shore.net/~cbo/

Angelyne
http://www.worldartists.com/world/angelyne.htm

See also...

The Bruno Watch
http://www.accsyst.com/writers/bruno.htm

The diary of a guy who lives across the road from Bruce Willis.

The Casbah
http://www.dsiegel.com

David Siegel's excellent (many would say classic) site offers advice on how to 'be' a celebrity. 'As casually as you or I breathe air, Siegel dispenses expert counsel: on HTML, on the principles of graphic design, on grammar and vegetarian cooking and even the best fertilisation techniques for women at the tail-end of their child-bearing years. For some reason, however, Siegel masks the true purpose of his site. Perhaps like the Pat Morita character in *The Karate Kid*, he believes his lessons are more effective if you don't quite understand what you're learning ... what they're actually being taught, through the thorough but veiled set of rules Siegel puts into practice at his site, is how to manufacture celebrity charisma, the preternatural sheen of Someone Who Matters ...'

Gossip, Scuttlebutt and Rumour

ON THE list of primary human needs, slightly below sex, food and sleep, there is gossip. I don't know about you, but I just can't get through the day without wondering if Demi Moore has converted to some kooky religion. Or if Gary Sweet has a chest-waxing problem. Or if Woody Allen has developed a liking for adults.

Living in the Era of Pointless Celebrity, we are fascinated and entranced by the not-so-secret lives of the rich and famous. Perhaps it's so we can feel better about ourselves, so we can mutter things like: 'Mr Film Star may be snorting coke out of Miss September's cleavage while I'm dateless and trying to stop my sofa from being repossessed, but at least my ex-wife isn't blabbing to the tabloids about my problems.'

The Web is a natural forum for all kinds of gossip. The first place to stop for the celebrity kind is **People** magazine. Why wait for *Who Weekly* to repackage the material from its sister when you can get it quicker and cheaper on the Web? (And doesn't this have interesting implications for the future of syndicated print journalism?) This site lets you read the main stories in the current issues of *People* and its sister publication *Entertainment Weekly* ('Liz Taylor Marries Again', 'Michael Jackson Shows Us Round Neverland'), and the magazines' sizeable celebrity archives. It also has a daily gossip section, and lots of little interactive gimmicks that let you do things like cast your Oscars vote.

Mr Showbiz has long been considered one of the best sites on the Web, and was a finalist in the 1995 Cool Site of the Year contest. This celeb-o-matic spot has quickly become something of an institution in Hollywood—local cafes give away Mr Showbiz postcards. To go with its '50s graphics, the site has a kooky theme song, special features, its own Celebrity Lounge

FAME

chat rooms and The Water Cooler, a regular poll space which has tackled tough questions like: Will George Clooney make a better Batman than Val Kilmer? Updated daily, it offers news, reviews, photos, bios, Oscars history and a gossip section called Scoop. Here's a sample:

> Bar Marmont, the legendary Chateau Marmont hotel's brand new watering hole, is Hollywood's latest hot spot. On a recent weeknight, actor Christian Slater entertained three young beauties at a table in the back, Mr and Mrs Wayne Gretzky shared a few cocktails with *Melrose Place* star Daphne Zuniga, and Gabriel Byrne and Counting Crows singer Adam Duritz (sans his *Friends* friend Jennifer Aniston) worked the room.
>
> What does the bar have that attracts such a star-studded clientele? Well, there's the faded-splendour ambience; according to one patron, the small, dark space has 'the feel of a four-star hotel in Shanghai during the war'. There's also Constance, the bald hostess in the leopard suit, who is one of Tinseltown's most famous transvestites.

Book my ticket, Ma, I'm leaving.

If you're the kind of person who harrumphs about invading the privacy of these poor, downtrodden rich people, then **Hollywood Online** might be more your speed. It doesn't so much traffic in gossip as information, but the lines between the two can blur. Hollywood Online is an attitude-free, star-studded affair, a site which leaves every stone unturned in its shameless attempt to glorify all that is the movies.

A great resource site, it offers all kinds of downloadable goodies: photographs, trailers and interactive press kits (a new fad). It has everything you could want to know about upcoming films and stars, and is guaranteed never to stray off the tasteful path. And because Australia lags behind the US in release schedules, most of it is news. Use its 'New' and 'Hot' sections to get the latest.

Hollywood Online's spiritual opposite is **Cyber Sleaze**. Here, in a special wing of his Metaverse site, former American MTV jock Adam Curry shovels his daily quota of goss, going a step or two beyond what most are willing to print. One week I dropped in, it carried a Tom Jones Australian sex scandal story, as well as items about rappers The Beastie Boys pleading with fans to return a 7 m inflatable penis stolen shortly after their 1992 world tour, singer Sinéad O'Connor growing her hair out for the birth of her new baby, and actress Geena Davis drinking reindeer blood to attract protective fairies.

If you're still hungry you could try **Somethin' Juicy**. It's fairly tame by some standards, but carries the odd gem. And you can have it delivered fresh every morning if you subscribe. Or visit the newsgroup **alt.showbiz.gossip**, where you can submerge yourself in the foetid pool of airport celebrity sightings and unsubstantiated career rumours: ''80s pop dweeb Debbie Gibson is dead!' 'The Pink Power Ranger has left the show!'

FAME

And if that isn't enough, try **alt.binaries.nude.celebrities**. No, on second thought, don't. It's much easier just to go to one of the dozens of naked famous people sites. But don't always believe what you see—there are a lot of Net artists pretty good at grafting famous heads onto other bodies. If the Net has given us nothing else, it has come up with Frankenporn.

Addresses

People
http://pathfinder.com/@@ZvHaz7FPcgEAQBNn/people

Mr Showbiz
http://www.mrshowbiz.com

Hollywood Online
http://www.hollywood.com

Cyber Sleaze
http://metaverse.com/vibe/sleaze/index.html

Somethin' Juicy
http://www.dnx.com/gossip/

Famous People Who Hang Out Online

THE WEB has been a gift for celebrities. It allows people whose fame has removed them from everyday society to get back into it, anonymously, cruise around and check out what the common folk are talking about.

Especially when we're talking about them. *Hitchhiker's Guide to the Galaxy* author **Douglas Adams** (e-mail address: *adams@cerf.net*) is a semi-regular visitor to the **alt.fan.douglas-adams** newsgroup. Adams doesn't reply to every question asked in the group (he's particularly good at ignoring anything with '42' in the title) but says he enjoys the direct feedback that the Net offers him:

> I have always made my various e-mail addresses freely available. I'm happy to be available by e-mail because it's much easier and quicker to answer than regular snailmail—which tends to pile up in huge backlogs which I then have to get a secretary to deal with. I guard my home address and phone number because I have my privacy, my family, my friends and security to think about. But cyberspace is—or can be—a good, friendly and egalitarian place to meet.
>
> One of the oddities about being a writer (as opposed to, say, an actor or a musician) is the long time lag between doing something and getting a reaction to it. A writer is constantly out of step with his/her audience, and the effects are often quite peculiar. Someone asks you to explain something you wrote a year or two ago, and sometimes you can hardly remember writing it.
>
> There's not much anyone can do about that (yet) but still the kind of regular contact I get with readers on the Internet helps to bridge some of the gap. I also enjoy corresponding with people in completely different areas of the Net. . . . I get the occasional 'Excuse me for asking, but are you the DA who wrote . . . ?' etc, which is fine, but I really like to leave it behind if I can.

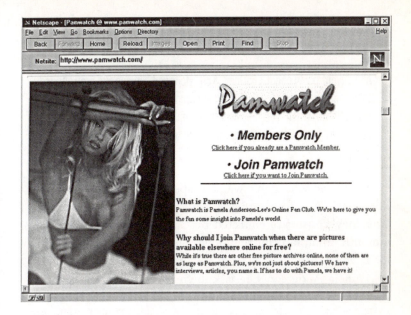

Adams is not alone. Net lore has it that many famous people don alternative identities and roam among their fans unrecognised, participating in discussions or hovering in the background of conversations about themselves—you could call it ego-tourism.

'Those who are worried about attracting kooks will keep their identities secret,' says Brian Smith, who runs a Website dedicated to the rock band **The Church**, 'but those who trust Internet users to be sensible aren't shy about it. Actress Sandra Bullock, for example, is known to use the Net a lot, doing all the things regular Net denizens do. But she keeps her identity hidden.'

The most famous and vocal newsgroup star is the unstoppable media tart Courtney Love, who has inspired more sightings stories than Elvis. Troy, a New Zealand student who regularly hangs out in the **alt.fan.courtney-love** newsgroup, says Love maintains a presence in the forum without either reading or posting to it directly.

> All relevant posts about Courtney, Kurt, Hole and Nirvana etc are collected by a woman named Carol from newsgroups and posted to Courtney in a digest form. When Courtney wants to reply to something she posts her answer to Carol who then posts it to alt.fan.courtney-love and the other groups.

For those who don't want to spend their whole lives monitoring the Net for words of Love wisdom, says Troy, 'All of Courtney's posts are collected by Carol and posted about once a month on alt.fan.courtney-love. So it is easy to get the whole lot if you want.'

Pamela Anderson Lee is known to regularly check out the **Pamwatch** Web site and actually mails to it. And **Madonna's Official Site** offers you the chance to e-mail her: 'I really want to know what you think of my new album. Talk to me! You can e-mail me at *madonna@wbr.com*.' Of course, it's probably the same as snailmailing her record company—some flunky will go through the messages and might pass on one in every thousand.

Though there are Websites and newsgroups dedicated to film and TV stars, supermodels, authors, comedians, politicians and sports people, it is musicians who have made the most sense of Net culture to date.

Midnight Oil was slogging its way around the backblocks of the United States in 1993 when drummer Rob Hirst first encountered the Internet. 'We kept ringing up our publicist in New York from Seattle or Albuquerque or wherever,' he recalls, 'and she'd say "I've heard all about the show last night—I've already got the songs you played, the audience reaction and the number of people at the gig."'

Without the band's knowledge, American Oils fans had set up a virtual community to trade information and gossip. **Oil**

Base has hundreds of pages of discographies, lyrics, live show lists and band minutiae. 'It turned out to be incredibly detailed and well researched,' Hirst says. 'We were quite taken by surprise by the amount of debate that was going on.'

Singer **Paul Kelly** has a similar story:

> In 1994, I was doing a little tour of the States. I had done a show in Los Angeles and the next day went to San Francisco. I was arriving at the stage door of the theatre for my sound check and this fellow asked if I was going to play 'Difficult Woman'. I had played it for the first time the night before in LA.
>
> I said: 'How do you know about a song I have never recorded and which I only played for the first time last night?' He found out about it on the Internet. He told me there were various discussions going on about concerts and he had spoken to someone that day who had given a little report of the concert the night before.

More and more, bands are discovering that thriving fan communities have beaten them to cyberspace, establishing a presence, creating discussion groups and Websites that range from simple and concise to incredibly detailed and eerily obsessive.

Boom Crash Opera maintains its own site, taking it seriously enough for bass player Ian Tilley to go to technical college to learn HyperText Markup Language (or HTML) — the computer language which enables you to create a site. Why do it themselves? Says guitarist Peter Farnan:

> The main thing was this feeling that with the way you express yourself expanding into new media, we were actually losing control of what we were. We got our own site up early this year [1995]. We didn't do all the multimedia authoring—we supplied the bits and pieces to the server and they put the thing up. Then we thought, 'That's ridiculous, we should be doing the work ourselves,' so we pulled it down and redid it. The

thing is, it should have the feel of the artists doing it rather than somebody else. Otherwise, it's just the equivalent of hiring somebody to do a glossy brochure for you.

Sydney band **Single Gun Theory**, which has always found larger audiences in Europe and North America than at home, has also used the Web to stay in touch. Its Website, authored by band member Pete Rivett-Carnac, has a bio, the latest news, videos, song samples, lyrics, a photo gallery, some merchandise, and directions to the band's favourite sites. Rivett-Carnac says:

> I just wanted to set up a web site for fun, to learn HTML, Java etc. (I'm really quite a dweeb at heart). Single Gun was a good excuse for me to spend some spare time doing that.
>
> For us, it means we don't have to mail out 'fan' info to people any more—well, not nearly so often, anyway. So *many* North Americans are on the Internet, and that's where our biggest 'fan' base is (sorry, even these days, I'm still slightly uncomfortable using the word 'fan'; hence the inverted commas).
>
> We just hate that 'pop star' crap. Even though we're not 'stars', we seem to be at a level of 'minor stardom' for some people, mainly in the US—which is kinda funny for us, shuffling off to work each day in our suits. Anyway, I just think it's good to keep in touch with the people who buy our records.

On the other side of the equation, Brian Smith says the feedback from The Church on his efforts was not exactly what he had expected:

> [Lead singer] Steve Kilbey's attitude to publicity and the whole 'rock star' thing, where everyone wants to know everything about you, is that it stinks. He wants his music to be the only thing people see of him. As you'd expect, this puts a dampener on a page devoted to information about the band. So he's politely interested, but doesn't want to actively

take part in the design or content of the page. He has, however, sent me a 'prose poem', which I've put on.

So far, I've learned about Web page design, of course, and that people are very grateful when you build the first Web page to cover a topic that's close to their hearts. If you want to attract a band's attention, then build the BEST Web page you can and keep it current—that way nobody will even try to outdo you.

Addresses

Douglas Adams
http://www.contrib.andrew.cmu.edu/~studarus/douglas_adams

The Douglas Adams Worship Page
http://www.umd.umich.edu/~nhughes/dna/

The Church
http://www.rucc.net.au/church/

Pamwatch
http://www.pamwatch.com

Madonna's Official Site
http://www.wbr.com/madonna

Oil Base
http://www.stevens-tech.edu/~dbelson/oilbase/

Paul Kelly Info Page
http://www.amws.com.au/pk/

Boom Crash Opera
http://www.geko.com.au/~bco/

Single Gun Theory
http://sgt.com.au/

See also...

The Hitchhiker's Guide to the Galaxy
http://www.connectnet.net.au/~abutt/hitchhikers.html

Australian site which catalogues the various manifestations of the *Guide* and links to other pages.

Heart of Gold
http://www.inmind.com/people/robbrad/fordp.html

Another, slightly larger list of links to sites dealing with *Hitchhiker's* and its author.

Ghostwriters Australian Web Pages
http://www.magna.com.au/~ghostie/gw_home.htm

Rob Hirst's *other* band.

Elvis Presley Is Alive and Well in Cyberspace

ELVIS PRESLEY turned 62 this year, if you want to believe the **alt.elvis.sightings** newsgroup. And if you don't, well, there's no doubt Presley has been just as interesting dead as alive. Elvis has become a kind of cultural blank slate on which we write our own mythology. People see in him what they want to: lover, fighter, holy fool, romantic, lecher, innocent abroad, good old boy, genius, kitsch object, idiot savant. Despite the vast amount of biographical detail amassed in the hundreds of books about him, our idea of Elvis remains diffuse and amorphous. Perhaps that is why Elvis continues to drive the collective imagination. Certainly, he is alive and well in cyberspace.

It occurred to me that it might be fun to check out a few Elvis sites. I started with **Disgraceland**, a 'cybermansion' and self-described humorous tribute to the man and his fans. I am not often floored by sites, but this one knocked me for six: room after virtual room of Elvisiana.

The Showroom features photos of 'the renowned Friz-Elvis, the world's first budgie Elvis impersonator!' Friz-Elvis turns out to be a suitably altered image of somebody's pet. Those wacky Internet artists—do they never sleep? Friz-Elvis, of course, has his own Internet fan club. A hunka-hunka birdee love!

The next room, Big Elvis, is a lovingly curated collection of Elvis sites on the Web, including a few from Australia. Here are straightforward Elvis pages, academic theories, oddities, impersonators, sacred sites, commercial outlets, art galleries, joke pages, anything even vaguely related to the King. The list has obviously been collated by an obsessive with a catholic sense of the importance of Elvisness and its many manifestations. There are more than 200 links and the list is growing at an unhealthy rate. Not even that Net faithful *The X Files* claims this kind of penetration. Here are just a few of the more interesting sites:

Eddie Fadal's Elvis Presley Museum. Fadal was a lifelong friend of Elvis and maintained a small museum of Elvis mementoes in Waco, Texas. Now it's gone virtual, with 'highly valuable and stimulating sights of some of our collectibles, such as the white shorts that Elvis wore to play racquetball'.

Who Killed Elvis? A serious essay on the zodiac's part in Elvis's downfall.

> When examining Elvis' natal chart my first hunch was that Elvis' moon in Pisces was the deadly fiend. Whatever else had happened to Elvis during his life (i.e. even if he never got that guitar at the drug store when he was 8) he would probably have ended up being an alcoholic or drug addict of some sort anyway, after his mother died, because he would find it so difficult to cope with the sudden loss of this solid emotional bond. People with Pisces Moon are very susceptible to drugs, and the worse the rest of their chart is, the more susceptible they become.

I knew there had to be a rational explanation.

The Elvis Theory. Elvis, obviously an alien, introduced rock 'n' roll to us. The young of Earth adopted it because it wasn't alien to them. They were Elvis's troops. It was music from their home planet. Yikes.

The Strange Case of the Lost Elvis Diaries. Reporter Jeff Parrish finds a note on his desk with the following message: 'I have the lost Elvis diaries and they can be yours . . . for a price.' With those words, Jeff finds himself in hot pursuit of a big story and knee-deep in intrigue. He enters a bizarre world filled with CIA agents, Elvis impersonators, and even the Mafia . . . all of them after the legendary lost journals of the King of

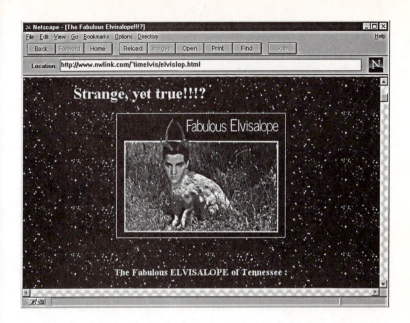

Rock and Roll. But are they for real, or is it all a don't-be-cruel hoax?

Zucchini Elvis. Seattle gardener Delroy Sykes was shocked to discover a zucchini growing in his garden that bore a striking and eerie resemblance to the late, great King himself. 'I was choked up and misty-eyed,' Sykes said. 'It was like a message from Elvis his self saying to me every thing would be okay in the world.' With dubious photo.

The Jeweler to the Stars. Mordechai Yerushalmi ran a jewellery store at the Las Vegas Hilton. Read his fascinating tale of the diamonds he almost sold to Elvis and how the King's passing cost him what would have been one of the most memorable deals of his life.

The Fabulous Elvisalope. An animal clearly related to Friz-Elvis the budgie. 'Elvisalopes are the rarest animals in

North America. A cross between a now extinct small deer, a species of rabbit and rockabillies, they are extremely shy and wild. Elvisalopes are easily recognised by their twitching legs, gyrating pelvises and characteristic sneer.'

Disgraceland's other rooms offer you the chance to check out memorabilia and photo collections, read Elvis headlines, catch up on sightings, join a fan club and even indulge in a spot of virtual cow tipping (a very Southern sport, perhaps Elvis's favourite). But the best is saved for last.

'Before you leave, why not pay your respects to the King by visiting the Disgraceland Chapel and Meditation Room?' Not only does the chapel have a new ceiling (yet more Elvis art, this time with his face grafted onto Michelangelo's best Sistine work), it offers another set of links, to Elvis churches. Yes, churches. They're all here: **The 24-Hour Church of Elvis**; **The First Presleyterian Church of Elvis the Divine**; and **The First Church of Jesus Christ, Elvis**.

Now, perhaps, we're finally getting to see Elvis in his true light. He may have been The Second Coming. A link to a comparison of the uncanny similarities between the lives of **Elvis and Jesus** offers further evidence:

> Jesus said: 'Love thy neighbor' (Matthew 22:39). Elvis said: 'Don't be cruel' (RCA, 1956).
> Jesus is the Lord's shepherd. Elvis dated Cybill Shepherd.
> Jesus was part of the Trinity. Elvis' first band was a trio.
> Jesus walked on water (Matthew 14:25). Elvis surfed. (Blue Hawaii, Paramount, 1965).
> Jesus's countenance was like lightning, and his raiment white as snow. (Matthew 28:3). Elvis wore snow-white jumpsuits with lightning bolts.
> Jesus lived in state of grace in a Near Eastern land. Elvis lived in Graceland in a nearly eastern state.

> Lord, I believe.

Addresses

Disgraceland
http://nwlink.com/~timelvis

Eddie Fadal's Elvis Presley Museum
http://info.acm.org/~yannone/elvis/elvis.html

Who Killed Elvis?
http://www.on.net/users/rob/psychic/elvis.html

The Elvis Theory
http://www.missouri.edu/~wleric/gallery/elvis.html

The Strange Case of the Lost Elvis Diaries
http://www.bookzone.com/bookzone/10000291.html

Zucchini Elvis
http://nwlink.com/~timelvis/zuchini.html

The Jeweler to the Stars
http://www.manifest.com:80/Jewelers/About/index.html

The Fabulous Elvisalope
http://nwlink.com/~timelvis/elvislop.html

The 24-Hour Church of Elvis
http://www.churchofelvis.com

The First Presleyterian Church of Elvis the Divine
http://pages.prodigy.com/NJ/zvqj45a/zvqj45a.html

The First Church of Jesus Christ, Elvis
http://jubal.westnet.com/hyperdiscordia/sacred_heart_elvis.html

Elvis and Jesus
http://www.mit.edu:8001/activities/41West/humour/Elvis_vs_Jesus.html

See also...

Elvis in Latin
http://www.cs.uoregon.edu/~bhelm/misc/elvis.html

The King is dead. The language is dead. Whammo! Perfect marriage. Dr Jukka Ammondt and the Finnish Broadcast Corporation Choir have released *The Legend Lives Forever In Latin*, an album of Presley songs in Latin. Check out 'Tutti Frutti' (Totus Potus), 'Blue Suede Shoes' (Glauci Calcei), 'Love Me Tender' (Tenere Me Ama), 'It's Now or Never' (Nunc Hic Aut Numquam) and 'Can't Help Falling in Love' (Non Adamare Non Possum).

The Doghaus Elvis Collection
http://www.doghaus.com/intro.html

'A virtual exhibition of bizarre, strange (some say psychotic) and unusual Elvis Presley memorabilia, souvenirs and collectables.' Includes 'Love Me Tender' conditioning shampoo, Elvis air freshener, King cologne, Elvis snowdomes, Elvis salt and pepper shakers and more.

The Net Court Room

Did Kurt Cobain Kill Himself?

TOM GRANT feels like a pariah. And well he might. He is using the Internet to say something many people don't want to hear. But he believes he has to say it. He believes Kurt Cobain, the lead singer and guitarist of Nirvana, did not kill himself. The Beverly Hills private detective believes Cobain was murdered.

Grant concedes that the idea sounds far-fetched. But unlike most people who come up with outlandish theories after celebrity deaths, he is in a position to cast doubt on the official version of events. At the time, and for some months afterwards, he was working for the singer's wife, Courtney Love. He was in Seattle the week Cobain died, looking for him at her behest. He searched the Lake Washington house 36 hours before the body was found, failing to notice, in the dark, the room above the garage where Cobain's body already lay. He has since spent most of his time investigating the case, refusing to let it close quietly.

Grant has been accumulating 'evidence' since the death, and is releasing it in stages on the Net, the only arena in which he believes he can get a fair hearing. The Net has offered him a way of routing around the mass media, of getting his material to the public without the obfuscation, misinterpretation and bias of journalists. For a year or so, his regular bulletins were being posted on the Net (where they create a fair amount of controversy) by a third party, but earlier this year Grant set up his own site, to make the line of communication even shorter.

He claims he has a pretty good idea who pulled the trigger and why, but does not want to put the cart before the horse. For the moment, he insists, he is concerned with basics:

I'M TELLING YOU, HE'S INNOCENT

> What I am out to prove is that it was not suicide, that this case was completely bungled by the Seattle police department and that it needs to be reopened. Everybody has been completely misled. Very few facts and details published in the media have been accurate. I am completely convinced that if it gets to the point where we are dealing with authorities which are honestly searching for the truth, not just trying to cover up their own sloppy work, this case will fall in a week. It's a very simple case to get to the bottom of.

So far, Grant's claims have been met with a wall of silence, which he knows does not make his case look any better. But he perseveres, insisting calmly:

> I am not a conspiracy nut. I have never seen *JFK*. I am the last person in the world that would want to hear stuff like this. I knew that, by doing this, I was going to put myself in a position of total embarrassment and humiliation. I feel naked out here, like a clown. At the same time, I keep reading about these kids killing themselves.

In the next room is a box of letters of support. When our interview is over, he sifts through them, scooping them out in handfuls until he finds the ones he's looking for, a small bundle from teenagers who say they were thinking of ending their lives until they heard what he had to say. These e-mail messages, these scraps of paper with their adolescent handwriting, keep Grant's zeal burning.

> It really doesn't matter that much to me how people respond to what I say. You can call me whatever you want. You can say I'm the biggest idiot on the face of the planet. I just have this need to inform the public.

Kurt Cobain's body was found in the 'greenhouse', a room above the garage, at his home in Seattle at 8.45 a.m. on 8 April 1994. The version of events which appeared in the media in the following weeks, based on police statements and word of

mouth, supports an open-and-shut suicide verdict. Distilled, it is this: Cobain was found with marks from firing the gun on his hand. His wallet was beside him, with the driver's licence carefully placed on top of it to aid identification. The door to the room was locked—the type of lock that worked from the inside, with a stool wedged against it. There was a suicide note beside the body. Says Grant:

> All these things that painted this suicidal picture of this guy, that he barricaded himself in there, wedged the stool against the door, left his driver's licence out ... they're not true. If the guy did commit suicide, then let's at least get the facts straight.'

Grant believes Cobain was not suicidal, that at the time of his death, he was leaving his marriage, his band and his public career, heading to the East Coast, where he planned to work with REM's Michael Stipe. 'He was in the process of leaving

Courtney,' Grant says. 'There is no doubt about that.' He says Love told him herself that Cobain had asked for a divorce.

THE CREDIT CARD

> Kurt had a credit card when he was at LA airport (on April 1). He used it to update his flight back to Seattle. The credit card wasn't in his wallet when he was found. That card was being used a few hours before the body was found—at the very least, a couple of days after Kurt was dead. The police never found out who was using it. The person using that credit card was trying to leave a trail. How can you close a case like this without finding out?

THE SCENE

Grant says Cobain did not barricade himself inside the room as the police and press reported. He produces the police report, which suggests the stool was on the opposite side of the room, next to an unlocked door which led out to a balcony. He also says the door could be locked by someone pulling it shut as he or she left.

THE DRIVER'S LICENCE

> In the police report it says the first officer, who observed the wallet lying on the floor, picked it up, opened it, took out the driver's licence and set it on top for a photograph.

THE NOTE

Grant believes the letter, written in a tight, left-handed scrawl, is open to interpretation. He says the 'so-called suicide note' to Courtney and daughter Frances was actually a retirement letter to fans. He points out that the body of the letter contains no direct reference to death, being principally an explanation of why he didn't want to be in the limelight any more. Grant also believes the note was written by more than one hand. He shows me a copy, pointing out the lines at the end: 'Please keep going Courtney, for Frances, for her life, which will be so much happier without me, I love you, I love you.' These lines, he says, appear to have been added later. They are in a different size.

THE GUN

The police report notes that 'there were marks on Cobain's hands consistent with the firing of the weapon'. 'I'd like to see them describe those marks,' Grant says. Grant believes no marks existed. He test-fired an identical weapon eighteen times:

> My hands were totally clean: no abrasions, no marks. That told me a little something, but I'd be the first to agree that that wasn't the weapon that he used—you can't say with certainty that the weapon he used didn't have something different about it that could have caused a mark. But I don't believe it did.

THE CORONER'S REPORT

Though the police reports have been made available, the coroner's report has not. Grant believes this is because there is no forensic evidence to prove Cobain's death was a suicide:

> When I first started speaking out, almost a year ago, I said that the coroner and the police would never be able to prove forensically that this was a self-inflicted gunshot wound. That's how much I am convinced that this was a murder. If I was wrong about this, they could have shut me down a long time ago.

Grant twice informed the Seattle police department of his suspicions, the day the body was found and a week later when he 'laid out fully' his problems with the case. He says he wasn't taken seriously, attributing the response to traditional police resistance to input from private investigators. He has since published more than 20 000 words relating to his investigation on the Net. The response has been muted.

Cobain's mother told reporters that Grant was just seeking 'his 15 minutes of fame', and has said nothing since. Courtney Love has not responded at all. The Seattle police department also declines to comment.

To believe or not to believe? Having spent a couple of hours with Grant, I have no doubt that he believes what he is saying. He is implacably serious and sincere. And who knows? He may be right. Nobody famous gets to rest in peace at this end of the twentieth century. Every celebrity death has its conspiracy theories, its rumours, its whisperings. In that light, it is hard to judge.

Still, Grant is simply asking questions about the conduct of a case. And some of those questions seem pretty reasonable:

> My motive here is pure and simple. I believe, whether anybody else does or not, that Kurt Cobain was murdered. There are kids out there killing themselves over a mirage. This suicide didn't happen. So if I can be sued for saying that or arrested or anything else, go for it. Because I'm not going to shut up.

Addresses

The Kurt Cobain Suicide Investigation Site
http://websites.earthlink.net/~tomgrant/

See also...

Yahoo:Entertainment:Music:Artists:Nirvana
http://www.yahoo.com/Entertainment/Music/Artists/Nirvana/

There are more than 50 Websites devoted to this band, all indexed here. The sites more specifically relating to Cobain and his death include:

Nirvana Frontman Kurt Cobain Is Dead
http://www.ludd.luth.se/misc/nirvana/misc/dead.html

Has another copy of the suicide note, easy to access when Grant's site is on the fritz.

I'm Sorry Kurt
http://web.dbtech.net/~jamiller/kurt.htm

A site which argues that Kurt would have been a whole lot happier if he'd just become a Christian and lived a decent life.

Kurt Cobain's Magic Talking 8-Ball
http://www.webcom.com/xcomm/cobain/

'If you've got burning questions about some of life's mysteries, you may find the answers through the Kurt Cobain Talking Eight-Ball. The Punk Poet of Grunge is standing by on the other side, ready to help you tackle the big questions.'

Why Tom Grant Should Not Be Believed
http://www.netcom.com/~dperle/nirvana/index.html

Web drifter David Perle has taken it upon himself to be the compiler of the equal and opposite response to Tom Grant. His site has extensive refutations of Grant's claims, and correspondence on the matter with Courtney Love (we think).

Nostalgia for the 1980s

THEY SAY that if you can remember the '60s, you weren't there. Well, I wasn't there and I remember them with appalling clarity, thanks to the relentless self-mythologising of the Baby Boomer generation, which has obliged us to live and relive the '60s ever since.

As for the '70s, the less remembered about them the better. Particularly because the early '90s were much too fixated on that era anyway.

And the '80s? Well, that much maligned decade is overdue for some spit-and-polish revisionism. It's had a very bad reputation since Michael Jackson and Madonna came to epitomise it. No decade deserves that. But if mainstream culture isn't ready to step back in time, the Net certainly is.

The 80s Server looks like early MTV fodder—all bright colours, cut and paste advertising layout and self-conscious wackiness. Think Toni Basil or Cyndi Lauper. The site pastes a cheery grin across the top of everything as it trawls through a variety of areas: entertainment, fads and fashions, icons, trivia and events.

It also has a timeline and a monthly feature—the last time I looked it was on the *Challenger* space shuttle explosion of 1986. This, by the way, did not offer a link to Chuck Farnham's Weird World's black-box 'transcript' of the last few moments of the crew's lives. Which gives you some idea of the prevailing aesthetic—this is the '80s writ nice.

Things get better, if cheaper, from there. **The Big Eighties** is less ambitious, a list of home pages of bands which supposedly defined the decade, from Adam Ant to Wilson Phillips (with detours along the way to a-ha, Mike and the Mechanics, Poison and Weird Al Yankovic). All in all, it's the kind of list you really wouldn't want to find your name on. Which is not

FAME

to say that there weren't great bands in the '80s. It's just that no-one has immortalised most of them on the Web yet.

The Cheezy 80s Page does a similar thing, but with a little more grunt. It includes among its attractions a list of pages of acts that really don't deserve Web recognition but have it regardless. Do we really need to be reminded of The Buggles? Do we need to do the safety dance one more time with Men Without Hats? Bananarama, Samantha Fox, Debbie Gibson, Huey Lewis and the News, Men At Work, Gary Numan, Real Life, Tiffany ... they're all here, all preserved in Net aspic. The site also links to **The Random 80s Lyrics Page**, which it describes as 'a source of much wisdom and enlightenment, and the true lyrics to *Take On Me*'.

There's a deeply attractive jellybean wallpaper on **Chucky G's 1980s Web Pages** (Ronald Reagan's favourite lollies, for those with short memories). The site covers bands, politics, movies, radio, TV, leisure activities and articles on the era.

Livin' in the Eighties looks back from what can only be described as a teen perspective. The list of the Top Ten films of the decade owes a lot more to John Hughes than Martin Scorsese. And Pee-Wee Herman knocks Robert De Niro out of the way in the best actor category. But at least the site goes a little wider in its search than some others, taking in TV shows (can you believe *ALF* has his own site?), cartoons, toys, food and drink (mmm, New Coke), movies, music, fashion, language, technology and various faddish recreation pursuits, from breakdancing to *Trivial Pursuit*.

Spiral into the Eighties with Jeff tracks through a lot of the same bands and movies, but it too is worth it for the side alleys, detours into arcana like the theme songs of *The A-Team* and *Knight Rider*, the Smurf fad and PacMan, among others.

While these sites are also fun, they highlight one of the more difficult cultural problems of the Net, which stems from the fact that it collapses our sense of geography. The Net doesn't care whether a site is from Ballarat or Bosnia. Unfortunately, however, the online community, in a semi-conscious way, does.

And the dominance of the US in that community is a problem, at least in these early stages of the wired world. There is, at present, a lack of global perspective. While other countries rush to catch up, the cultural heart of the Web is American. Certainly all these '80s sites carry an American perspective. Which is both a little sad, and distorting. Then again, imagine what the inevitable Australian site will be like: Bob Hawke after the America's Cup victory in 1983, INXS and Pseudo Echo, the recession we had to have…

Addresses

The 80s Server
http://www.80s.com

The Big Eighties
http://galaxy.einet.net/editors/douglas-bell/rock/eighties.html

The Cheezy 80s Page
http://www.mit.edu:8001/people/tobye/cheezy80s.html

Random 80s Lyrics Page
http://itg-pc1.acns.nwu.edu/cgi-bin/lyric

Chucky G's 1980s Web Pages
http://www.acm.org/~cgrosvenor/1980.html

Livin' in the Eighties
http://www.rpi.edu/~boothj/eighties.html

Spiral into the Eighties with Jeff
http://chat.carleton.ca/~jmain/eighties.html

See also...

Steven Berke's Break Dancing Home Page
http://weber.u.washington.edu/~bock/bd/bd.html

Graffiti, history, culture, fashion, videos and how-to-do-it demonstrations of one of the great lost arts of the era. As the late night slow dance is to marriage, so is the break dance to the emergency spinal care unit.

Tom's Solution to the Rubik's Cube
http://sdg.ncsa.uiuc.edu/~mag/Misc/CubeSoln.html

Does anyone still care? You bet they do. Nothing that left-brain-oriented and nerdy could go away quietly. At this site you can find out all there is to be known about Rubik's '80s phenomenon.

Classic Arcade Games
http://coinop.org/sharkie//vids.html

The launch pad for anyone interested in video games of the era. It offers tours of the St Louis Coin-Op and Video Game Museum, gives details on video game auctions and archives a bunch of classic advertisements for the machines.

Ed's Eighties Page
http://www.users.interport.net/~efishman/index.html

It turns out also to be the home of 'Eileen and Eddie's Wedding Page'. Indeed, when I dropped by, there was no '80s material at all. And judging from the pix, our hosts aren't exactly octogenarians. Maybe it usually has other things available. Maybe not. Another Web mystery.

Once Upon a Time in the Eighties
http://www.engl.virginia.edu/~enwr1016/index.html

A hypertext document which presents a timeline of some of the events of the decade by linking to fourteen essays by students at the University of Virginia.

AUSTRALIA

What Does the Rest of the World See of Australia?

WHAT would happen, I wondered, if I plugged the word 'Australia' into the Net's search engines, those marvellous little programs that head out into the electronic jungle and bring back a list of sites that seem to match your request.

It seemed like a dutifully patriotic thing to do, particularly given that tens of thousands of foreigners do the same thing every time they want to find something out about this country.

So what does the cyberspace picture of Australia look like? First up, I learned that more than 70 000 documents on the Web had 'Australia' somewhere in their title or abstract. I decided to look at the first 300.

What did I find? Mostly that everyone out there is having the same idea. And that idea goes something like this: 'Sooner or later the Internet will be in every home and people all over the world will use it to find out what Australia is like. When that happens, *I* will be there to give them what they want … and maybe sell a few services off the site as well.' Everywhere you look on the Net, there are would-be Australian ambassadors and tourist agencies. First cab off the rank in my search was **Exploring Australia**: 'The Wonders from Down Under', the Australia Announce Archive tourism site, which explains how to get a visa for Australia, suggests that if you have a specific question about the region you should post it to the newsgroup **rec.travel.australia+nz**, and offers a series of links to Australian sites and daily news services.

The **Guide to Australia** project, maintained by NSW's Charles Sturt University, aims to compile links to every available Australian information source on the Web, to 'grow into an on-line, hypertext encyclopaedia'. Sounds quixotic, slightly mad even, but the Guide is as good as it gets. For better or worse, primary school kids doing school projects will never need to open a book again. Its General section offers background info on the country, our population distribution, currency, daylight saving times, financial dealings, and industries. It also has fact sheets from the **Department of Foreign Affairs and Trade** on each state.

The Geography section has interactive and static maps of Australia, **oceanographic analysis**, links to our **Antarctic** bases and guides to the states and territories. If you're interested in the Environment, there is weather info (including daily satellite images) from the **Bureau of Meteorology** and links to sites dealing with such issues as **biodiversity**, **threatened fauna**, vegetation monitoring by satellite, **Greenpeace** and the **Environmental Resources Information Network**.

The Communications and Media sections offer everything from lists of Australian newsgroups and Websites to radio and television stations and newspapers. And in the **White and Yellow Pages**, the whole population's addresses and phone numbers are online. There's also a Culture section, which looks at **Australian Art**, music and **Literature**. And a huge range of Tourism links for the country, specific states, regions and cities. The Travel file has flight schedules for **Ansett** and **Qantas**. The numerous Government and History links include the **Australian Bureau of Statistics** and a full copy of the **Constitution**, And the Guide also lists other index sites, including **The Australia Index** and **Internet Directory Australia**.

For views from the outside, **Lonely Planet: Destination Australia** offers a tribute to 'the richness of Australia's natural treasures and its cultural diversity', and although it stops short of putting a whole guidebook online, it has more than enough info to tweak the imagination of the would-be traveller, with sections on our environment, history, economy, and culture, as

AUSTRALIA

well as advice on the practicalities of getting around once you're here. For a more individual perspective, **G'Day Australia** is the travel journal of Gerhard Ortner, an Austrian in love with the outback. His site chronicles his 1994 trip from Darwin to Melbourne, with more than 90 photos.

An American outfit called **The Oz Channel** offers a very cool Vegemite site as part of its service. Alan Sipole's Vegemite Page has a fascinating history of the spread, as well as an art gallery (Le Veg Louvre) featuring works such as Botticelli's The Birth of Vegemite and Michelangelo's David. There's an interactive play centre which allows you to display your own Vegemite art or download Vegemite images, a merchandise store, and The Kitchen, a storehouse of Vegemite recipes.

Working my way down the list, I came across sites catering to more specialised interests, such as **Diving in Australia**, various genealogical societies, a handy **Timezone Converter**, and information about **The Australia Telescope National Facility**, a collection of radio telescopes in New South Wales. I found out about **Australia's Bid to Hold the World Science Fiction Convention in 1999, InterWine Australia** ('Australia's 24-hour, international cellar door'), migration patterns, cricket results, churches online, backpackers' guides, a Canadian article on the Australian women's hockey scene, and a guide to local vegetarianism, **Australia's Wonderland**.

And slowly it dawned on me that I really should go out the front door and see some of it myself.

Addresses

Exploring Australia
http://www.aaa.com.au/Exploring.html

Guide to Australia
http://www.csu.edu.au/education/australia.html

Department of Primary Industries and Energy
http://www.dpie.gov.au/

Oceanographic Analysis
http://www.aodc.gov.au/EAC/EAC-title.html

Australian Antarctic Division
http://www.antdiv.gov.au/

Bureau of Meteorology
http://www.bom.gov.au/

Biodiversity
http://www.csu.edu.au/biodiversity.html

Threatened Fauna
http://mac-ra26.sci.deakin.edu.au/

Vegetation Monitoring by Satellite
http://www.erin.gov.au/land/monitoring.html

Greenpeace
http://www.sofcom.com.au/Greenpeace/

Environmental Resources Information Network
http://www.erin.gov.au/

Telstra White and Yellow Pages
http://www.telstra.com.au/

Australian Art
http://ausarts.anu.edu.au/ITA/AusArts/

Oz Lit
http://www.vicnet.net.au/~ozlit/index.html

Ansett Schedules
gopher://cis.anu.edu.au:70/11/FAQ-ext/Airlines/

Qantas
http://www.anzac.com/qantas/qantas.htm

Australian Bureau of Statistics
http://www.statistics.gov.au/

The Australian Constitution
http://info.dpac.tas.gov.au/features/ausconstitution.html

The Australia Index
http://sin.csu.edu.au/australia/

Internet Directory Australia
http://www.ida.com.au/

Lonely Planet: Destination Australia
http://www.lonelyplanet.com/dest/aust/aus.htm

G'Day Australia
http://ebweb.tuwien.ac.at/ortner/australi.html

The Oz Channel
http://www.ozchannel.com/

Diving in Australia
http://bronte.cs.utas.edu.au/diving/

Timezone Converter
http://www.arch.adelaide.edu.au/tzconvert.html

The Australia Telescope National Facility
http://wwwatnf.atnf.csiro.au/ATNFHomePage.html

Australia's Bid To Hold The World Science Fiction Convention in 1999
http://www.maths.uts.edu.au/staff/eric/ain99/

InterWine Australia
http://www.wineonline.com.au/

Australia's Wonderland
http://kangaroo.ida.com.au/nsw/sydney/Wonderland.html

Aboriginal Sites

TREVOR MARANDA, of the Burra Burra clan of the Gundungurra Aborigines, had one thought when he put together **The Gundungurra Tribal Council** Website in January 1996. 'Education,' he says. 'Solely, only education. Allowing others who may not have ever realised the "true" history of the invasion of this country the chance to find out about it. Hopefully through education, people can respect our culture, and our continuing struggle in regards to land rights.'

Visitors to his site can read about the blood-soaked history of the Gundungurra, whose traditional land extended over a vast area of New South Wales, from the Burragorang Valley, which now holds Sydney's water supply, south to Goulburn, and westwards to the Lithgow region.

The site also contains the tribe's Dreamtime story of the creation of the Blue Mountains, Cox's River and the Jenolan Caves, as well as links to sources of information on Mabo and to indigenous groups worldwide.

Maranda is funding the project himself in the hope that his example will encourage other Aboriginal communities to get wired. So far, he says, responses to the site have been mostly positive—and mostly from overseas. Many people are taking the opportunity to explore the cultures of other countries online. The more global the medium, the more locally specific the interests it can serve. And one of the first things Net wanderers visiting Australia seem to want to know is how to find out about Aboriginal culture.

There is a fair (and growing) amount of Aboriginal material online, but at the moment, there's no overview site. The closest thing to one is the **ANU Aboriginal Studies Virtual Library**, which will look a little dry and academic for some, but seems to contain the best set of resources. It has sections on general information, history, native title, language, art and culture, and world indigenous studies. Its sizeable collection of links is easy to understand and well annotated, but not much to look at.

The **Council for Aboriginal Reconciliation** also has a large site, whose strongest point is its Reconciliation and Social Justice Library. Here you will find documents, reports, newsletters and other materials, from the Deaths in Custody royal commission, the Aboriginal and Torres Strait Islander Commission, the Australian Institute of Health and other bodies concerned with Aboriginal legal rights, health and welfare. The trip through the Deaths in Custody section, which catalogues the details of each case, is a particularly moving one.

On a smaller scale, **The Koorie Home Page** hosts a group of short essays on Aboriginal history and culture. Simple overviews are provided of art, lifestyles, social control, self-determination, assimilation, land rights, population changes and cultural survival.

If it's land rights you're most interested in, the Australian National Library provides a biography and a collection of the papers of Eddie **Mabo**, which it purchased in 1995 from his widow. The **Native Title Act of 1993**, which banished the concept of *terra nullius*, the idea that no-one owned the land before white settlement, can also be found online, as can a **Native Title Case Archive.**

An Adelaide gallery, **Tandanya — The National Aboriginal Cultural Institute**, has a site devoted to Aboriginal art, with online exhibitions, as well as a permanent collection of samples of the work of various artists. The site of the remote **Maningrida** community in the Northern Territory sells sculpture, bark paintings, weaving and didjeridus, all made by artists from out-stations. Maningrida Arts and Culture, an organisation established in the early 1970s, provides an outlet for more than 200 traditional and contemporary artists living within an

AUSTRALIA

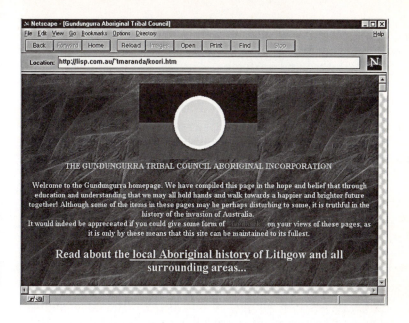

area of more than 10 000 square kilometres. Margaret Carew, the site coordinator, says:

> We really just set the site up to see what sort of response we could get from art buyers, and also to introduce local people here to the new technology.
>
> As far as selling art goes, we have sold some, but it hasn't been a huge amount. By far the most interest from buyers has been in didjeridus—from the spiritual set in America. This was something we did not expect, but sales of didjeridus has pretty well covered the cost of our Internet account. We have also sold bark paintings to private buyers in Pittsburgh, Washington, DC, and Oslo through the site.

For older and less portable art, the **Australian Rock Art Research Association** has a site with plenty of discussion and study of the paintings, as well as an archive of articles and photos. If you just want to look at pictures, there's a site for that too: **Rock Art**.

The **Didjeridu WWW Server** turns out to be a US site set up to 'serve the interests of the growing population of didjeridu players around the Net world'. Fortunately, the site appreciates the instrument's history and meaning, and has links to Aboriginal-studies resources addressing 'wider issues such as Aboriginal culture, spiritualism and their political repression' as well as the simple facts of where to get a didge, how to play it and where to contact others doing the same.

The best known indigenous music group, of course, is **Yothu Yindi**, whose Website allows you to watch video clips, listen to song samples and read up on the background of the musicians, their homeland, and their people, the Yolngu. 'Australia's indigenous people are custodians of the oldest surviving culture on the planet,' the site points out. 'Today's Aboriginal cultures represent an unbroken chain linking back into human prehistory, and are among the last remaining people on Earth with a natural way of life essentially unchanged by the rise of Western civilisation.'

Oldest culture, newest medium.

Addresses

The Gundungurra Tribal Council
http://lisp.com.au/~tmaranda/koori.htm

ANU Aboriginal Studies Virtual Library
http://coombs.anu.edu.au/WWWVL-Aboriginal.html

Council for Aboriginal Reconciliation
http://www.austlii.edu.au/car/

AUSTRALIA

The Koorie Home Page
http://webnet.com.au/koori/homekori.html

Mabo
http://www.nla.gov.au/1/ms/find_aids/8822.html

Native Title Act of 1993
http://austlii.law.uts.edu.au/au/legis/cth/consol_act/nta1993147/

Native Title Case Archive
http://www.arts.uwa.edu.au/AnthropWWW/ntcases.htm

Tandanya — National Aboriginal Cultural Institute
http://chopper.macmedia.com.au/Tandanya.html

Maningrida Arts and Culture
http://www.peg.apc.org/~bawinanga/mac.html

Australian Rock Art Research Association
http://sunspot.sli.unimelb.edu.au/aura/Welcome.html

Rock Art
http://liswww.fste.ac.cowan.edu.au/student/Michael/cave1.html

Didjeridu WWW Server
http://www.nd.edu/~sborman/didjeridu/

Yothu Yindi
http://www.YothuYindi.com/

See also...

Kam Yan: Indigenous Australia Today
http://www.abc.net.au/ipu/

The ABC's indigenous television show. The site provides background info, screening times and a list of Aboriginal links.

Australian Aboriginal Writers
http://www.vicnet.net.au/~ozlit/aborigwr.html

Part of the huge OzLit site. It has about 100 writers on its list, most with their own pages, with short biographies and recommended reading guides.

Kamilaroi/Gamilaraay Dictionary
http://coombs.anu.edu.au/WWWVLPages/AborigPages/LANG/GAMDICT/GAMDICT.HTM

Gamilaraay is a rich language with a vocabulary of many thousands of words and quite a complicated grammar, used by the natives of this area of NSW. 'This Web dictionary does not contain all the words of the language. Due to the impact of colonisation in northern New South Wales, Gamilaraay stopped being used daily in the first half of this century, and as a result much knowledge has been lost. But the dictionary does bring together much of the material collected by researchers and others over the past 40 years.'

Aboriginal Trail at the Australian National Botanic Gardens in Canberra
http://osprey.erin.gov.au/anbg/aboriginal-trail.html

An online booklet explaining the walk. It details plants the Aborigines used for food and medicine.

Links to Aboriginal Resources
http://www.bloorstreet.com/300block/aborl.htm

An American site which collects links to indigenous sources the world over.

Politics and the 1996 Net Election

IT WAS the year of the Net election, the first time since the explosion of the World Wide Web that this country had gone to a federal vote. And on the Net, the competition was pretty funny. It was put up or shut up. Everybody wanted to be the first to have the biggest and best site.

Just like the real world, the Net has gold rushes, lemming parades and peer group pressure. In fact, the latter has been one of the main forces in its development. Thousands of businesses and organisations have established Web sites for no real reason other than the fact that the competition was doing it. Millions of dollars have been thrown at the Web by people whose main fear is being left out of something.

Exactly that kind of fever gripped Australia in early 1996. Parties and organisations rushed to put up sites for the national poll, even though only about three per cent of Australians were online at that point. Mind you, a three per cent swing was going to be enough to change government—every voter counted. Such was the boom in political sites that by the time the election actually rolled around, you could do everything online except cast your real vote—you could cast plenty of fake ones though, on various sites offering pre-poll polls. Sooner or later, the odds are that we *will* be able to vote online, but the process of authenticating identity has some way to go first. You could check out the info on every seat in the country at the **Australian Electoral Commission** site, as well as wade through previous results and find out exactly how to have your own say on Vote Day.

The Democrats were, proudly, the first party online, with their basic policy documents up long before the campaign was a sniff on the breeze. **The Labor Party** site was the most impressive of the official party ventures during the poll, with enough push to get policy documents and speeches, economic facts and an aggregation of poll results in the year before the campaign all online. The John Howard Unplugged section covered (vainly as it turned out) Coalition gaffes and a Soapbox section allowed surfers to have their say, often with the predictably funny results. 'During Campaign '96', the site claims, 'there was an average of 11 000 hits and 40 Mb of files downloaded each day'.

The Liberal Party got its page up in week two of the campaign. It too had policy documents and speeches, but added the touch of making all federal candidates available by e-mail, something Labor had not managed to do (though you could message Keating). And **The National Party**, bless 'em, got their suitably daggy site up late in the campaign.

You could find out more about **The Greens**, **The Women's Party**, **The Natural Law Party** (anyone for enforced meditation and yogic flying?) and the **No Aircraft Noise** folk, who got cartoonist Patrick Cook to come up with a cute little downloadable game, *House Invaders*, which allowed the player to squash as many planes, cockroaches and politicians as possible. And if you won, you got a few seconds of peace and quiet.

It being the Net, of course, you could also find material from groups you (and I recognise this is subjective) might consider distasteful, from the very mildly so (**Australians for Constitutional Monarchy**) to the extreme (**The League of Rights**). Ahh, free speech. Always a pretty thing. At least the Net has a way of balancing itself. Also online was **The Australian Republican Movement** and the **Opponent of the Australian League of Rights**.

The media were not going to be left out either. The **Sydney Morning Herald**, **The Financial Review** and *The Age* all created Election '96 sites, as did the **ABC**, which bravely provided a live feed of results on election night (something a few sites

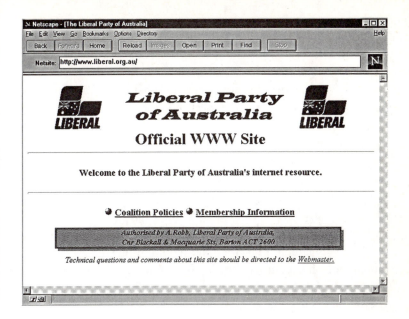

tried, with, as surfers reported, more technical difficulty than success). Unexpectedly, these sites found that a significant proportion of their audience was made up of grateful expatriate Australians, Net-connected in faraway places, looking for information on which to base their postal votes. Archived material from these sites can still be accessed.

Since the election, things have been a lot quieter on most of the party sites. The Democrats remain the most committed of the major parties to the medium, with a site that regularly updates the activities, campaigns and media releases of their representatives. The site actually has interesting ramifications for democracy lovers—for a small financial outlay, the party is able to keep in touch with the wired part of its constituency, to explain what it is up to in an immediate and accountable way. Where other parties present themselves as monolithic, broadcasting to the people from behind a high wall, the

Democrats have understood that the Web can be more intimate and one-to-one in its communication. It can feed ideas both ways.

Many of the smaller sites have not changed at all since the poll. Strapped for cash, demoralised, too busy or just taking long holidays, it is clear that the party Web machines will crank up closer to the next vote. Oddly enough, considering the landslide Coalition win, neither the Liberals nor the Nationals have made a lot of use of their sites. Both have made their policies available, but really function as no more than electronic libraries, no longer seeking to engage and include the Net drifter. The Labor site is not much better.

There is much that the Net could offer to the political climate of this country: the chance for people separated by geography to share ideas, a venue for robust debate, a place parties can come to get immediate feedback, the chance for them to let us know what is going on, to give us all access to the decision-making process . . . the list goes on. Sadly, it remains to be seen whether the major players have the vision to see it as anything more than just another marketing tool.

Addresses

Australian Electoral Commission
http://www.aec.gov.au

Australian Democrats
http://www.democrats.org.au/

Australian Labor Party
http://www.alp.org.au

AUSTRALIA

Liberal Party
http://www.liberal.org.au

National Party
http://www.npa.org.au

Australian Greens
http://www.peg.apc.org/~ausgreen/

Women's Party
http://www.ednet.com.au/community/awp/

Natural Law Party
http://www.vicnet.net.au/~NaturalLaw

No Aircraft Noise Party
http://www.ozemail.com.au/~nonoise

Australians for Constitutional Monarchy
http://www.mq.edu.au/hpp/politics/acm.html

League of Rights
http://www.adfa.oz.au/~adm/politics/LOR.html

The Sydney Morning Herald Election '96 Web Site
http://www.smh.com.au/elect96

The Financial Review
http://www.afr.com.au/content/election/index.html

ABC Online — Election '96 Home Page
http://www.abc.net.au/election/

See also...

aus.politics

The local politics newsgroup. Prepare to flame or be flamed. Appears to be inhabited mainly by ideological predators. If you believe in something, you'd better have a good reason ready. This vigour is good, but it tends to mean that only the occasional discussion thread actually goes somewhere before breaking down.

The Australian National Library's Commonwealth Government Page
http://www.nla.gov.au/oz/gov/ozgov.html

'If you can't find it here, it's probably not on the Net,' the site boasts. It's an archive of federal and state government department activity. You can find press releases, speeches and policy documents all carefully preserved in their full-text form. Most ministers have their own home pages.

Queer Resources

NICK MASKILL, webmaster of **Cyberqueer**, an 'e-zine and info-park of queer Australia', reckons the gay and lesbian community is quicker on the uptake with new technology and more wired than its heterosexual counterpart. It also has a higher average disposable income and is more inclined to spend money on entertainment. Maskill says that what makes the Net particularly attractive for gays is its lack of censorship and regulation, and its ability to connect people. He explains:

> If I was gay and lived in China, or many places around the world, the Net would be the only source of information about being gay, coming out, AIDS and many other things. If I was in rural Australia (or anywhere without a strong gay network) then the Web, newsgroups, mailing lists and e-mail would quickly become my main source for support, communication and exploration.

Maskill constructed Cyberqueer with Lisa Pears (formerly of *geekgirl*). They opened their doors last December. He says the site resulted from his Net addiction—he was looking for a way to turn his obsession into a full-time job when he alighted on the idea. The first discussion with Pears took place at 4 a.m. at last year's Sleaze Ball in Sydney. A few months later, Cyberqueer was up and running.

'We wanted to create a popular site that was both informative and entertaining,' Maskill says. 'There are great Websites out there, as well as a great queer culture that we have access to. We want to utilise the Net and its technology for queer initiatives such as video IRC and live broadcasts of queer events, but like everyone else we are waiting for more bandwidth.'

While it waits, the site has plenty to make it worth bookmarking. It boasts feature articles, interviews, profiles, gossip, photo albums of major events, columns, raunchy personals, classified ads, advice and guides to gay and lesbian resources on and off the Web.

All those resources prove Maskill's point. The gay community is very well catered for online. It's almost surprising how many local sites have sprung up covering gay culture and lifestyles. The **Sydney Gay and Lesbian Mardi Gras**, 'the world's premier gay and lesbian festival', has a site. And gay and lesbian newspapers such as Melbourne's **Brother Sister** and Sydney's **Capital Q** have online incarnations.

The **Australian Queer Resources Directory** is 'a library of things that may be of use to the Australian GBLO communities'. It contains news clippings, papers, articles, reviews, event announcements and resources lists. The directory, which is maintained by the Sexuality Project of the Australian Student Christian Movement, has links to information on HIV and AIDS, the struggle against Tasmania's anti-gay laws, local and world news, gay humour, reviews of books, plays and films, and **The Australian Good Tranny Guide**, an online book which offers advice on everything from medical services to support groups to friendly shops and businesses.

Another hub of local activity is **Pinkboard**, a meeting place for community groups, businesses, and venues. It offers classifieds, personal ads, what's-on guides, photo galleries and a 'graffiti wall' where users leave e-mail gossip about the Mardi Gras and the Sleaze Ball.

GayLawNet, the home page of David Allan, is dedicated to 'answering your questions and providing you with the simplest access to a gay lawyer'. **Digital Queers Australia** is a group of computer businesspeople determined to improve access to technology for gays by 'donating time, products, expertise, or funding' to community groups. 'We want to promote positive images of queers as capable and efficient users

AUSTRALIA

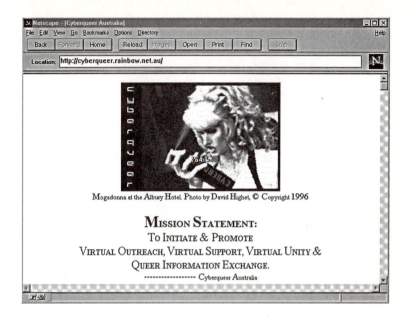

Mogadonna at the Albury Hotel. Photo by David Highet, © Copyright 1996

MISSION STATEMENT:
TO INITIATE & PROMOTE
VIRTUAL OUTREACH, VIRTUAL SUPPORT, VIRTUAL UNITY &
QUEER INFORMATION EXCHANGE.
-------------------- Cyberqueer Australia

of high technology,' the site says. 'Computer users are not boring nerds, and queers are not completely glossy!'

Queer Vision is a gay-owned and operated broadband service 'established as an alternative to commercial television networks, where gay and lesbian programming rarely sees the light of day'. The service intends to use the Internet (as the technology grows more powerful and penetrates more of the home market) as a tool for broadcasting queer TV to the world. Its site previews some of its plans, which include comedy, drama, lifestyle, erotica and home shopping channels.

Even **The NSW Police Gay and Lesbian Liaison** unit has a Website, offering explanations of laws, tips on staying safe, the findings of a study on gay hate crimes, facts on various initiatives and programs of the unit, and contact details for its officers. The site is run by Marrickville liaison officer Terry Harvey, and was set up in August 1995 as part of an officers' course at the Goulburn Police Academy. Harvey says:

The NSW Police Gay and Lesbian Liaison Officers page is a world first for the NSW Police Service. When it was established, it was the only page of its type on the Internet. The NSW Police Service leads the world in its efforts to improve the relationship between members of the gay and lesbian community and the police.

The liaison officer's page provides a mailbox for people wanting to ask questions, information about safety and links to other community organisations. The major benefit is that the page allows those people who would not normally seek advice from police to do so in a totally relaxed, non-confrontational manner.

Addresses

Cyberqueer
http://cyberqueer.rainbow.net.au

Sydney Gay and Lesbian Mardi Gras
http://www.geko.com.au/~mardigras/

Brother Sister
http://werple.mira.net.au/~leto/news/index.html

Capital Q
http://www.ipacific.net.au/capq

Australian Queer Resource Directory
http://ausqrd.queer.org.au

The Australian Good Tranny Guide
http://ausqrd.queer.org.au/austg/austg.htm

Pinkboard
http://www.pinkboard.com.au/

AUSTRALIA

GayLawNet
http://www.labyrinth.net.au/~dba/

Digital Queers Australia
http://www.geko.com.au/digiqueers/index.html

Queer Vision
http://www.queervision.com.au/

NSW Police Gay and Lesbian Liaison
http://www.eagles.bbs.net.au/~gllos/

See also...

aus.culture.lesbigay newsgroup FAQ
http://just.net.au/~justnet/lesbigay/faq.html

Macquarie University National Centre in HIV Social Research
http://www.bhs.mq.edu.au/nchsr.html

A site documenting the research activities of the centre, particularly the National Priority Program focusing on Education and Prevention for Gay and Homosexually Active Men. 'The research program addresses a range of issues concerning sexual identity and sexual practice with particular reference to gay and homosexually active men, both gay community attached men and men not so attached.'

HIV Electronic Media Information Review
http://florey.biosci.uq.oz.au/hiv/HIV_EMIR.html

A storehouse of material from various publications. 'Articles on HIV/AIDS are presented from local or overseas sources as a resource and educational exercise. We do not advocate any particular treatments or therapies. Articles presented do not necessarily represent our personal views, or those of our employers.'

Sport

OK, SO THE most exercise I ever get is moving the mouse about on its little pad. Or waddling off to the kitchen to put the kettle on. Or rummaging about in the biscuit tin looking for something with mock cream in it. So I have more than a love of doughnuts in common with Homer Simpson.

That doesn't mean that, like any other male Australian, I don't have my Sport Guy side, that I don't become a sweating, obsessive idiot during summer cricket season and a shivering, obsessive idiot while the footy is on in winter.

So what if I'm out of shape and uncoordinated? Sport is *about* people who can't play. Sport is for watching, for thinking about, for getting hot under the collar about. The players come and go, the teams change, but fandom goes on.

Only a couple of hundred guys alive will ever know what it's like to play cricket for Australia, to walk out onto the pitch at the hallowed MCG, or Lord's, and belt a ton or bowl a blinder. And those guys will never be able to explain it. For the rest, the hundreds of thousands, the millions of us, sport is a different experience. But no less an experience.

Darryl Harvey's AFL Page shows exactly why the best Websites are put up by fans. **Grandstand — The Offical AFL Home Page** is nowhere near as interesting, or as broad in its scope. Harvey's site covers every angle, from local competitions and results, to a weekly wrap-up, to archives of previous years. You can download free football tipping software, or find out how the code is being preached overseas, in countries such as the US, Canada and the UK. Harvey also maintains the best resources list for official and unofficial club home pages (again, the rule of thumb is to stay unofficial — they're usually lower on production values, but higher on spirit and passion).

Other links include: **Darren's Excellent Adventure**, which

AUSTRALIA

follows the pain and the glory of Darren Bennett, a former AFL player now punting for his life in the US gridiron scene (read his diaries, check out the latest stats); the **CenterBet** Sports Betting Agency; tributes such as **Jazza's Gary Ablett Web Page** ('anything & everything on the Champion Full-Forward from Geelong'); various tipping competitions; other AFL pages and to newsgroups **rec.sport.football.australian** and **aus.sport.aussie-rules**.

By comparison, rugby league has been a little slower out of the blocks, though perhaps this is because of the widespread disenchantment about the future of the game—fans have been hard pressed to muster enthusiasm in the last couple of years. **The Australian Rugby League Page** has covered the ongoing battles over who will steer the game into the next century (and who will get the TV rights), but it has mercifully been more concerned with the actual on-field contests. Its site offers photos, regular news stories and score updates, and a history of the game in Australia. The **Official ARL Site** gives the sanitised view.

For a more global perspective, the **International Rugby League WWW** has the best collection of links to dozens of club and fan sites, from the local outfits (let's hear it for Don Tebbutt's nostalgic **Newtown Jets Home Page**) to newsgroups **rec.sport.rugby.league** and **aus.sport.rugby-league**. **Rick Eyre's Rugby League Page**, a dead giveaway in the red and black of the North Sydney Bears, is another good source of league links.

If it's rugby union you're looking for, **Tim's Rugby Information** keeps an index of local happenings and sites, while an American site, the **Rugby URL Index**, offers the broader view.

Cricket fans are well catered for. **The Ultimate Cricket Page** has a lot of photos, scores and links, but it's **The Australian Cricket Page** which really has the goods for Web sports fans. Here you can get news and schedule information, have your say on the feedback page, read match reports, follow columns like Between the Creases (snippets of news and commentary) or find out how to pick up live, ball-by-ball coverage of games through the Internet. There's a section detailing the history of the game and its rules, as well as a library of links to other cricket sites, many from fans in non-cricket-playing nations, staying in touch with the global cricketing community

The Sydney Cricket Ground has its own site, at which you can find statistics of games from 1881, a history of the turf and exactly why 50 dozen towels were at the heart of its most important turning point. The State Library of South Australia has a **Donald Bradman Page**, showcasing its collection of memorabilia donated by the great man.

The **Candela Motorsport WWW Information Service** offers information on just about anything that moves: speedway, rally, indycar, Formula One, drag racing, NASCAR ... even go-karting gets a guernsey. There are news services, photo galleries, chat rooms and a very impressive collection of links. If you just want to relive the highlights of the 1996 **Australian Grand Prix**, there's a site for you too.

Golfers have a couple of excellent places to visit. **The Home of Golf** is well above par, with a weekly news column, coaching tips, a library and a clubhouse in which to drown your digital sorrows. **GolfWeb** too offers a wealth of information and tips.

Basketball fans can dribble on to **The Unofficial NBL Home Page**, which has articles, scores, ladders, teams, stats, up-to-date news and a hall of fame. Track pounders will be glad to know **Athletics Australia** has its own site.

Sports from **Ten Pin Bowling** (download bowling games!) to **Lacrosse** (any game in which you're armed with a stout stick is good by me) have Australian homes. Punters, of course, are not left out. The **TAB** site will give you the lowdown on various race meetings of today, tomorrow and yesterday. And **Australian Network Racing** provide details of 'Australian horse racing, betting, horses, trainers, jockeys, stud services, tipsters, raters, horse ownership via syndication services and details of forthcoming events on the Australian horse racing calendar'.

Addresses

Darryl Harvey's AFL Page
http://www.footy.com.au

Grandstand—The Offical AFL Home Page
http://www.cadability.com.au/AFL

Darren's Excellent Adventure
http://www.nflaussie.com/

CenterBet Sports Betting/Odds
http://www.centrebet.com.au/

Jazza's Gary Ablett Web Page
http://www.deakin.edu.au/~bennet/

The Australian Rugby League Page
http://www.ozsports.com.au/league/

The Official Australian Rugby League Site
http://www.arl.org.au/_arl.html

International Rugby League WWW
http://www.cooee.com.au/~msivis/irlwww.html

Newtown Jets Home Page
http://www.ozemail.com.au/~dtebbutt/Jets/index.html

Rick Eyre's Rugby League Page
http://www.ozemail.com.au/~reyre/sport.html

Tim's Rugby Information
http://www.monash.edu.au/cc/staff/ecn/tim/WWW/rugby.html

The Rugby URL Index
http://darkwing.uoregon.edu/~benc/sites/all.html

The Ultimate Cricket Page
http://www.odyssey.com.au/sports/cricket.html

AUSTRALIA

The Australian Cricket Page
http://kangaroo.ida.com.au/sport/cricket/

The Sydney Cricket Ground
http://www.scgt.oz.au/scg.html

Donald Bradman Page
http://dino.slsa.sa.gov.au/sslnew/bradman/

Candela Motorsport WWW Information Service
http://www.dragnet.com.au/candela

Australian Grand Prix
http://www.ozemail.com.au/~mawdes/melbgp.html

The Home of Golf
http://www.golf.com.au/

GolfWeb
http://www.golfweb.com.au/

The Unofficial NBL Home Page
http://natsem.canberra.edu.au/private_web_home_pages/joshp/nbl/nbl.html

Athletics Australia's Web Site
http://www.ausport.gov.au/aths

Ten Pin Bowling
http://www.its.newnham.utas.edu.au/users/mbyrne/

Australian Lacrosse Homepage
http://www.ais.com.au/lax/lax.html

TAB
http://www.tabcorp.com.au/tab/

Australian Network Racing
http://www.geko.com.au/~anr/

See also...

Beyond the Black Stump Sports Page
http://werple.net.au/~lions/sports.htm

As good a place as any to start. It has a huge collection of links to sports sites from around the globe, in particular those of interest to Australians. You find places that cover athletics, Aussie Rules, cricket, golf, hockey, various motor sports, basketball, rugby (union and league), tennis, ten pin bowling and pro wrestling (how wrestling snuck under the heading 'sport' is beyond me).

OzSport Review
http://kangaroo.ida.com.au/sport/review/

A Website designed to offer up-to-date results from all kinds of Australian sports, 'as well as articles about the sports and sportspeople that you all love and hate'. Its service features news bulletins about events, That Was the Week That Was summaries and a regular Notes'N'Quotes column. It also links to a bunch of specific-sport sites.

Sports Photography Library
http://www.ozemail.com.au/~sporting/

For those who like to be reminded of what they've seen.

THE DIGITAL HUMAN

Finding Community in Cyberspace

THE SLOW deterioration of our sense of community has been an issue for most of the twentieth century. The car increased personal freedom and gave us mobility, but by taking away the advantages of living close together, it tore apart the web of community.

Television did the same by keeping us in our houses. Even as it gave us the impression that we were sharing experiences, it was isolating us. Technology, as Neil Postman wrote in *Technopoly*, both gives and takes away. Even something as seemingly benign as air-conditioning has exacted its price. In the heat of summer, people are less inclined to sit outside, on porches or in yards, chatting with neighbours.

Popular mythology has it that computers are the latest anti-social force. They cut us off from human contact, make us individual rather than group animals. Users are pictured as sad little people sitting alone at their screens, cut off from the real world. But what if computers, and the Internet in particular, could help restore our sense of community? What if our experiences in the online world could teach us something about the values of human relationships? What if the Internet could be part of the solution rather than part of the problem?

Is it possible? I suspect the answer is, as usual with Net questions, 'yes', 'no', and 'maybe'. The Net insists on being all things to all people. Some use it for entertainment, some for information. But many use it to connect with the people around them, whether they're a few metres or thousands of kilometres away. A sense of community is there for anyone who wishes to look.

Some find it in Internet Relay Chat, the vast, sprawling network of live talk rooms. Others find it in the Usenet newsgroups. I find that in the anarchy of those areas most threads are lost and most connections superficial and fleeting. They're fun and often useful, but little real conversation takes place there. It's just a lot of people baiting, hectoring and bragging on the virtual stage.

More interesting experiments in community are taking place on a smaller scale, in bulletin boards and conference systems such as the **WELL** (the Whole Earth eLectronic Link) in San Francisco. These are like a cross between Usenet and a club. Each is a collection of conference areas, subdivided into topics. Each topic is a conversation of some sort, a collection of posts that is moderated and steered by an unseen host. **David R. Woolley**, who wrote the '**Conferencing on the Web**' chapter in *The World Wide Web Unleashed*, defines them as:

> A form of group discussion that uses text messages stored on a computer as a medium for communication. For true conferencing, some structure is essential. In particular, the system must support 'threading', the ability to sequentially read the messages that make up one discussion. You need to be able to read all the way through the conversation about where to get the best sushi in Boise without having celebrity gossip and announcements about used stereo equipment for sale mixed in.

The main difference between conferences and newsgroups is scale. Think of newsgroups as large, open spaces where all kinds of animals roam about. Think of conferences as smaller, more comfortable spaces, like salons.

I like to hang out at **Cafe Utne**, a Web-based conference at The Utne Lens, a sister to *The Utne Reader*, one of America's best (and in Australia hardest-to-find) magazines. As the software develops, more and more Websites are setting up conferences within their walls, turning drifters into communities. At the time of writing, the Cafe, which has been open since November 1995, was running more than 30 conferences

THE DIGITAL HUMAN

on themes from sex and relationships to arts and entertainment to the repercussions of the information age.

By way of example, the InfoAge conference has more than twenty topics from software design to censorship to the pros and cons of virtual communities to the successes and failures of web conferencing. Those taking part in the discussions have found their way in from all around the globe. In the first weeks, there were Americans, Canadians, Brazilians, Japanese and a couple of Australians. There are places to swap travel tips, recommend books or films, argue about world events or just hang out and see what the discussion of the day is about.

The Cafe describes itself as an informal gathering place for people who:

- want a fun, relaxing and harassment-free atmosphere,
- like discussing ideas & issues in a thoughtful and respectful manner,

- contribute pointers to what's best on the Net,
- are willing to help make this online community work for everyone!

It is a carefully constructed world. You have to join to get access, and Cafe policy is keeping the male/female ratio at 2:1 (if you want to complain, head over to the Feedback conference). The Cafe works because, unlike the IRC and news groups, it isn't a free-for-all. *The Utne Reader* and Utne Lens attract certain types of people. In bringing readers together and introducing them to each other, the Cafe creates a ready-made community of like-minded people. Even in the first couple of months, you could feel a sense of community beginning to grow. I watched a hesitant Japanese lurker join in on a conversation, stumbling nervously on the keyboard for fear of embarrassing himself. The warmth and generosity of the welcome he received surprised and delighted me.

Being a regular in a conference is like being in the middle of an experiment. Where it will lead is anyone's guess. But it's interesting to feel people striving to look outside their own experiences and viewpoints, to see what others are thinking. In the Cafe Utne virtual community, there is a respect for others, a calm, friendly, enjoyable love of company. There are people finding each other and finding themselves, learning to see the value in what makes us different as well as what makes us the same. It's a very good start.

Addresses

Conferencing on the Web
http://freenet.msp.mn.us/people/drwool/webcon2.html

David R. Woolley's chapter on conferencing from the book *World Wide Web Unleashed*. Check out his Website on the software technicalities of conferencing at http://freenet.msp.mn.us/people/drwool/webconf.html

It keeps an eye on the latest technical developments. You can jump from Woolley's site to each of the sites using the various pieces of software, so it's a good way to find your way around them.

The Utne Lens
http://www.utne.com/lens/big.html

The WELL on the Web
http://www.well.com

geekgirl and Women Online

AUSTRALIA'S (and the world's) first cyberfeminist fanzine wasted no time in making its point when it appeared at the start of 1995. Splashed across the cover of the first issue was this slogan: 'Put down that pony and pick up a computer!' It was a clarion call to all women who felt they were being left out of the technological revolution, who felt it was just another case of the boys with their toys, telling the girls to go and play somewhere else.

And the call was widely heard. **geekgirl**, produced by Rosie Cross on a shoestring from her home in inner city Sydney, has become one of the most popular Australian sites on the Web. While other businesses have thrown tens (even hundreds) of thousands of dollars at their sites, Cross has proved that talent will out, that it's the quality of the ideas that counts.

This funny, sharp and *smart* zine looks great, too. And although it has a small 'p' political slant, it doesn't push obvious barrows.

> Barrows are for gardeners. There is no philosophy, unless it's a pragmatic desire to continually challenge existing power structures. The Net over the last few years has changed dramatically. Even so, there are these really awful barriers to overcome, and one of them is the concept of gender neutrality.
>
> *geekgirl* tries to stay away from manifestos and philosophies. I like the motto 'Grrrls need modems!' and choose to distribute or publish the views from a diversity of women and men who all represent different views or politics. I guess I personally like to demystify the technology and encourage everyone to get online.

geekgirl's first issue featured interviews with the American author–prankster St Jude, Britain's self-styled cyberfeminist

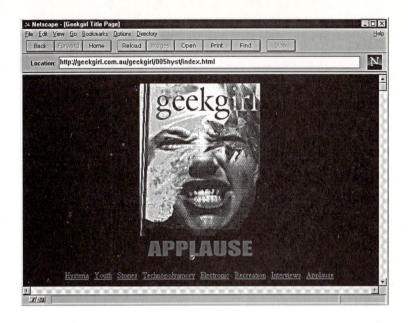

Dr Sadie Plant, and our own VNS Matrix, a group of South Australian artists 'on a mission to hijack the toys from techno cowboys and remap cyberculture with a feminist bent'. Subsequent issues have tackled all sorts of themes, but have continued to offer humorous coverage of life, politics and arts on the Web. Cross is more than satisfied with the result: She says proudly:

> I definitely feel the grrrowl of *geekgirl* has been heard around the world, having successfully highlighted issues about sexism and harassment—but also in not representing women as victims or terrified technophobes.
>
> As a package, I think *geekgirl* is a working model for heterogeneity and also a benchmark of cyberfeminism. I think *geekgirl* has been a foundation for political debate. It has certainly given a lot of people ideas and been archetypal in encouraging more women and grrrls to hop on board.

Cross says she does not believe that women are excluded

from technology. She thinks it's just harder sometimes for them to find a foothold, 'given the old prejudices of gender bias in education and the way some women have been discouraged to use machines'. She argues that empowering women helps both sexes and says many men on the Net don't like the 'boys are technophiles, girls are technophobes' stereotypes either:

> Generally men hog machines. They huff and puff and pretend in many instances they know what they are doing when they don't. They often say they like machines when they don't because it's expected of them, and they generally find it hard to share skills. These are not innate traits of the male species. They are based on competition and societal expectation. The interesting thing which is developing due to the nature of information technology communications is that men . . . demonstrate another side to their expected character. Men like being feminine. It takes the load off always having to be the one with the answers and techno know-how.
>
> There is a lot of tacit support from men regarding the issues of feminism. When you think about it, it's to their benefit to be supportive. Women who don't like women or don't see the political necessity of feminism can be far more venomous, spiteful and hurtful than men can be! You've never been flamed on the Net till you have been flamed by another woman who hates feminists! Needless to say, I like having more women online because it sorts out these problems in an organic way as opposed an Us vs Them scenario. More women online means more diversity and creativity of expression in digital space.

geekgirl, says Cross, has helped to legitimise the use of infotech by women. It has encouraged more women to take the digital plunge and, she hopes, 'made educators concerned enough to reassess how they teach computer skills to girls and how the myth of technophobia and lack of interest in machines is fostered in schools.

'In the ol' days in 1989, women were about 2 per cent of

those using the Internet. Now it's a grrrowing 34% and there are just the most wonderful resources online for women.'

Unlike many Web zines—see Resource File on zines—*geekgirl* is also available as a hard-copy magazine, from newsagencies, record and book stores. Cross says she continually reassesses the future of the hard-copy version, because something always seems to go wrong with it. On the Web, you can fix the hitches and glitches—the paper version is final.

Carla Sinclair, LA-based author of *Net Chick*, a full-tilt, high-speed trawl through the feminist regions of the Web, says women thinking of getting wired should just do it. *geekgirl* is one of the best places to start, she adds.

> I love it. I am always telling people to go there. Not only is it good because it has great pieces of writing and a fun attitude, but it also has links to other spots. Once you're there, you can start surfing to other places.
>
> Of course, I have to say go to **The Net Chick Clubhouse**, because that's my site. And have you seen **Webgrrls**? It's a list of women's sites. They're compiled by Aliza Sherman, who calls herself Cybergrrl. It's in alphabetical order and you can click on someone's name and it takes you to their home page. I like that. You get to know other women that way. It's a good way to start networking with other people who are on the Net.

Another women's site is **The Black Stump Girl Page**, part of the extraordinary Australian Black Stump site. Here you'll find hundreds of links to services for women online, split into categories: artists, books, business, fame, fashion, feminism, motoring, music, health, sports and resource lists. From **Women and Cars** to **The Girl Scouting Home Pages** to **Pleiades—An Internet Resource for Women**, you'll find plenty to pique your interest here.

Sinclair points out that the key to the Web is understanding that you're not just clicking on to a site, but to part of a network. The best sites all link to like-minded places. One of the joys for the drifter is that for every door you open, more present themselves in front of you.

Addresses

geekgirl
http://geekgirl.com.au/

The Net Chick Clubhouse
http://www.cyborganic.com/People/carla/

Web Grrls — Women on the Web
http://www.webgrrls.com/

The Black Stump Girl Page
http://werple.net.au/~lions/women.htm

Women and Cars
http://www.theautochannel.com/mania/women/

The Girl Scouting Home Pages
http://www.emf.net/~troop24/scouting/gsusa.html

Pleiades — An Internet Resource for Women
http://www.pleiades-net.com/

See also...

FeMiNa
http://www.femina.com/

'A comprehensive, searchable directory of links to female-friendly sites and information on the World Wide Web.' Classified listings, site reviews and a Women's Site of the Week pick.

Glass Wings
http://www.glasswings.com.au/GlassWings/welcome.html

Katherine Phelps, who wrote the book *Surf's Up: Internet Australian Style*, has been running this webzine/hangout for yonks. It has a shopping mall (ugly but necessary, I suppose, to fund the rest of the site), games and lots of discussion of sexuality and sensuality.

Australian Institute for Women's Research and Policy
http://www.gu.edu.au/gwis/aiwrap/AIWRAP.home.html

The institute is 'the first gender issues research centre in Australia to focus on the links between academics, government, industry and the wider community in the development of policies affecting women and gender issues. AIWRAP is committed to creating a dialogue between women's issues researchers and policy practitioners in private enterprise, the government and the community. Through this dialogue, AIWRAP will provide timely and useable research expertise to enhance the status of women in Australian society.' Can be a little dry, but has acres of research and well-maintained lists of links.

VNS Matrix
http://sysx.apana.org.au/artists/vns/

At the other end of the market, the Matrix gals are never dull. Four artists from South Australia, they 'investigate and decipher the narratives of domination and control which surround high technological culture, and explore the construction of social space, identity and sexuality in cyberspace'. Mythbusters, media hackers and all-round troublemakers.

Women's Web
http://www.womweb.com/index.html

'An online community for women and men who want to learn more about women's business, issues and lives.' *Working Woman*, *Working Mother* and *Ms* mags make up the heart of the site. It's a bit light on links, though.

Women's Web World: The Feminist Majority Online
http://www.feminist.org/textmenu.html

An American nonprofit organisation that promotes women's rights. Loads of research, publications, news and events listings, with a well-maintained library of links.

Women's Wire
http://www.women.com/

A San Francisco Webzine with more of a sense of humour than Women's Web World. It offers news and entertainment sections, its own comics, profiles and the chance for surfers to participate in various discussions.

Women's Resources
http://sunsite.unc.edu/cheryb/women/wresources.html

A comprehensive crunchdown of hundreds of Websites relating to women's issues, from health to sport to gender issues to cool-chick films.

NrrdGrrl!
http://www.winternet.com/~ameliaw/

A groovin' site for anyone who has been told she is 'too smart, too loud, too opinionated, too tall, too short, too fat, too thin, too brash, too shy, too sexy, too plain, too bitchy, too nice, too needy, too aloof, too weak, too strong, too independent, too sensitive, too serious, too fickle, too cute, too silly, too demanding, too much, too ANYTHING, too EVERYTHING'. Is that you?

The Friendly Grrrls Guides to the Internet
http://www.youth.nsw.gov.au/rob.upload/friendly/index.html

Rosie Cross's excellent, comprehensive Web tour. Get your ticket free.

Body Modification

POP CULTURE is like the universe as pictured by the Big Bang theory—forever expanding. The centre grows and grows, but the fringe is always there, moving further and further out. As the mainstream subsumes trends and fads, the fringes either lift the stakes or find new margins. As tattooing, for example, became fashionable enough for office workers, nice girls and youth group coordinators early in the '90s, piercing underwent a resurgence. Then when it seemed everyone was getting something pierced, scarification became the new extreme (though there were noticeably fewer takers). What's next is anyone's guess—maybe minor amputation, say the tip of a finger.

Fiddling about with the body (in the new, rather than old sense of the phrase) has been very much 'in' this decade. Though the interest appears to have subsided slightly over the past year or two, plenty of suburban breakfast table conversations still include questions along the lines of: 'Dad, can I borrow $100 to get a surgical-steel stud driven through my tongue/ear/nose/eyebrow/lip/navel?'

For online piercing fans, or just the curious, **BME: Body Modification Ezine** covers its subject with an exemplary zeal and fastidiousness. You will never again need to wonder what a man with a few dozen studs and rings in his penis would look like. The site covers piercing, tattooing, scarring and branding, other types of modification (surgery, 'transhumanism', bodybuilding), and ritual and temporary modifications. It has archives of historical material, and interviews and profiles of the major figures in the scene.

Be warned, the sensitive may find some of it off-putting. As one of the unpierced, I have to admit that there are pictures here that made me break into a sweat and cross my legs.

Sometimes even the names are enough: 'Olivier's chest implants, fully healed', 'Arm surface impaling', 'Genital bisection — bisected corona and subincision', 'More of the human Christmas tree', 'Total male nullification'.

This is not to say I disapprove — I just can't see any of it going with the frock I was planning to wear on that date I was talking about. And I keep imagining myself setting off those metal detectors in airports.

Another place to find information on body redecoration is **The rec.arts.bodyart FAQs**. The online archive of this newsgroup contains simple guides to many of the procedures, and a Yellow Pages–style list of the people who perform them. The newsgroup's philosophy is that: 'You have control over what you do with your own body. Others should not tell you what you can or cannot do with your own body ... What you choose to do should be your own choice, neither forced on you by others, or rejected by those whom you love.'

Tattoo lovers are well catered for on the Web, too. **Tattoos.com Ezine** claims to have the largest gallery of skin art in cyberspace. Certainly it takes an eternity to work through its hundreds of photos. It also lists studios, keeps an archive of tattoo-related articles and has links to many places like the **Electric Ink Tattoo Salon**, a Rhode Island tattoo parlour which offers portfolios of the work of its artists, as well as its very own tattooing FAQ, written with refreshing candour by *needlemeister* Chris Borge:

> Does it hurt? Of course it hurts, we're sticking needles into you. Generally speaking it's an annoying kind of pain, not unbearable but also not a pleasure. (There are those who enjoy it, but they're another story entirely.) The least painful areas are generally the outside of the arms and legs. Chest and back are somewhat more painful and usually the sternum and the ribs are the worst. Genitals, I think you can figure out for yourself.

THE DIGITAL HUMAN

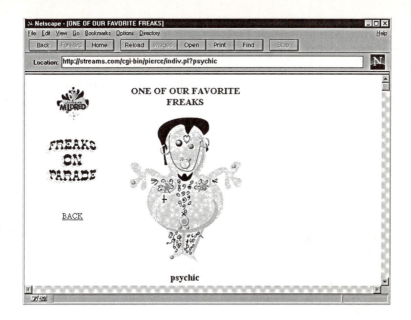

A good rule of thumb is that any place that feels good to be touched is going to suck to be tattooed.

Dawn's TatZine is a specialist online mag for women. It's a big download, but worth the wait: 'If you're sick of those tattoo magazines that seem to portray ALL tattooed women as being sleazy, leather-clad chicks, then this is the site for you! Don't you think that it's about time that a Tattoo/Fashion magazine was created? I know I do.' Dawn Collopy offers tips for keeping your tattoo vibrant and interviews other women about their tats.

Of course, there are always going to be people like me who can't bear the thought of being pierced or punctured. For us, there is a neat, clean, hygienic alternative, **Piercing Mildred**, a Web game which 'offers you the chance to exact body modifications such as exotic piercings and scarification without all the muss and fuss' by arranging various bits and baubles on the cartoon Mildred. The game is sophisticated—you have a limited amount of money to buy your piercings and tattoos, which can be quite imaginative, and they come with their own, inbuilt 'variable chance of infection'. Hit the 'Heal' button and any problems clear right up. If only it was like that in real life.

Addresses

Gauntlet International
http://www.gauntlet.com/

BME: Body Modification Ezine
http://freeq.com/underground/bme/

The rec.arts.bodyart FAQs
http://www.cis.ohio-state.edu/text/faq/usenet/bodyart/top.html

Tattoos.com Ezine
http://tattoos.com/

Electric Ink Tattoo Salon
http://www.tiac.net/users/cborge/

Dawn's TatZine
http://shoga.wwa.com/~dcollopy/

Piercing Mildred
http://streams.com/pierce/

Death—No More Taboos

THE NET doesn't like taboos. It's a safe bet that whatever society deems should not be talked about in polite company will be talked about here. And loudly. What was covered will be brought into the light. What was closed will be forced open.

So it's not a surprise that death has more than its fair share of Web sites. Some are real cheery, like **The Death Clock**, which asks you for your birth date and your sex, then uses average life expectancies to calculate the number of seconds you probably have left to live. If you're feeling bad after it gives you the figure, check out the celebrity archive—at least you might be due to outlive Madonna.

Less threatening is **Find-a-Grave**, which lets you search through an alphabetical and geographical listing of the final resting places of supposedly noteworthy people. Or the **Dead People Server**, which asks the question, Is there a better celebrity than a dead celebrity?

The best-known dead person on the Net is Joseph Paul Jernigan, a murderer who met his maker on 5 August 1993. On that day, after his appeal failed, he was executed by lethal injection. Usually, executed criminals' bodies are released to families or buried by the state, but Jernigan had signed an organ donor's card. Thanks to the toxicity of the barbiturate that killed him, however, his organs were unusable, but Jernigan's body attained a new lease of life of a different kind though the **Visible Human Project** at the National Library of Medicine in Maryland. It was X-rayed, embedded in gelatine, frozen, cut into four blocks, and then sliced into 1871 pieces (yes, much like ham at the deli). Each 1 mm thick layer was photographed, and the pictures now make up the core of the project's biomedical image library.

In November 1994, some of these images were made

available on the Net, and Jernigan became an overnight, posthumous celebrity. The reason for the excitement was that the scans of Jernigan's body parts can be taken to pieces and reconstructed. They can be run, slide by slide, as an animated tour, or viewed in sections. Only a fraction of the whole body is available on the Web; you have to apply to the library to download all the scans, and/or those of Jernigan's less famous female counterpart, who has been sliced into more than 5000 sections. CD-ROM versions are also available.

If it's your brain rather than your eyes that needs stimulating, **Kearl's Guide to the Sociology of Death and Dying**, is an exhaustive, annotated list of serious death resources on the Net, those concerned with how we die and how we cope with dying.

'Death is the muse of our religions, philosophies, political ideologies, arts and medical technologies,' writes author Michael Kearl, a sociology professor at a Texas university. 'It sells newspapers and insurance policies, invigorates the plots of our television programs, and—judging from our dependency on fossil fuels—even powers our industries.'

The largest and best set of death-related resources is housed at **DeathNET**. This crusading site, which began in January 1995, is a comprehensive archive of all aspects of death and dying, with special interest in euthanasia and suicide. Thanks to our prudery and denial, most of these resources, it points out, are not readily available from any other source. The site was created by John Hofsess, executive director of the Right to Die Society of Canada, in collaboration with Derek Humphry, author of the controversial suicide guide *Final Exit* and president of ERGO! (Euthanasia Research and Guidance Organisation) in Oregon.

> DeathNET offers the world's largest collection of 'right to die' materials and services on the Internet. It gathers together a wide array of

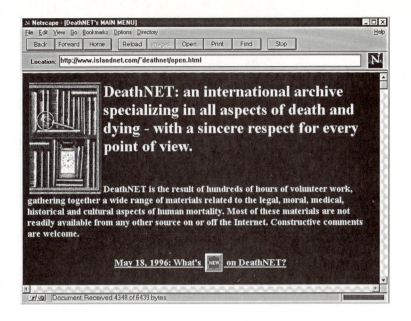

information dealing with specific illnesses and severe disabilities—especially those of a life-threatening nature. It provides connecting links to medical libraries and other online services dealing with bereavement, care-giving, emotional support and counselling.

There are more than 800 files in the DeatNET library, and more than 200 links to other medical and health-related resources. It houses publications such as *Beyond Final Exit* and *Departing Drugs*, which contain information not available in book stores. The service has so far run into criticism from many right-to-life groups, and maintains a media monitoring section to create 'a public record' of how the mass media treat 'right to die' stories and issues.

Death and Dying houses all ten chapters and hundreds of thousands of words of *The Natural Death Handbook*, another suicide and euthanasia guide. It covers questions from how to care for someone dying at home to how to draw up a 'living will', how to prepare for dying, alternatives to euthanasia, and how to organise a funeral without using undertakers. It also contains many personal accounts of brave and 'conscious' deaths.

For the more Gothic, romantic view on death, it's impossible to go past **The Dark Side of the Web**, a supermarket-sized site with more than 1100 links to all manner of things connected with dying, from apparitions and crucifixes to haunted houses, the occult, pagan rituals, artistic images and movies. Its 'Cemeteries, Funeral Homes and Death' starts off with **After Death: A Description of What Happens**, and ends up at **The World Wide Cemetery**, which reveals itself to be a serious attempt to help people come to terms with loss. When a person close to us dies, it points out, we use media to notify others of the passing. So why not use the Net, shared globally by more than 30 million people?

The virtual monuments in the cemetery 'will not weather with the passage of time' and can be visited by people from around the world. The idea is that they will allow us to commemorate the lives of our loved ones in ways that traditional newspaper death announcements or stone inscriptions can't. Photographs, moving images and sounds can be included with a monument. People can create hypertext links among family members. It's the kind of place you go into cynical and come out from looking for a hanky.

Addresses

The Death Clock
http://www.ucs.usl.edu/~rkc7747/death.html

Find-a-Grave
http://www.orci.com/personal/jim/index.html

Dead People Server
http://www.scarletfire.com/dps

The Visible Human Project
http://www.nlm.nih.gov/research/visible/visible_human.html

Kearl's Guide to the Sociology of Death and Dying
http://www.trinity.edu/~mkearl/death.html

DeathNET
http://www.islandnet.com/~deathnet/

Death and Dying
http://198.68.36.114/GIB/death.html

The Dark Side of the Web
http://www.cascade.net/darkweb.html

After Death: A Description of What Happens
http://www.uio.no/~mostarke/forens_ent/afterdeath.html

The World Wide Cemetery
http://www.io.org/cemetery/Overview.html

See also...

Museo de las Momios
http://www.sirius.com/~dbh/mummies/

Guanajuato, Mexico, the birthplace of muralist Diego Rivera, is also known for its mummies. 'Until recently, to be buried in the small cemetery there, one must pay a burial plot fee which must be renewed by descendants of the deceased. If the fee can not be paid, the corpse is dug up and placed behind glass in a museum, and because of some sort of magical properties of the soil, the exhumed bodies are surprisingly well preserved—with hair, skin and often clothing still intact.'

The Obituary Page
http://catless.ncl.ac.uk/Obituary/

Another of the many virtual cemeteries. Visit the memorial garden, register a death, check out their links. It also has a pets' corner.

Dead Man Talkin'
http://monkey.hooked.net/monkey/m/hut/deadman/deadman.html

A series of columns written by Dean Carter, a death row inmate at California's San Quentin (he was convicted of killing four women in 1984). Carter gives an insider's view of what it's like waiting to die. 'I haven't decided how I feel about lethal injection yet. We are supposed to have a choice on cyanide gas or lethal injection and when asked which one I would choose if I am ever executed, I never have an answer. I think that it has been made too clean and clinical to kill someone.'

The WWW Post Mortem Page
http://www.best.com/~gazissax/silence/altfunin.html

A death site index. It gives site quality rankings, from four headstones down to one.

The Death of Rock and Roll
http://weber.u.washington.edu/~jlks/pike/DeathRR.html

Jeff Pike was so curious about the relationship between rock and roll and death that he wrote a book about it: *Untimely Demises, Morbid Preoccupations and Premature Forecasts of Doom in Pop Music*. The hypertext-laced Web version sorts through the deaths of dozens of rock figures, and asks why models, politicians, film stars, wrestlers, race drivers and stunt pilots don't have such life-threatening jobs.

The Cardboard Box
http://www.funeral.net/info/cdbd.html

The way to go out. Why not try what they delicately describe as a 'non-protective casket'? What were you going to protect yourself against anyway? The Interlake Casket & Urn company offers this cardboard coffin. Sturdy. Handy. Cheap.

Blow Yer Brains Out
http://www.islandnet.com/~moron/deterrent/roulette.html

'So you've had a bad day at the shithole you work in and while you have romanticised about killing your boss, you just can't get it together to go grab your fifteen minutes of fame. Your lover left a long time ago and the only mail you ever receive is from bill collectors and lawyers. You've got no food, no money, no clean clothes, no friends and you think you've got scabies. You've thought about ending it all, but think that it's an awfully big step.' Here's the gun. All you have to do is click on the trigger and the site tells you if your one in six chance made you a winner or a loser. I missed.

Bad Hair Days

THE DAMN thing got me again. One minute you're innocently clicking on a curious sounding hypertext link and the next, well, it's four hours later and you've trawled through 117 places that would have seemed totally unconnected before, but now seem all of a piece.

My journey began at **Mullet Watch**. The site name interested me because I have a thing about fish. Thinking it might be a library of fascinating ichthyological sightings (as one would), I ventured aboard. Clicking on 'What is a mullet?', I was met with a photo of country and western star Billy Ray Cyrus and the declaration 'This is!' Oh, the horror! As it turned out, they were only talking about his hair. The site explains:

> A mullet is long at the back and short at the front. It is an unusual haircut because, even though it is never in fashion, it is always worn with pride. It is not a natural haircut. Your hair doesn't grow into a mullet. You have to have it cut that way on purpose. A mullet is not long hair slicked back. A mullet is two haircuts in one. A mullet is a work of art!

Ash Wakeman, Sydneysider and self-appointed 'Mullet Watch maintenance man', invites mullet spotters the world over to contribute sightings. Some of the better-known mullets, he says, belong to comic characters Bishop and Longshot from *The X-Men*, magician Penn Jilette, singers Nick Cave and Michael Bolton and TV actor Ken Wahl. The mullet is not gender-specific. Princess Di often sports the female equivalent (the femullet).

Wakeman became interested in mullets after reading an article in *Grand Royal*, the house zine of rap act the Beastie Boys. He and his flatmates (who are also mullet obsessed) have

THE DIGITAL HUMAN

named February 14 International Mullet Day. The highlight of their yearly celebration is the announcement of the Wahls, awards given to mullet wearers and watchers. Here are some of their notes on the 1996 awards:

> The Wahl for Celebrity Mullet of the Year is a three-way tie between Jonathon Taylor Thomas, Zacharey Ty Bryan and Taran Noah Smith. The three obnoxious kids on *Home Improvement*. Stupid names = stupid show = stupid hair.
>
> The first Mullet Watch Hall of Famer is none other than spunk Brad Pitt. Brad is not known for his mulletness and is a surprising choice. However, it was felt that the very fact that the sexiest man in the world (I think Bill Murray should hold that title) once had a mullet gives hope to Mulleted guys the world over.

Somehow, Mullet Watch got me thinking. How many other hair-related sites are there out there? I'm sure it says something about Net users that most of the 100-plus links I've checked out have something to do with . . . male-pattern baldness. But let's look at those that don't. **Hair Trek** takes as its subject *Star Trek Voyager's* Captain Kathryn Janeway (Kate Mulgrew), who has a very assertive hairstyle. The site allows you to transpose other styles (Farrah Fawcett, Whoopi Goldberg) onto her head. Cute.

Unsurprisingly, **Hair: The Musical** has its own unofficial pages, with the history of the show, explanations of the plot, information on the original cast, sound and photo archives, and a list of current productions. **The Official Hair Dyeing Page** is packed with information drawn from the successes and failures of its two authors. **Lily's Retro Eighties Hairdo Hall of Shame** is one woman's tales of 'a decade of embarrassments'. With photo accompaniment, she describes her various 'dos in bemused terms, from the 'cross between Siouxie Sioux and a feather duster' to the purple number—'high saturation and high maintenance'.

And then they just get odd. **Planet-Hair-Ium** offers hair horoscopes, inviting you to click on your sign and 'find out what solutions the stars have in store for you (and your hair) this month!' Thankfully, it tells me which will be my Good Hair Days in the month. Only two. Seems about right.

The Bob Haircut Pages, turns out to be just a library of photos of women with that haircut, from '20s actress Louise Brooks to Teri Hatcher and Phoebe Cates. Ditto **The Long Hair site**, which does more than blur the line between fandom and fetish:

> This page is dedicated to those beautiful ladies who decided to wear their hair very long. I myself adore long hair on ladies, especially when the hair goes down to the waist or even beyond—if it is shiny and healthy. So I thought it might be a good idea to set up a Web page, to share my fascination with other long hair lovers. My intention is to give those

of you who adore long female hair the possibility to enjoy its erotic beauty without the need of nakedness.

Call me old-fashioned, but I just felt soiled. I chose instead the possibility of enjoying clicking out.

Addresses

Mullet Watch
http://www.zeta.org.au/~ash/mullet/mullet.htm

Hair Trek
http://www2.ari.net/gene/janeway/janeway.html

Hair: The Musical
http://www-leland.stanford.edu/~toots/Hair/hair.html

The Official Hair Dyeing Page
http://www-leland.stanford.edu/~mizraith/dyeing.html

Lily's Retro Eighties Hairdo Hall of Shame
http://www.well.com/user/lilyb/hairdo.html

Planet-Hair-Ium
http://www.yoursalon.com/salon/yourproblem/planet.html

The Bob Haircut Pages
http://www.informatik.tu-muenchen.de/cgi-bin/nph-gateway/hphalle9/~kuerten/spec/bob.html

The Long Hair Site
http://www.tlhs.org/

See also...

The Beard and Moustache Home Page
http://www.sys.uea.ac.uk/~dmh/Beards/Beards.html

The home of facial hair on the Net. It has its own club, a beard photo and cartoon gallery, a beard discussion page, a regularly updated events list and a collection of members' pages. It also keeps tabs on the 1997 World Beard and Moustache Championships.

Beards
http://members.aol.com/Beardguy/beards.htm

'Welcome to the home of excellent Beards!' it proclaims. And yes, it's face fuzz heaven. 'Beards don't always get the respect and appreciation they deserve! These pages highlight some of the many excellent beards I've seen.'

The Snazzy Beards Page
http://www-scf.usc.edu/~psilvia/beard.html

A tribute to men 'and women' who have developed what the curator refers to as 'snazzy beards', such as Sigmund Freud, Jerry Garcia and author Frank Herbert. 'Like MIAs, left-fielders, and sociologists, people with snazzy beards often do not receive the recognition that they deserve.'

Bald Is Beautiful
http://pubweb.acns.nwu.edu/~pfa/bald.html

Home of the Baldness Hall of Fame, Proud Bald Men on the Web, Bald Pride and various organisations, it has music by, for and about bald headed men, and a collection of files on bald animals, bald humour, bald literature, bald places and bald plants.

BELIEFS

Alternative Alternative Religions

CONTEMPLATING **The First Church of Jesus Christ, Elvis,** I experienced what can only be described as an epiphany. Kneeling before the beatific picture of His Kingliness, reading aloud the scripture—*'And Elvis so loved the world that he died, fat and bloated, in a bathroom. He very pointedly did not rise from the dead three days later, but was nonetheless seen across the world by various and sundry housewives'*—it became obvious to me that religion and cyberspace were made for each other.

But not that old-time, mainstream religion. No, the Internet, the home of the individual pursuit, the benefactor of the niche group, the friend of the small concern and the idiot collective, is the perfect breeding ground for new (and ever stupider) faiths.

A pilgrimage to **GodWeb** converted me once and for all. GodWeb, 'the newest, hottest religion on the electronic frontier … a collaboration of all the brightest up-and-coming faiths', brings together many Net congregations, promising to package and deliver the 'power of polytheism' for all of us.

'The problem with monotheistic faith is its lack of flexibility,' the site preaches. 'It's impossible for one God to adapt to numerous cultural, economical and political interests, so you end up with your Godhead spread too thin over a dozen interest groups, caught in the middle of political debate, and branded with stereotype.'

Assembled here are **The Church of The Holy Scab**, **The Intergalactic House of Fruitcakes**, **The Virtual Vatican** and **The Cult of the Forked DaggarJon**. The Scab disciples prostrate themselves before the altar of grossness. The Fruitcakes, 'the Last True Faith on this pathetic little planet', worship something called Otis, in myriad ways.

WITNESS THE NOT SO TRUE BELIEVERS

> Every week we choose a sacred object of worship. This object may never have been worshipped before and cannot have appeared in *Time* magazine. The object is celebrated in a two colour (read 'black and white') Xerox collage, which we mail to all members of the House, and anyone else who wants one. This object is worshiped for a week by our followers and then ignored thereafter.

Pope Violence the First of the Virtual Vatican believes in bad moods, while the people of the DaggarJon, 'the first Netscape-enhanced religion', are much less fussy about their spiritual modus operandi: 'Believe whatever you want, and still have a place in the afterlife. Do as many or as few sacraments as you like. No special places of worship required.'

Dear reader, my search for spiritual guidance did not stop there. I spent time, quality time, at **The McChurch Tabernacle**, which argued that if God does exist, 'He should be prevented from contact with impressionable children' because He 'would be the type of personality who would be likely to peer at the children entrusted to His care from the dark side of a one-way mirror, occasionally sending cryptic messages to individual children, expecting them to figure it out for themselves or face dire consequences.'

On the other hand, 'McChurch is a REAL religion, complete with iconographic images suitable for worship, a martyred saint, snappy advertising slogans, and easy to understand spiritual truths that make McWorship as easy as picking up a burger and fries on the way home from work! Easier, in fact! McChurch has a great deal to offer to average middle-aged housewives, unemployed door-to-door encyclopedia salesmen, cynical solipsists, and under-achieving responsibility dodgers . . . in short: PEOPLE LIKE YOU!'

Something told me they weren't taking my quest for enlightenment seriously. I had the same feeling at **The Grand Holy Unorthodox Church Ironic**. From the catechism:

BELIEFS

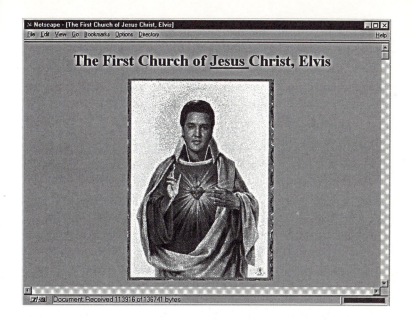

Irony is the force which truly controls the universe. Look around you. At any given moment, improbable and even silly things are occurring at an incredible rate. The only possible explanation is that some divine intelligence is coordinating everything. It just happens that this divine intelligence, which we call Tod, has a really warped sense of humour.

The Church of the Bunny is also meant to be funny. And isn't. The **First Church of the Mad Scientist** describes itself as 'wacky', which is always a sign that you should turn your browser around and head the other way.

The First Church of Virus proclaims itself a 'memetically engineered atheistic religion'. Really, they're just a bunch of non-believers who are looking for converts: 'The name was chosen to be deliberately antagonistic, to put people on their guard and let them know this idea was designed to infect them. Call it truth in advertising.'

The Church of Euthanasia is either deadly serious or deadly funny, depending on which way you want to look at it. And if you can't bring yourself to look at it either way, then its ambiguousness can also be enjoyable and thought-provoking:

> At the core of the church's theology is the belief that every aspect of the deepening global environmental crisis, including climate change, reduction of biodiversity, poisoning of the water and atmosphere, and topsoil erosion, directly results from the over-abundance of a single species: *Homo sapiens* ... Euthanasists support only voluntary forms of population reduction, including suicide, free abortion, and sodomy, which they define as any sexual act not intended for procreation. They are also fiercely vegetarian, and support cannibalism for those who insist on eating flesh.

You can check out their *Snuff It* e-zine, links to related sites, and essays on such things as 'Butchering the Human Carcass'. Or contribute to their fund to start a Suicide Assistance Hotline.

More seriously, **The First Church of Christ, Abortionist** was founded by Carnegie Mellon University staff and students in April 1994 to provide moral leverage against the Christian far right in America. It argues that society must recognise that 'the foetus is not a person, and that we cannot afford to presume an inalienable right to breed'.

The religion that makes the most sense to me is **The Church of the SubGenius**, 'The world's only admittedly for-profit, non-tax-deductible religion!' This is a bit of a worry, given that, as far as I can tell anyway, it's not meant to make sense. An ongoing satire, it uses slogans, epithets, parables and general blathering to send up our belief systems.

Subscription to the SubGenius belief system promises us all the chance to eliminate compulsive urges such as:

smoking, lethargising, overeating, insomnia, the inability to take drugs, constipation, old age, sex and money problems, baldness, illness, the Work Instinct, assouliness, and painful shortage of SLACK!

This is a certified religion of scorn and vengeance directed at all of THEM, the enemies of us Outsiders. It is 'self-help' through scoffing and blaspheming, frenzied fornication and the Tumping of Graven Images. The Church of the SubGenius is the ultimate secret order, the superior brain cult for those who 'know better' but who demand in the LUST for GRINS a spectacular, special-effects-laden belief system—a 'stuporstition.'

Just right for the Information Stuporhighway.

Addresses

The First Church of Jesus Christ, Elvis
http://jubal.westnet.com/hyperdiscordia/sacred_heart_elvis.html

GodWeb
http://www.urich.edu/~jtd3h/godweb.htm

The Church of the Holy Scab
http://www.creative.net/~thoth/church/

The Intergalactic House of Fruitcakes
http://www.tiac.net/users/ighf/

The First Church of the Binary Revolution
http://www.txmusic.com/church/church.htm

The Virtual Vatican
http://www.netwalk.com/~popev/

The Cult of the Forked DaggarJon
http://www.urich.edu/~jtd3h/pregod.htm

The McChurch Tabernacle
http://mcchurch.org/

The Grand Holy Unorthodox Church Ironic
http://www.io.com/~chimera/irony.html

The Church of the Bunny
http://ourworld.compuserve.com:80/homepages/bunnychurch/

First Church of the Mad Scientist
http://wilmot.unh.edu/~mca/madscience.html

The Church of Virus
http://www.lucifer.com/virus

The Church of Euthanasia
http://www.paranoia.com/coe/

The First Church of Christ, Abortionist
http://www.contrib.andrew.cmu.edu/org/fcca/

The Church of the SubGenius
http://sunsite.unc.edu/subgenius/

See also...

Weird Religions
http://www.physics.wisc.edu:80/~shalizi/hyper-weird/kooks.html#weird-religions

A list of newsgroups and Websites devoted to fantastic faiths.

Altar of Unholy Blasphemy
http://www.paranoia.com/~goat/altar

Only to be visited if you have a strong spiritual constitution. Starts off being a call to arms, a demand that we all shake free from the shackles of society and use our own strength, integrity and moral resolve to move through life. By the second page, it's into full-on (shock me now, Lord) Christian-baiting.

Finding God In Cyberspace
gopher://una.hh.lib.umich.edu/oo/inetdirsstacks/religion%3agresham

For the mainstream religious, this is a large, dry, academic guide to where to find things. If you haven't actually lost God (I leave him on top of the fridge, so I will always know where to find him), it may not be of much use to you.

The Great God Contest
http://www.islandnet.com/~luree/contest.html

The rules are simple. Any religion in the world is invited to enter its god, who will have to undertake three challenges. The winner will be the god who completes them in the shortest time.

Astrology

THE AMERICAN author, and everyone's favourite lexicographer, Ambrose Bierce, once defined astrology as 'the science of making the dupe see stars'. More than a century later, both astrology and Bierce's **Devil's Dictionary** are alive and well, and nestling cheek by jowl on the Net.

Bierce's book, out of copyright since the early part of the century, has been almost wholly reproduced online by an obsessed Norwegian. Astrology sites come to us from all over the globe. The biggest and best index of stargazing links is **Astrology on the Net**, a directory to more than 200 Websites. Most of these want one thing: your money. To get you to hang around long enough, though, most are willing to cough up some simple horoscopes. So there are plenty of places to get a straight, simple daily or weekly forecast for free. Any of the following—**Dell Horoscope Magazine**, **The Psychic Center**, **Astrology By Moonlight**, **Internet Horoscopes**—will provide the service. You will also find varying amounts of background info on the art of stargazing (but not as much as you could find at the **Resource Guide to the History of Astrology**), before the inevitable hard word is put on you to pay for a more in-depth service.

If you're going to spruik, you might as well do it with a little panache, so my favourites are the celebrity astrologers. Chief among these, it seems, is **Jonathan Cainier**, whose column appears in the *Daily Mail* newspaper in England, and who is strongly recommended by many sites around the Net. His site offers weekly forecasts for each of the twelve signs of the zodiac, in text and audio format. Of better value is the self-proclaimed 'Astrologer Extraordinaire', **AdZe MiXXe**, one of those charming media creations who constantly refers to himself in the third person. Part stargazer, part shameless

BELIEFS

self-promoter (and not necessarily in that order), MiXXe runs a bright and bustling site which offers everything from financial predictions to sex advice. He proclaims:

> On the public record, I've successfully predicted the collapse of the Tokyo Stock Exchange, the stock market high of 1996, the fall of the Berlin Wall, the dissolution of the Soviet Union, Hurricane Andrew, the fall of Marcos and Baby Doc, the ice storms of 1993–94, the Blizzard of 1996, Frank Sinatra's success with *Duets*, Clinton's victory over Bush and many, many others.

This guy must be good. *No-one* would have thought Frank Sinatra was capable of another No. 1 hit.

On MiXXe's site, you will find today's horoscopes, astrological news and the star charts of the rich and famous. ('It's not talent, it's not luck, and it's not education that had made Bill Cosby a success. It's his Stationary Saturn and corresponding work ethic.') MiXXe even has his own e-zine, which offers background information on stargazing, his tour of the planets and sun signs, a glossary of terms and much more. A humour section offers Light Bulb Jokes of the Zodiac ('How many Taureans does it take to change a light bulb? Taurus gets bulbs that don't need changing') as well as Bosses of the Zodiac, the slightly risqué Condoms of the Zodiac and Excuses and Flu Bugs of the Zodiac.

Not content with being a funny guy, MiXXe also flaunts his depth by including information on Jung and astrology as well as a catalogue of astrological references in the Bible and Shakespeare ('The stars above us, govern our conditions' — *King Lear*). You can also browse the inevitable merchandise files, ask questions of AdZe's Oracle or check your compatibility with your partner or a celebrity, living or dead.

The other celeb worth checking out is **Kramer, Fishing Guide to the Stars**. Dubbing himself the 'astrology home buoy', this folksy prognosticator, who offers weekly forecasts and a variety of paid services, treats the whole job with a refreshing lack of reverence:

> The biggest problem with astrology is astrologers. Too many of the practitioners of this intuitive and interpretive art form are serious. Extremely serious. Way too serious. These are PEOPLE we are talking about, and humankind is essentially funny, right to the core. So lighten up. If you find an astrologer who takes him/her self too seriously, run away. The real key to astrology is learning information for yourself. Keep what works; toss the rest. While that may be a bland truism for life, it really applies in this field.

Of course, this being the Net, there are also those who don't take it seriously enough.

The folk at **Humorscope** do have their moments, though ('Cancer: Due to forces beyond your comprehension, you are

BELIEFS

about to be squirted out of the Universe like a watermelon seed. Sorry.') as does the wonderfully named Cosmopolis Panopolus, whose **High-Tech Horoscopes** have a similar ring ('Cancer: Much to the embarrassment of your family and the chagrin of your friends, you will discover that you really like country music.')

And this being the Net, the more specific your interest, the more likely you are to find it covered. There are individual sites for regional variants, **Asian Astrology** to **Aztec Astrology** (the latter an Australian site which generates an Aztec horoscope for the day). There are sites for those who want to link astrology with the stock exchange, such as **AstroEcon**, which explores 'the relationship between the mass psychology of modern investors and astrological cycles'.

Perhaps the oddest of all is **Guru to Go**, a star guidance service … for lesbians. I would have thought sexuality didn't make a lot of difference in zodiacal terms, but this site offers specialised advice on personal relationships, business and financial matters for gals who like gals. The only hitch is, you have to e-mail them first.

Addresses

The Devil's Dictionary
http://www.cs.uit.no/~frankrl/Devil/dd_.htm

Astrology on the Net
http://www.astrologer.com/website.html

Dell Horoscope Magazine
http://www.bdd.com/horo1/bddhoro1.cgi/horo1

The Psychic Center
http://dev-com.com/~ninefuture/

Astrology by Moonlight
http://www.masterm.com/astrol.html

Internet Horoscopes
http://www.tis.co.uk/tis/horoscop/index.htm

Resource Guide to the History of Astrology
http://nickel.ucs.indiana.edu/~lness/guide.html

Jonathan Cainier's Daily Forecasts
http://www.bubble.com/webstars/

AdZe MiXXe, Astrologer Extraordinaire
http://www.adze.com/

Kramer, Fishing Guide to the Stars
http://www.io.com/~fgs/

Humorscope
http://www.teleport.com/~ronl/horo.html

Cosmopolis's High-Tech Horoscopes
http://www.xmission.com/~mustard/cosmo.html

Asian Astrology
http://users. deltanet.com/~wcassidy/astro/astroindex.html

Aztec Astrology
http://www.maths.utas.edu.au/People/Michael/Aztec.html

AstroEcon
http://home.cynet.net/astroecon/

Guru to Go
http://www.pimps.com/guru.html

Lifestyles International Astrological Foundation Famous Celebrities
http://www.lifeintl.com/celeb.html

See also...

alt.astrology

Web-O-Rhythm
http://www.qns.com/html/weborhythm/

A biorhythm generator on the Net. Give it a little biographical info and it plots your intellectual, physical, emotional and intuitive cycles, displaying them in a nice little graph that, in my case, always seems to be heading in the same direction as the English cricket team's batting averages.

Personal Biorhythm Generator
http://www.facade.com/Occult/biorhythm/

Much the same.

Learning the Tarot — An Online Course
http://www2.dgsys.com/~bunning/top.html

A step-by-step guide.

Astarte's TarotWeb
http://plains.uwyo.edu/~kraftboy/tarot.htm

An introduction to the Tarot, with an FAQ, explanations of the decks and all sorts of tips and details on how to get the most out of them. Plus the choice and care of your deck, a regular newsletter, a bulletin board for discussion and links to other Tarot sites.

I-Ching
http://www.facade.com/Occult/iching/

For those of us trying to understand the forces that affect our lives. This site performs an I-Ching reading. Think hard on a problem or a question facing you and click on the button to cast the coins. Then spend the rest of your life trying to understand the answer.

Conspiracy Theories

CHRIS CARTER, creator of *The X-Files*, the television program that specialises in (and capitalises on) the surging paranoia levels of the '90s, says he is not surprised at all that the show struck a chord with the public. 'I had anticipated the paranoia and weirdness out there,' he adds, 'but I wasn't prepared for the prevalence of a basic distrust of authority and the government.'

Says the show's co-star, Gillian Anderson: 'It has become almost trendy to admit, discuss, lecture about one's distaste and frustration with the government and the government's tendency towards secrecy and cover-ups.'

Is the whole world still recovering from Watergate and the Cold War? Or, more likely, is it just the cumulative effect of the news media telling us so often that governments lie that we no longer believe them capable of truth? We're living in a time when all of the traditional pillars of society—the judicial system, government, religion—are no longer seen as reliable. People have lost faith in them.

The Net provides a breeding ground for this kind of thinking. It's no surprise that conspiracy theories have flourished. If you build a medium that allows everyone to be his own publisher, then you have the perfect vehicle for crappy, kooky, downright stupid ideas. The Web is a haven for hundreds of flavours of lunacy that would never be published in any other medium, except maybe on the kinds of handbills that are handed out by wild-eyed people at student rallies.

Then again, many of the great thinkers of history have been thought of as kooks. Undoubtedly, good will come from the Net loosening up the trade in ideas, but the signal-to-noise ratio is very low.

The 50 Greatest Conspiracies of All Time began as a book by American writers Jonathan Vankin and John Whalen, but is now a Website too. Well, parts of it are. The book covers everything from the idea that the CIA created LSD in mind control experiments, to America's supposed biological warfare experiments, to the assertion that Jack the Ripper was a member of the royal family, to the oft-stated theory that the moon landing was a hoax, to the idea that Jim Morrison is alive and as well as he could be. Four chapters from the book are reproduced online, along with six new ones, dealing with aliens on the Moon ('That's one small step for . . . guess what, Buzz? We got company!'), the Dead Sea Scrolls cover-up, the CIA, and others.

The site also boasts the best collection of related links on the Web, offering directions to a slew of conspiracies, from the antique to the freshly minted. There are those who believe that there was more to the **Waco** siege than was let on, and that the destruction of the Federal Building in **Oklahoma City** couldn't possibly have been the work of one bomb. There are still those who believe **Paul Is Dead** (his recording career continues to lend weight to the theory) and those who will never give up on the idea that the Warren Commission got its **JFK** verdict wrong. **Fair Play** magazine, by way of example, is a bi-monthly site that keeps the Kennedy conspiracy flame burning: 'It has been said that the American people are the only jury that Lee Harvey Oswald will ever have. It is our responsibility, then, to examine with utmost care and objectivity the evidence for and against him, and to reach an independent verdict.'

A one-stop shop for the curious, **Conspiracies** is a huge, online library of these alternative beliefs. Did J. Edgar Hoover influence the outcome of the Warren Commission investigation into JFK's death? Was AIDS invented by the US government for use in warfare? Does Russia (those pesky Russkies!) have

BELIEFS

an operational Star Wars defence system? The questions go on forever. So do most of the answers.

Theorising is not purely an American pastime, though. **Nexus** is an Australian-based magazine that explores what it calls little known facts, 'suppressed information'. Its editor, Duncan Roads, says conspiracies are nothing to be afraid of—they make the world go round.

> Virtually every best-selling action book or movie is based on a conspiracy of some form. In fact, as you well know, there are conspiracies everywhere, of all sizes, happening all the time—it is how our society works. *Nexus* magazine is not a conspiracy magazine. We do, however, cover subjects and stories that often cause the reader to assume there has been a conspiracy. For example, we have found evidence of at least two dozen very successful treatments for cancer that have been suppressed!

> The subject of suppressed health news is but one of many subjects covered in *Nexus* magazine. Other topics have included: cars which run on water; suppressed archaeological discoveries; the history of banks; free-energy cover-ups; how the CIA runs heroin and cocaine; mind-control technology and how it is being used; and UFOs, the unexplained. We gain our information from researchers, doctors, magazines, newsletters, computer networks and books.

Predictably, and mercifully, not all Web sites take things seriously. The **Department of Conspiracy Investigation and Propagation** 'was created by President Nixon to fill a much-needed void. Previously, conspiracies in America were a haphazard, slipshod, and unregulated affair. With the creation of the DCIP, America leapt ahead of international competitors in the conspiracy field. The Department's charter is to "Investigate unknown, and therefore unregulated, conspiracies; to regulate and co-ordinate existing conspiracies to ensure minimum duplication of effort and maximum efficiency; to obfuscate and derail foreign investigation of domestic conspiracies; and to promote the creation, funding, and perpetuation of existing domestic conspiracies."' It offers a collection of its current plots, greatest hits of the past and the chance to register your own conspiracy.

One of the favourite conspiracies of the hobby watchers is that of the Illuminati, the shadowy group of history and government manipulators (they supposedly gained control of America last century and have yet to relinquish their phantom reins) that makes the Masons look like the Boy Scouts. **The Bavarian Illuminati** has its own mock home page: 'The Illuminati have a long and glorious history of world domination. From the days of Atlantis to modern day software corporations [there are dozens of world domination conspiracy jokes at Microsoft's expense on many of these sites], our goal has remained unchanged.'

The site has spurious histories and outlines of current projects, such as its attempt to change the UN uniforms: 'Due to a clerical error, United Nations peacekeepers do not have the Illuminati logo on their helmets. You can help correct this by writing to your U.N. representative and requesting that this oversight be remedied.'

The Illuminati Home Page also purports to offer information on this group, but its contribution to world politics comes mainly in the form of a parodic song, to be sung to the tune of 'Eleanor Rigby':

> Illuminati . . .
> Hide their assassins' instructions in newspaper text . . .
> Who will be next?
> They're all around us . . .
> Underline every third word in the Times and you'll see . . .
> How can it be?
> The Illuminati . . . They're watching me, I know.
> The Illuminati . . . They're everywhere I go.

American cable channel Comedy Central has the cutest entrant in the humour category. In its Web Sites We'd Like to See section, it offers **Oliver Stone's Paranoia Web Site**. You enter your name, the name of a dead politician, a war and a country and whammo! It generates a conspiracy theory for you.

And then there are those which are just, well, odd. Like **The Lisa Marie Presley Page**, which raises the startling allegation that the publicly known Presley is not the King's daughter. 'Lisa Marie disappeared in 1977 and has not been seen since,' it insists. 'The evidence consists of scientific reports, recorded conversations, documents and more.' Making nebulous claims about the Church of Scientology's involvement, the site says Presley is living in Europe with her two daughters.

If nothing else, this theory makes the whole Michael Jackson marriage make sense.

Addresses

50 Greatest Conspiracies of All Time
http://www.conspire.com

Waco
http://www.ucalgary.ca/~dswan/conspiracy.html#waco

Oklahoma Bomb Conspiracy Page
http://www.westworld.com/~myndex/okbomb/okbomb.html

Paul Is Dead
http://catless.ncl.ac.uk/Obituary/paul.html

The JFK Assassination Home Page
http://www.thuntek.net/~rharris/jfk.html

Fair Play Magazine
http://rmii.com/~jkelin/fp.html

Conspiracies
gopher://wiretap.spies.com/11/Library/Fringe/Conspiry

Nexus
http://www.peg.apc.org/~nexus/

Department of Conspiracy Investigation and Propagation
http://www.conspiracy.org/

BELIEFS

The Bavarian Illuminati
http://www.illuminati.org/

Illuminati Home Page
http://www-swiss.ai.mit.edu/~boogles/Illuminati/

Oliver Stone's Paranoia Web Site
http://www.comcentral.com/sightings/ostone.shtm

The Lisa Marie Presley Page
http://www.docs.uu.se/~y89hbo/presley/lisa.html

See also...

Covert Action Quarterly
http://MediaFilter.org/MFF/CAQ_Contents.html

Founded in the 1970s by CIA renegade Philip Agee and associates to expose the activities of their former employer. As with *Nexus*, not enough of the magazine is available on the site (a few articles from the current issue and a limited back catalogue), but what is there is worth checking out. Unlike most operators in the area, this one offers solid and well-researched material.

Sovereign's WWW Content Page
http://Syninfo.COM/Sov/index.htmlx

'Here you will find news and events that the national and international media would never be allowed to print, information that you need to know to protect yourself in the upcoming changes going on around us right now. Covering subjects like One World Government, Militia, Patriot, AIDS, Sovereignty, Right to Keep and Bear Arms, Spirit, Awareness, Liberty, Congress, News, Rights, Solutions & more.' A seriously huge site. It's also the home of Publius Press, which publishes the work of Ralph Epperson. His *Conspiratorial View of History*, a 30-year effort, looks at many other conspiracies and argues that: the driver shot Kennedy, God definitely exists, Russia has wooden missiles, and the Turin Shroud is genuine (there was a scientific conspiracy to prove it false!).

The Trilateral Commission
http://www.trilateral.com/

'A worldwide conspiracy of wealthy families and financial institutions. Through our control of the money supply, we ensure that our members attain the highest offices in the most powerful countries in the world.' In 1996, they say, their main project was 'working on getting Bob Dole elected president'.

Atom Bomb
gopher://wiretap.spies.com/00/Library/Humor/Misc/conspire.txt

A text-only, spurious FAQ of the 'real' events surrounding the dropping of the atomic bomb, taken from **rec.humor.funny**: 'Is there any evidence that a thermonuclear device exploded over Hiroshima in 1945? No, absolutely none. According to leading historians and physicists, the thermonuclear bomb was not invented until years after the supposed detonation over Japanese territory.'

National Conspiracy League
http://www.infi.net/~knolled/

Conspiracies as baseball trading cards. Collect the set. With links to 'Conspiracy's Greatest Hits!' and the current players of the left and right.

UFOs and Aliens

I BELIEVE there are aliens among us. I believe they share our planet, walking our streets undetected. The person next to you right now might be one.

I believe that if you try really hard (and use modern marketing technology), you can spot them as they make their tiny, revealing cultural mistakes. They are the ones who think *Hey, Hey It's Saturday* is funny. They are the ones who barrack for Carlton. They are the vegetarians who choose the lifestyle because they think vegetarian food tastes better.

If you're searching for extraterrestrial life or intelligence, the Net is as good a place as any to start. Cyberspace could easily be considered an extraterrestrial world, teeming with life. The intelligence, of course, is much harder to find. Begin your journey at the **SETI** Institute, the official, scientifically responsible end of the UFO hunting spectrum. The Website of the Search for Extra-Terrestrial Intelligence offers information about the Institute, its many education programs, other initiatives and developments in the scientific/space community, The Big Search itself (I'll save you the trouble: the answer is roughly 'Not yet'), and a Frequently Asked Questions file.

Perth's Ron Bertino hosts what he calls the **World's Biggest UFO Archive**. And indeed, he may not be kidding. If nothing else, his site links to more than 50 alien-related Web ventures, from the perfectly sane to the completely loopy, from legitimate science to crackpot theory (sometimes hard to tell apart). Here you'll find everything from crop circles to Face on Mars theories.

Bertino keeps his own library of hundreds of UFO-related documents and also has photo albums of the famous 1947 Roswell alien 'autopsy' and other sightings. Check out the shots of flying saucers, little green men and 'possible alien structures

TAKE US TO YOUR LEDERHOSEN

on the moon' (yes, Ron, and they could just be rock formations).

You might as well visit one of the many **Roswell** sites while you're on the theme. After all, this is the conspiracy that just won't go away. And it *is* easy to believe that there was an alien spaceship crash in New Mexico in July, 1947, that the American government did autopsies on the four dead creatures, and that the film of those autopsies, the one piece of hard evidence that UFO watchers are desperate to have to prove their theories, was smuggled out and released to the public 50 years later from England by the mysterious Mr Ray Santilli. It's also easy to believe in Santa Claus—you get better presents that way.

When the Roswell film was shown on television in 1995, one of its owner's claims was that special effects people had said they believed the footage was real. Well, one SFX outfit, **The Truly Dangerous Company**, begged to differ. And it put up a Website to show exactly how easy it would have been to make the film. If nothing else, it's worth stopping by the Autopsy Bleeps and Blunders section and playing Spot the Goof.

But there's more. In 1994, **The World Wide Web Virtual Library: Unidentified Flying Objects** set itself up as a clearing-house for UFO documents and now functions as a text-based library of curious happenings. It's not as good or as comprehensive as Bertino's, but between the two sites, you'll cover more terrain than you could have imagined.

For recent material, **The Internet UFO Group Media Page** will keep you in touch with all the latest news and headlines in the area, and archives transcripts of television and radio reports about sightings and information. You want to see the KGB files on long covered-up UFO sightings in Russia? Here is the place.

The **Department of Interplanetary Affairs** offers a neat

BELIEFS

line in conspiracy theory (the shadow government, the Illuminati, are out to get us all) but is worth it for the fact that it manages to get UFOs, New Age philosophy, major paranoia and NASA's 'disinformation' campaign about the moon and Mars into one site.

The Swiss **Spirit** site is much more benign in its attempt to link UFOs to the phenomenon of the New Age, and ultimately more amusing. It's just a pity they couldn't link them to the phenomenon of decent grammar: 'The UFO-Phenomena is just one way of meeting other realities into daily-consciousness, besides ie. Out of Body Experience, Meditation (Higher-Self integration), Channeling and other influences of so called Paranormal, which is just the border of our own understanding of reality.'

Some sites actually claim to have an alien hand in them. **Messages From Distant Children** invites you to read the latest

201

messages from across the galaxy (I'm not sure how SETI missed them) before dragging you into a complex, circular discussion. Reality, this curious site warns, is only the sum of popular beliefs.

I hope that someone out there will get around to visiting us one of these days (and frankly, if I had my personal choice, it would be Athena, the spunky green alien who fell in love with Dr Smith on *Lost In Space*). But despite the acres and acres of words and pictures on these sites, and the vast libraries of documents, none of them ever seems to come to grips with the big UFO/alien questions:

1. Why do they always abduct non-credible witnesses?
2. Why are they always spotted by individuals in desolate areas rather than, say, by millions of us as they hover gently beside the Sydney Harbour Bridge during New Year's Eve fireworks displays?
3. Why don't they stick around? The weather's good.
4. If they're so smart, what are they doing here?

Addresses

SETI
http://www.seti-inst.edu/

World's Biggest UFO Archive
http://www.iinet.com.au/~bertino/index.html

The Roswell Incident
http://www.execpc.com/vjentpr/jroswell.html#evidence

The Truly Dangerous Company
http://www.trudang.com/autopsy.html#CONTENTS

The World Wide Web Virtual Library: Unidentified Flying Objects
http://ernie.bgsu.edu/~jzawodn/ufo/

The Internet UFO Group Media Page
http://www.best.com/~schmitz/IUFOG/iufog-media.html

The Department of Interplanetary Affairs
http://www.maui.net/~daryl/enmar.html

Spirit's UFO Phenomena
http://www.spiritweb.org/Spirit/ufo.html

Messages From Distant Children
http://www.users.interport.net/~mstanley/index.html

See also...

alt.alien.visitors

If they are here, this is their newsgroup.

Schwa
http://www.theschwacorporation.com/

In the dictionary, the schwa (the symbol is an upside down 'e') stands for the indeterminate vowel. Here it means something similar, the unknowable, society's amorphous fears and hatreds, our inarticulate loathing. An alien image stolen straight from Whitley Strieber (and not dissimilar to the figures at the end of *Close Encounters*) stares at you from the home page. This is a deeply cool subcultural collision, a non-linear, comic-style tale of alien invasion and paranoia from American artist Bill Barker. Really, it's an exploration of what it means to be 'the other'. It keeps the visitor in a permanent state of delighted unease. And of course, once you're hooked, you can participate in the self-defeating parody of consumerism and blow all your cash on the Schwa merchandise.

Yahoo: UFO Information
http://akebono.stanford.edu/yahoo/Entertainment/Paranormal_Phenomena/UFO_Information/

Another overall set of listings. Yahoo cheekily groups them in its Entertainment section, but we'll let it off.

The Roswell Index
http://www.roswell.org/

Home of stacks of info on the incident (it's not convinced by the footage, but maintains there is enough other evidence), and also the International Roswell Initiative, a petition-based project to have Roswell taken seriously by the world.

UFO Photos
http://www.oslonett.no/home/torealf/ufo.html

A Norwegian site which offers just about every UFO photo you've ever seen. Real? Fake? Who cares?

Urban Legends

DESPITE what you may have heard, not all the best Websites are built for people with no attention span and an addiction to digital pyrotechnics. Not all the best sites have trendy little Java doodads, fun forms to fill out, games to play, downloadable sound files, video movies, animations or wacky ways to navigate. Not all of them even have photos or graphics.

Tape my mouth closed and call me an old-schooler, but fabulous design doth not a cool site make. It doesn't even get it close. What makes a site work is content. Imagination. Perspective. Uniqueness.

The Urban Legends Archive has no pictures at all. No gimmicks, no tricks. Just text and a layout which even its kindly mother would describe as bare-bones rudimentary. And yet it is one of the most fascinating, compelling and undeniably cool sites I've ever been to, the kind of place you visit meaning to stay for five minutes, but where you end up spending the whole afternoon, occasionally leaning back from the computer screen and yelling to whoever else is in the house (i.e. the dog, last night's washing up): 'Hey, honey, you've got to come and read this.'

A natural for the Net, which is by nature a haven for rumour, scuttlebutt and plain bullshit, the archive examines some of the most widely circulated, but often unsubstantiated, stories of our time. Did you know, for example, that in need of a little cash and exposure, Barbra Streisand made a porn movie early on in her career? Or that hunky Sylvester Stallone did the same thing?

Did you know that bears are more likely to attack menstruating women? Or that there is a tiny fish in South America, the candiru, which swims up the warm urine stream of those

'WHATEVER YOU DO, DON'T LOOK BACK'

who relieve themselves in the water and then, once inside the body, releases its spikes?

Did you know that the crew of the *Apollo 13* spacecraft had suicide pills that they considered taking when everything went wrong on their mission? Or that more than a dozen people have died when the faulty vending machines they were rocking fell on them?

In each of the above paragraphs, the first statement was a myth. The second was true. That's one of the beauties of the archive—it's not always the ones you believe that turn out to be true. (I would have been happier, though, if the story about a man who attempted to repair damage to his scrotum with an industrial staple gun had not been confirmed.)

Most of the material is drawn from the tales, assertions and rumours that are the main traffic of the popular **alt.folklore.urban** newsgroup. The best and most comprehensive of these posts are lovingly repackaged on the site. The contributors explore each story, explaining it in detail, then set out to corroborate or debunk it, looking for its origins or any evidence supporting it.

Alt.folklore.urban's FAQ defines an urban legend as a story which 'appears mysteriously and spreads spontaneously in varying forms; contains elements of humour or horror [the horror often 'punishes' someone who flouts society's conventions]; makes good storytelling; and does NOT have to be false, although most are'. Its site catalogues hundreds of them in the following handy categories: animals, celebrities, classics, collegiate, death, Disney, drugs, food, language, legal, medical, miscellaneous, movies, politics, products, religion, science, sex, songs and television. In its own way, it captures many of the themes of our time, our fears, our foibles and our collective guilts. It provides another kind of social history, a glimpse into our collective unconscious.

BELIEFS

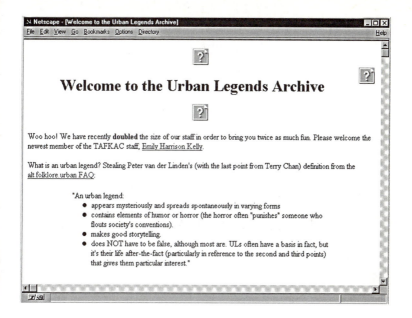

Perhaps the oddest thing is to realise how many of these rumours and stories have taken hold of you. I remember reading in folklore academic Jan Harold Brunvand's *The Vanishing Hitchhiker* a number of ghoulish stories I had heard at slumber parties in high school or around campfires at night as eerie noises drifted in from the bush. They were often almost identical, with different window dressing to suit the audience.

Anyway, it's not just the ghoulish, killer-in-the-backseat tales of fear and retribution that make the archive worth a visit. There are lots of more-benign stories you may have thought were true that the archive claims are not. For example:

If you put a teaspoon into an open champagne bottle, it will *not* prevent the fizz disappearing.
Sesame Street's Bert and Ernie are *not* gay.
Eskimos do *not* have more than 50 different words for snow.

Walt Disney is *not* cryogenically frozen (OK, I didn't really believe this one, but I wanted to).

Cartoon pirate Captain Pugwash did *not* have a crew that included Master Bates, Seaman Stains and Roger the Cabin Boy (the cabin boy's name was Tom). Wow. I'd been spreading the Pugwash stories for years. Any site which has the power to change what you believe is cool by me.

NB: The candiru fish is about 40–60 mm long and only 4–6 mm wide. A total leg-crosser of a fish, it is more likely to attack women owing to their larger urethral opening. It can be removed by surgery or by use of the xaqua plant or the buitach apple, which will kill the fish and dissolve it. Just thought you might want to know.

Address

The Urban Legend Archive
http://www.best.com/~debunk/

MEDIA

Abundance vs Scarcity

A FRIEND of mine, who makes a good part of his living through his ability to pass himself off as a specialist in a number of fields, reckons the growth of the Internet could mean the death of the expert. His logic is simple. From time immemorial, the expert (wise man, court magician or statistician) has been the reservoir of knowledge. A large part of the expert's authority has derived from his or her ability to remember, or retrieve, information that others don't have access to. He has been a giant dam in the river of information. But the info-flow is changing. All those little tributaries are starting to route around the dams and head for the sea.

The Net lends itself to the spread of extraordinary, obsessively detailed and catalogued (and often arcane) information. And despite initial appearances, not all of it is about *Star Trek* or *Monty Python*. **The Internet Movie Database** has more than 75 000 separate entries. More than 200 000 people are referenced in its library, with details of just about every film-maker, actor, composer and cinematographer you've ever heard of, as well as those you haven't. Pretty much anyone who ever saw a script being photocopied or walked past a location shoot gets a mention.

If it's contemporary music you're interested in, try the **Ultimate Band List** or the **Yahoo Artists List**. Last time I looked, the latter contained links to 10 905 separate band sites. That's an open door to more information than you could pull together in a couple of years of phoning record companies or scanning magazines. And speaking of magazines, **The Electronic Newsstand** collects their Web sites for our use. The number of mags offering virtual versions passed 2000 earlier this year. Some are pretty stingy, but many put a substantial percentage of their contents on the Web.

These resources are not even scratching the surface of the thousands of academic papers and research libraries connecting with each other online. And though the pedigree of material available on the Net has been questionable, its foundations appear to be solidifying with every passing day. More than once the Net has been called the modern equivalent of the Library of Alexandria. And the suggestion that it could one day contain almost every word ever written is not an unlikely one.

If we all have easy access to far more information than we have had before, I'm betting that the role of experts will change. They will still be needed for their ability to see patterns, to make sense of numbers, to analyse and comment, and to contextualise. But their days as info gatekeepers are coming to an end.

This is just one of the changes likely to be brought about by a basic shift that the Net (and the digital age) presents. In many areas, it moves us from a model of scarcity to one of abundance. When information was hard to come by, it lent itself to control. It could be stored and guarded. Until now, 'limited bandwidth' has made the spread of information difficult. The printed word—books, magazines and newsspapers—the primary model for information distribution, has always racked up the bills. All of its forms are expensive to make, to distribute and to buy. The Net offers theoretically unlimited bandwidth. It makes savings left, right and centre—print and distribution costs go out the window (more on that in the next chapter). It has the potential to make all kinds of previously expensive information affordable.

The Web is not concerned with size. Web newspapers and magazines are not limited by problems of squeezed editorial space. Stories can be as long or as short as they want to be. Sites can be as big as the imaginations of their creators. The **Australian Broadcasting Corporation** site is a good example.

MEDIA

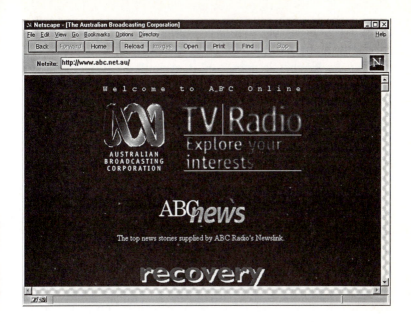

If cyberspace were a real, physical place, the site would have its own postcode. Stitching together thousands of web pages, it has been a major undertaking for Aunty. 'And this is just the tip of the iceberg,' says site coordinator Thomas Ashelford. 'The web is elastic. It's not like TV or radio, where there are a limited number of frequencies and a limited number of hours in the day. It's just gonna keep on growing.'

The ABC home page offers four ways to access its reservoir of material. You can head into the site via 'TV', 'Radio' or an overview called 'Explore Your Interests', which allows you to search by subject. If that seems too vague, the fourth path is at the bottom of the main screen: a shortcuts finder, a quick-fix device which allows you to jump directly to any one of 28 destinations. Choose from the TV and radio schedules, a bunch of collections of links, *24 Hours* magazine, the various radio networks and programs, a handful of television shows and ABC

Shopping Online. The site is not just about spruiking its own products. There's a fair whack of self-promotion, but beyond the details of what is going on at various programs, some of the sites are working to add value through the Web, making use of the bandwidth.

The transcripts of youth current affairs program *Behind The News* (it reaches a million students each week) are useful for teachers, who can print them out and distribute them in the classroom. Similarly, Radio National archives transcripts of its happy family of Report programs (*The Health Report, The Law Report, The Education Report, The Media Report* and *The Business Report*). Thus, should you fail to report at one of the Report times, you can pick up on what you missed at your later convenience. Transcripts of radio have long been available to the public, but never in such an easily accessed way. You used to write or phone and wait for an eternity. You also had to pay. But that's the difference between abundance and scarcity.

The *Quantum* pages offer another example of the extra uses that can be found for research. They provide the story material, as well as additional information in the way of contact addresses for those interviewed, often with e-mail addresses and phone numbers.

Another venture that highlights the difference that the abundance model can make is **The Internet Pizza Review Home Page**, brainchild of Melburnians Felicity Jones and George Seremetidis. The site is an invention of stupendous simplicity, but admirable vision. Simply put, its aim is this: to use the vast Internet community to review every pizza joint in the known universe. What could be easier? There's an undeniable bravery, ambition and romance in this idea that just gets to me. Right now, there are two people out there trying to provide an electronic bible for crust-lovers the world over. If they can achieve this feat, the pizzophiles will know that, wherever their journeys might be taking them, there will be a decent ham-and-pineapple at the end of the road.

The pizza review site, which was born in December 1995, invites you to offer your verdict on a local pizza establishment. The review, it says, can be as short as you like, but no longer than 100 words (to make it easier for readers). The visitor to the site can scan the reviews by establishment name, location or rating. Jones says she dreams of having every pizza joint on the face of the Earth reviewed, even if cataloguing them all presents a challenge for her sanity. OK, pizza-reviewing might sound like frippery to you, but if you stop and think about it, this site is interesting as much for what it represents as what it actually is.

The Internet Pizza Review Home Page, like *The Spot* and an increasing number of others, is a prime example of the potential of the Net to do that which has previously not been possible. It is truly a Net venture. No other form of media could have handled such a venture without massive funding and input. It's totally based on the abundance of the medium. And that begs the question of what kind of media entities we will see on the Net that we haven't seen before. What kind of new models will spring up to take advantage of the changed conditions?

The goalposts are moving. We've had scarcity. We've made a lot of money from it, built an economy on it. But the model we're moving towards now is almost the complete opposite. Those who are looking to the Net for their potential income would do well to keep it in mind.

Addresses

The Internet Movie Database
http://ballet.cit.gu.edu.au/Movies/blurb.html

The Ultimate Band List
http://american.recordings.com/wwwofmusic/ubl/ubl.shtml

The Yahoo Artists List
http://www.yahoo.com/Entertainment/Music/

The Electronic Newsstand
http://www.enews.com/

ABC Online
http://www.abc.net.au

The Internet Pizza Review Home Page
http://www.guru.apana.org.au/pizza.htm

The New Distribution Network

WHEN *Wired* magazine's digital guru-in-residence, Nicholas Negroponte, was in Australia in early 1996, he revealed that one of the projects at the Massachusetts Institute of Technology Media Lab, which he heads, was the digital book. Negroponte said the experiment, if successful, would put an end to the common complaint that computers are not portable enough to compete with newspapers, magazines or books. The digital book, he promised, would look and feel as much as possible like a paper-based book, though the pages would be a little plasticised. A chip would be embedded in its spine. The book would be blank, until such time as its owner—that is, you—downloaded content into its pages. Then, when you'd finished reading whatever your choice had been, you could dump the 'book' back into your computer and download another. Then another. One of the Media Lab's books could be a whole library. It's a curious thought, and one which no doubt makes old growth forests around the world breathe a sigh of relief (and Swedish bookcase manufacturers howl in disgust).

Negroponte has a broader point. Though books are beautiful artefacts, we are fast approaching the time when they will not really be necessary. Books are mostly written on computers—some read as if they were written *by* computers. They exist, in their original form, as digital information. Negroponte argues (at great length in his book, *Being Digital*), that the conversion of digital information into something physical, something we can touch, is often a waste of time. He believes the transition from bits to atoms can be unnecessary. What we know as books could be stored and sold as digital information, downloaded either from a store or, more likely, from the Web. Think about it. Millions of copies of the same book could be reproduced and distributed anywhere in the world at almost no cost at all. The digital book would mean that, in the case of novel and non-coffee table books at least, the printing industry could theoretically be rendered obsolete. Books would not disappear, but they would probably become more of a luxury item, sold at a premium.

A similar potential future exists for recorded music. Music these days is mostly recorded digitally. Then it gets printed onto lumps of plastic and sprayed with a metallic film: voilà, the compact disc. We have turned bits into atoms. Then we turn it back into bits in our CD player. Again, isn't the whole middle section unnecessary? You don't actually need the plastic thing. You don't need the atoms. Why not just shop by computer? Why not load that digital music into its memory, and then feed it to your amp and speakers? Think about that scenario. Who needs a CD player? Who needs a CD plant, or boxes to put them in, a warehouse for the boxes, trucks to drive them around, roads for the trucks to drive on? Who needs the CD store? Who needs retail at all? You want a cover? Print it out on your own machine. At that point, who needs the record company? What stops the artists making the music directly available through a collective site or their own sites, letting you download it for some kind of fee. Imagine what album prices would be like if the company didn't take a cut.

Record stores can see the Net—and its potential to rewrite the rule books of production and distribution—coming. More and more you will find that the big stores are about what they call the 'retail experience'. They are repackaging themselves and their products. They are trying to be cool places to go. They are trying to offer something different. They are trying to be a leisure destination. Because they know that they are soon going to be technologically, if not socially, redundant. It's going to be fascinating to see just how much the Net changes things. For info and culture junkies, the collision of the concept

MEDIA

of abundance with economic models based on scarcity, particularly in the media, will provide endless interest.

The television industry is based on a scarcity of frequencies. There are only six free-to-air channels available—they just can't fit any more into the broadcast spectrum. The radio world is similarly limited. What could the Net do to these industries if it, as seems inevitable, becomes the major method of delivery? Here's one possible scenario for TV. There will still be networks and they will still make programs. But they might behave more like video stores. They might say: 'We will make the fifth episode of the latest remake of *Pride and Prejudice* available on Sunday night at 7.30.' Come Sunday, you could watch the evening schedule live. Or you could download the program at that time (or any time after). That way, you could build your own evening from thousands of downloadable choices, from hundreds of networks—why wait two or three years for that new series you know is screening in the US? And if reading the TV Guide seems like too much work, 'intelligent' software programs might go hunting through the thousands of program choices and highlight things you might be interested in.

With TV, it's all some way off yet (though one Californian company was demonstrating live TV feed on the Net as early as 1995), but the future of radio is already happening. Using the **Real Audio** software, people are listening to about 60 radio stations on the Net, from **Net Radio**, 'The world's first 24-hour, live, Internet-only radio network', to **Kick AM** in Sydney and **Kiss FM** in Melbourne. In mid 1996, the Real Audio site launched *Timecast*, a service that enables users to customise their daily news broadcast intake. You can choose which broadcasts you'd like, from a variety of news and entertainment sources. It then delivers them digitally at your command. Another site, **Audio Net**, lists all the stations available on the Net, with recommended highlights (there's a lotta sport out there). It also offers programs on demand—everything from celebrity interviews to food and wine.

I happen to like a show on **National Public Radio** in America. Once a week, Harry Shearer, who does many of the voices on *The Simpsons*, hosts an hour of chat, satire and political analysis. If I could listen to that in Australia, I would. Chances are that soon, I'll be able to. The technology is already there to make it possible for us to listen to any radio station in the world, at any time. You're homesick for Belgian FM? That can be taken care of. Sure, the sound quality is pretty crappy at the moment, but that will change. The software will improve.

Of course, though the technology that has given us the Net makes these things possible, there's no guarantee they'll actually happen. Those in control of the media now have too much at stake to just go quietly and meekly into an era of global markets, where their control is diminished. All kinds of international deals will have to be done, and governments will increasingly be called upon to attempt to protect industries. That's one of the most interesting things about the Net. It doesn't matter how simple and obvious a direction the technology is taking—people can always screw it up.

Addresses

Real Audio
http://www.realaudio.com/

Net Radio
http://www.netradio.net/index.html

Kick AM
http://www.kick-am.com.au/

Kiss FM
http://kiss.source.com.au/

Audio Net
http://www.audionet.com/

National Public Radio
http://www.npr.org/

The Newspaper in a Wired World

TECHNOLOGY and myth feed off each other. The Internet, with its attendant phobias, paranoia and evangelism, provides plenty of sustenance, and has thrown up dozens of myths already. Here's one of my favourites, lifted from a disgruntled e-mail comment on something I wrote in **The Sydney Morning Herald**: 'I don't care whether I buy my news from **CNN** or the SMH,' the person wrote. 'I just want to be able to read it. I firmly believe that once a practical news reader is available, the publishing industry and all its inherent logistical problems will be a thing of the past. Goodbye newspapers.'

You hear and read about the impending death of newspapers a lot these days. I have to say, and not just because I want someone to continue paying my rent, that I don't see it happening. I believe newspapers can, and will, survive well into the digital age.

It seems to me that they're in as good a position as any medium to do so. They are already the most interactive, the closest to the new media paradigms. As with the Net, you approach a newspaper as a collection of information sites, in your own time and with your own hierarchy of interests. Newspapers are non-linear, easily personalised experiences. It's hard to find two people who read them in the same way, in the same order.

If newspapers are in trouble today, it has more to do with their failure to spot shifts in their readership than with competing technology. It has more to do with shooting themselves in the foot than with being shot.

The doomsayers seem to be missing the point that the media world is increasingly about options. It's about more, not less. Media beget media and at the moment, there's so much begetting it looks like the Old Testament out there. Check out your

local newsagency. You'll need a bulldozer to work your way through the thicket of Net-related magazines on the market. Last time I looked, Australia was producing four of its own and importing more than a dozen.

I read somewhere that 2000 books were published in 1994–95. Video was supposed to kill cinema. Instead, it made audiences more cinema-literate, then sent them back to the cinema in droves to impress themselves with how much they knew.

Basically, newspapers, like television and radio, will mutate to suit the new age. They're not an intermediate technology like the CD-ROM, the eight-track cartridge, or Betamax video. They are adapting already—they always have done. The idea that the Net will mean curtains for any medium is based on an image of the media as fully formed and fixed in stone. In reality, almost all the media are in constant flux, realigning, desperately trying to mould themselves to the changing landscape. Even the *Sydney Morning Herald*, a 150-year-old daily broadsheet, one of the larger, slower-moving press institutions, looks a lot less like it did a decade ago than you might think.

The success of the Net will surely have serious ramifications. It will change the way many people access information. It will change the way that information can be usefully packaged. It will change what readers want and when they want it. It will move the goalposts.

It might shrink newspapers. It might decrease the number of people who want to receive their information from them. It might also increase it, as people develop more specific tastes and info-diets. It might spell bad news for dailies but good news for weeklies. Whatever happens, you can be sure that the Net will force papers to improve, to change and compete. If they don't, they will deserve to die.

You can also be sure that, just as we've seen in the case of pay-TV, the companies that end up running online news services will turn out to be those that were running their off-line equivalents. It takes enormous capital and resources to set up a news service. It also takes some kind of credibility. And on the Net, with so much information disembodied, that is very important. So when it comes to news, people will prefer information which comes with a brand name they trust (or distrust less than most).

What newspapers have (on their good days) is the ability to sift piles of information, edit out the redundant, irrelevant and unreliable, and present the useful bits in a meaningful context. The biggest problem on the Net, aside from the limitations on how information can be displayed on a screen and the difficulty of reading your computer on the bus or at the beach, is that the piles of information it offers have little context, less meaning, and even less editing.

When newspapers first arrived, they were providing information for an information-starved populace. In many ways, they're now doing almost the opposite, providing a filtering system for people who have *too much* information. And if that isn't a definition of the Net's problem, I don't know what is.

Newspapers were actually very quick to work out that they had to find a footing in cyberspace, and 1996 has been a real watershed year. Newspapers on the Net have suddenly become highly visible, with many committing significant staff and resources to their online production. As I write, more than 200 have made the leap. Some, like **The Washington Post**, also made the mistake of not attempting to understand the philosophies of the medium they were venturing into. In a project with the **Los Angles Times** and a handful of smaller papers owned by the same publishing company, the *Post* asked users to pay for the privilege of accessing its information. The **New York Times** also asked for cash up front. The ventures stiffed—it's not hard to understand why when the Net offers so many *free* alternatives. Competitor **USA Today** offers a no-strings-attached Web news service which includes everything down to the crosswords, as well as archives of things such as weather and sporting achievements.

In Australia, the *Sydney Morning Herald*, **The Age**, **The Australian Financial Review** and **The Australian** offer limited news services. Most of the English papers are online too. Indeed, they are leading the race. Chunks of **The Guardian** and **The Daily Telegraph** are available on the Net. So are the complete **Times** and **Sunday Times**, and **The Financial Times**—updated *four times a day*.

Depending on your interests and language skills, you can also dial up papers ranging from France's **Libération** to Peru's **La República** to the **Cambodia Times**. Access to such newspapers is a joy for info-junkies. On the morning after the 1996 Cricket World Cup final, I was able to get the details and local colour from Sri Lanka's **Daily News** as the Sydney papers were hitting the streets. And even though Australia lost, it was nice to taste the winners' exultation in Elmo Rodrigopulle's front-page story: 'Sri Lanka conquered cricket's Mount Everest when they bashed the Australians by 7 wickets'.

Similarly, the weekly **St Petersburg Press** makes for an enjoyable read, filling in the passer-by on the comings and goings in one of Russia's most beautiful cities. The last time I dropped by, the front page boasted a picture of a lot of scrawny bodies sunning themselves, with the following explanation: 'The first full week of spring brought glorious sunshine and a 0°C heat wave that had these hardy souls shedding duds to catch those rays.'

Newspapers, which are really pretty similar the world over, provide a comfortingly familiar model for our information consumption. Most of us don't want to spend our lives chasing down bits of random information and putting them together to make something. We want and need people to help us do it.

And here we run smack-bang into another myth, that of the personalised newspaper. Whenever people talk about the future of this form, they wax enthusiastic about how we'll be able to choose the categories of news we want and get a personalised newspaper delivered to us electronically every morning (see CRAYON in the next section).

This will work for many people, but for others it simply won't. Like market research, it is based on the idea that you can sell people what they wanted yesterday. But while most readers may have some fixed interests, we usually don't know what we're interested in until we see it. The personalised newspaper will have to take account of this.

Meanwhile, the Net will provide for some, newspapers for others. And others still will stick with magazines, TV, radio or, more likely, a diet comprising servings from all the media food groups. I think it's safe to say that, barring serious media stupidity, which is always possible and usually likely, we'll be buying papers, watching TV and listening to radio (the latter two through the Net, eventually) for a long time to come.

Addresses

The Sydney Morning Herald
http://www.smh.com.au

CNN
http://www.cnn.com

The LA Times
http://www.latimes.com

The New York Times
http://www.nytimes.com

The Age
http://www.theage.com.au

The Australian Financial Review
http://www.afr.com.au

The Guardian
http://www.guardian.co.uk

The Times and Sunday Times
http://www.sunday-times.co.uk

The Daily Telegraph
http://www.telegraph.co.uk/

The Financial Times
http://www.ft.com/

Libération
http://www.liberation.fr

Daily News (Sri Lanka)
http://www.lanka.net/lakehouse/anclweb/dailynew/select.html

The St Petersburg Press
http://www.spb.su/times/index.html

La República
http://www.rcp.net.pe:80/LaRepublica/

The Cambodia Times
http://www.jaring.my/at-asia/camb_at_asia/camb_times/ct_list.html

See also...

Newslink
http://www.newslink.org/

The best guide to newspapers available online.

Keeping Up With the News

SO WHAT can you get on the Web in the way of daily news without turning to the online versions of newspapers? The truth is, a hell of a lot.

Yahoo has its own daily service, which uses Reuters wire copy to provide a digest of the top ten stories of the moment, accompanied by a list of the day's earlier winners. Each of these items is a couple of hundred words of simple text. It has separate digests of items in specific news areas: world, technology, sports (with scoreboards) and entertainment. The bias is predictably American, but there's usually enough here to include something of interest.

In its **Daily News Links** section you'll find an index of dozens of similar news services, all updated at least once every 24 hours, and many more often than that. Business services dominate, but I'm sorry, you'll have to track those yourself — stock quotes are not my speed. General news, politics, entertainment, science, sports and weather sources abound.

Most of these attempt to emulate newspapers in structure and style. **WWW WorldNews Today** goes the whole way. It's a large Net-only newspaper, published seven days a week for free. It has a dozen or so major sections, all of which have their own little nooks and crannies. As in a real newspaper, you have to learn where to find everything (those damn crosswords keep moving), but once you do, there's plenty to keep you occupied and up to date. Coverage ranges from the main headlines to news of entertainment, people, fashion, style and travel.

Newslink bills itself as 'the most comprehensive news resource on the World Wide Web'. You have to register for access to the site (which always makes me a little uneasy — I get flashes of junk e-mail lists), but once you're through the door, there are 3000 links to newspaper, magazine, broadcasting and news sites.

At this point, it becomes very easy to regulate your media diet, to make it more specific. You can head off to the **Canadian Press** service or the British **Press Association**, both of which offer at least a little balance to the American domination on the online news.

If you want to narrow your focus even more, the breezily titled **Internet Disaster Information Centre** tries to track world disasters as they happen, by linking to and from sites covering the action. Of course, the problem is that when it's quiet, it's very quiet.

The Omnivore also links together news sources from around the Web, but **The Daily News, Just the Links** does this even more effectively, allowing you to tour the globe via the local news outlet in whichever country you select. Check out the **Daily News From Iceland** ('Cold weather ahead') or the **Estonian News** service—leave your e-mail address and it will mail you regular bulletins. If you want to, you can even get the latest **East African News**. In Swahili.

What this site achieves by functioning as a jumping-off point, **The One World Daily News Service** matches by being the destination. This huge and amazing site offers global news by country (it now covers more than 80) and theme (more than twenty, ranging from children's rights to global warming to the problem of land mines). It's hard to think of a medium other than the Net that would allow such ambitious scope. One World's site is multifarious almost to the point of being kaleidoscopic, but needs to be updated more often.

From the macro to the micro, if you're looking for the information that falls through the cracks of the other services, or is deemed unsuitably bizarre, then **Chuck Shepherd's News of the Weird** is the place to park your Netmobile. All Chuck's

MEDIA

newspaper columns (he's syndicated through a series of American papers) are archived here, going back five years. No gimmicks or flashy graphics, just Chuck's eye for the awry.

> In November 1995, Christopher Conley, 14, received a $50 000 settlement from Lifetime Products, the manufacturer of a basketball-goal net. Conley, of Nashua, New Hampshire, had sued because his teeth had gotten caught in the net as he went up for a dunk shot, resulting in the need for massive dental work (*USA Today*, 11-3-95).
>
> In January 1996, the Supreme Court of Israel rejected the appeal of inmate Amir Hazan, 35, that he be allowed to keep an inflatable doll in his cell. Prison officials had turned him down, claiming the doll might be used to aid an escape attempt or to conceal drugs—and also that inmates might fight over it (*Reuters wire copy*, 1-23-96).

If you're looking for the information that was *forced* between the cracks, the stuff that may have been shuffled out of sight or hidden under the carpet on purpose, try **Project Censored**, an initiative by a Californian professor and a panel of journalists who every year nominate the ten stories, events or themes they think have been most under-reported in the American media—such as the failure of the National Institute for Occupational Safety and Health to notify more than 169 000 workers who had been exposed to hazardous materials that they faced an increased risk of cancer and other serious diseases.

Not everything is bad news, though. There are alternatives to doom, gloom and desperation. **Good News of the Week** (notice it's of the *week*, not the day—things aren't looking up *that* much) is a simple site which brings you stories proving that somewhere in the world, something positive is happening. Read about peace talks that are actually working, bits of useless bureaucracy being dismantled, lives being saved.

My favourite, however, is **CRAYON** (CReAte Your Own Newspaper).

'Creating your own newspaper is simple,' it promises. 'Imagine going to your local paper office and telling them exactly what you do and do not read, and then the next day they deliver to your door a newspaper that is customised just for you.' You come up with a name for your paper (a motto is optional), then wade through the hundreds of news sites from around the web that the CRAYON folk have linked to: US news, world news, politics, editorials and opinion pieces, weather reports, business, information and technology, health and fitness, sports, cartoons, horoscopes, almanacs, lottery results, births and deaths, and trivia of all kinds. You simply tick off those you want and ignore those you don't. By choosing along the lines of your own interests, pretty soon you have a working, personalised paper. When the arduous choosing is over, you take a deep breath, save your collection of links, keep it on your computer and voila! Every day, it updates itself as the various sites grow and change.

CRAYON, which has been operating since March 1995, is an elegantly simple idea and makes you think about the nature of the Web, but whether it will lead to anything is another question. It's a copyright nightmare, of course, and some companies have requested that their links to it be removed. But many have not. The material was placed on the Web for free, and CRAYON is free, so what's the harm?

Addresses

Yahoo Daily Headlines
http://www.yahoo.com/headlines/

Yahoo Daily News Links
http://www.yahoo.com/News/Daily/

WWW World News Today
http://www.fwi.com/wnt/wnt.html

Newslink
http://www.newslink.org/

Canadian Press
http://www.xe.com/canpress/

The PA NewsCentre
http://www.pa.press.net/

Internet Disaster Information Centre
http://www.disaster.net/

The Omnivore
http://way.net/omnivore/index.html

The Daily News, Just the Links
http://www.cs.vu.nl/%7Egerben/news.html

Daily News From Iceland
http://www.centrum.is/icerev/

Estonian Daily News
http://www.viabalt.ee/News/ETA/

East African News
http://www.africaonline.com/AfricaOnline/cgi/show-cur-cal.cgi?harari

The One World Daily News Service
http://www.oneworld.org/news/news_top.html

Chuck Shepherd's News of the Weird
http://www.nine.org/notw/archive.html

Project Censored
http://zippy.sonoma.edu/ProjectCensored/

Good News of the Week
http://www.nrv.net/~dsower/goodnews.html

CRAYON
http://www.crayon.net

MEDIA

See also...

Evolution in Action
http://iquest.com/~rfreynol/ev/

Dark humour, light heart. It's another collection of news clippings from around the globe of dumb things people do on their way to the Pearly Gates.

Not the Front Page News
http://www.OntheNet.com.au/~sdavis/nn.htm

Another site specialising in bizarre happenings from around the globe. The site curator offers a mailing list service for those who would like a little regular oddity in their digital letterbox.

Wired, HotWired and the Digital Backlash

FIRED, Tired, Mired . . . the headline writers are going to have a fabulous time sending up **Wired** magazine when the great digital backlash begins. Oh, pardon me, it already has. Check out both online issues of **Retired**, a parody which announces itself with slogans like 'The magazine that's deader than grunge and twice as trendy' and 'We make *Mondo 2000* look like *Scientific American.*' Beneath the fluorescent masthead are cover lines for imaginary features, summarising the kinds of viewpoints the site creators think *Wired*, a 'vapour-media' mag, represents:

> *High-Tech Toaster Ovens—What Will They Think of Next?*
> *Glossy Ads*
> *Cruisin' The Net: IBM Has a Homepage!*
> *IRC Whoopee: We Talk Poo-Poo-Pee-Pee with Someone Who Might Be a Girl.*

And then there's **Underwired**, which offers feature articles such as 'Type Design vs Legibility—Who Gives a Shit?' Turn the page and you'll find an ad for NotWired, then a parody of *Wired*'s contents list.

Charity may well begin at home, but *Wired*, a magazine which, if nothing else, has generated an enormous interest in cyberspace among people who don't drop the word 'Pentium' into every third sentence, is copping it from the online crowd in spades. As is its online partner, **HotWired**.

This was fairly predictable. If you stick your head above the trench, you'll get shot at. And *Wired* hasn't just been sticking its head up, it's been out there in a sequinned frock and fluoro wig, dancing on the corpse of the Industrial Age, shouting, 'Look at me, I'm a star!' Unsurprisingly, this has got up a lot of people's noses. *Wired* is drawing fire, basically, for

MEDIA

not being everything to everybody. This too was pretty much inevitable. The magazine broke a mould. Instead of basing itself on other computer mags, it took as its models earlier publishing icons: 1960s *Esquire*, 1970s *Rolling Stone* and, from the 1980s, *The Face*. Like them, it attempted to be a self-aware, lifestyle-oriented *zeitgeist* mag — to set the trends rather than chronicle them. With fractured graphic design, loads of attitude and a self-appointed mission to proselytise about the digital world, *Wired* set out to be what *PC Week* and *Macworld* could never be. It set out to be sexy.

By breaking through to the mainstream, non-techie market, it legitimised the exploding popularity of the Internet and set agendas for the media. *Wired* said that anyone could do this computing thing. It made it sound easy, taking away the fear factor. Sure, it replaced that with an almost religious zeal, but which is worse? *Wired* has put consumerism before gizmology, people before technology, and, yes, breathless over-excitement before calm, rational thought. And now, having achieved extraordinary success, the magazine is under attack.

Partly this is just what happens in publishing: sales lead to sniping. Partly it's because most great magazines enjoy only a couple of years of greatness before they start to decline anyway. And partly it's because there are a lot of fragile egos thinking they haven't had enough credit for their part in the digital revolution, that *Wired* ought to be sharing more of the glory around.

The critics are not hard to find. *Mondo 2000* founder R.U. Sirius, for example, took a few pot shots in his first column for the excellent *21.C*. He accused *Wired* of being, essentially, a wolf in sheep's clothing—a corporate, conservative, advertising-driven monolith passing itself off as a flag-waving revolutionary. Taking the argument much further is a savage online essay, '**The Killer App**: Wired Magazine, Voice of the Corporate Revolution', by Keith White, who says:

> *Wired*'s distinctive look of maimed typography and fluorescent hues may be interesting, but the magazine's truly marvellous feature is its business–cultural mission. *Wired* is technology's hip face, an aggressive apologist for the new Information capitalism that speaks to the world in the postmodern executive's favoured tones of chaotic cool and pseudo-revolution . . . *Wired* works, on the most basic level, by tweaking its readers' anxieties, constantly reminding them that they are hopelessly behind the times on the latest developments in technology and underground hacker culture. It simultaneously offers careful instruction in vocabulary, name-dropping, thinking and purchasing to allow readers to retro-fit their resumes, apartments and lifestyles.

Meanwhile, parodies of *HotWired*, the online sister to the magazine, are also appearing. **HowTired**, a satirical stab at the service, comes complete with inscrutable stick figure logos and self-consciously abstruse text: 'Amorphous globules of locution resound with trendy flashes of obfuscated clarity. Ambiguity renders inanity unintelligible. An argument grandiloquently articulated is but faintly refutable.' Make of it what you will.

HotWired was at conception, and remains, one of the most interesting sites on the Net, a working model of the publishing mode of the future. It's a marketplace of ideas, a constantly growing and changing arena for an endless number of mind performers. HotWired is technology-based, but not technology-obsessed. When the Communications Decency Act was signed into law in February 1996, HotWired's Netizen page was a major force behind the Citizens' Internet Empowerment Coalition's lawsuit to overturn it, with a sign-up campaign that brought thousands of 'signatures'. Pop, HotWired's arts and entertainment section, keeps tabs on happenings in the worlds of art, television, zines, movies, music, books, CD-ROMs and less classifiable things. Its commentary section boasts musings from software designers, digital commerce experts and self-styled grumps like Brock N. Meeks, a journalist who specialises in Net politics. World Beat travels the globe for evidence of the Wired World that everyone is predicting, and it also offers handy travel hints and directions to Web resources. Club Wired is the regular home of online live chats with the famous and infamous as well as a series of ongoing discussions. There are features, archives and important issue-related articles regularly updated for the user. And if it all sounds a little dry, the Cocktail section shows you can try to change the world and still find time for a dry martini.

HotWired does all this with humour. Any site that links you to some guy's **Anti-Web Page**, on which he provides a list of ten reasons why the Web will die, has something going for it. If there's going to be a backlash, you might as well have fun with it. Now where was that martini again?

Addresses

Retired
http://www.islandnet.com/~moron/deterrent/deter.html

Underwired
http://www.covesoft.com/underwired

Wired
http://www.wired.com

HotWired
http://www/hotwired.com

The Killer App
http://www.voyagerco.com/misc/killerapp/killerapp.html

HowTired
http://www.howtired.com

Chris Gregg's Anti-Web Page
http://www.gatech.edu/3020.new/mmm/cgregg/

See also...

An Interview With Wired Founder Louis Rossetto
http://www.shift.com/ShiftProd/cgi-bin/DisplayPage?SITE=Shift&KEY=shift2-3.wired.wired&TRACKID=MC_

The TiReD-WiReD Server v1.1
http://www.2d.org/TiReD-WiReD/tired-wired.cgi

A silly, absurdist send-up of the Wired In—Out list. 'The TiReD-WiReD Server utilises a Patented AI Algorithm to accurately predict the whims of Generation-X (No relation to Racer X). This list is approximately 79.0473937988281% more reliable than the guy at WiReD. Tired—Paul Anka, Wired—pinwheel. Tired—flora, Wired—boot. Tired—tampon, Wired—tapeworm...'

Microsnot Corporation
http://www.microsnot.com/

Nothing to do with *Wired*, but it is a parody, of Microsoft and Bill Gates. And Lord knows, we can't get enough of those.

WORLD WIRED WEIRD

A Case for Bad Taste

FIRST, a few words of warning. If you think *To The Manor Born* was funnier than *The Young Ones*, stop reading. If you think the live organ donation scene in *Monty Python's The Meaning of Life* overstepped the mark, stop reading. If you can honestly say you have never even thought about slowing down when passing a traffic accident, stop reading. Oh, and if you've just eaten, you might think about stopping too.

Because I want to talk about **Dan's Gallery of the Grotesque**, one of a number of Websites which explore the limits of taste. It's not pretty, kiddy-friendly stuff. Subtitled 'The Premier Forensics Exhibition on the Web', Dan's Gallery boasts a range of photographs depicting suicide, homicide, horrific accidents, war casualties and various other horrors. Sometimes the Net is not for the faint of stomach. The Gallery arrives on your screen with a disclaimer stating that some people might find the contents disturbing. It suggests that children really ought to be accompanied by an adult.

More than 500 000 users visited the gallery last year, 2 000 on the first day I attended. It presents itself as a museum, complete with floor plan of the various areas, information booth and gift shop.

'My Gallery of the Grotesque is a metaphor for the squalid, degenerate world that was born out of our own self-indulgence and apathy,' Dan writes in an introduction. 'Witness here the fabric of our society unravel: we pervert the suffering of others as the fodder for our own debased entertainment. We place those who commit the most deviant acts on pedestals for all to idolise, and we care little for those most in need.'

The Gallery, he claims, is a subversive work, as offensive as the reality it mirrors. By creating it, of course, Dan has his postmodern cake and eats it too. Presenting these images in the context of 'art' turns the site into a commentary on our media-dominated world, a world which exalts serial killer Jeffrey Dahmer and turns the O.J. Simpson trial into the latest Big Top attraction. Dan's Gallery is meant to be viewed as the blackest of black comedies. It asks you to consider your reaction and, more subtly (or perhaps this is me over-reaching), your *complicity* in the success of this type of tabloid journalism. One hand invites you in, the other slaps you for coming.

As with Quentin Tarantino's *Pulp Fiction* and Oliver Stone's *Natural Born Killers* and the fabulous Belgian film *Man Bites Dog*, there is a fine line between parody and glorification. It's a tough call which way such films or sites fall, and almost always a personal, subjective one.

But Dan's Gallery of the Grotesque would by no means be the only speaker at a Tasteless Sites of the Net conference. Another boundary pusher is **The Vomitus Maximus Museum**, which has a skull and crossbones on its home page, along with a lengthy warning to the easily offended to turn and head back the way they came.

Like Dan's, this museum is presented as a series of gallery rooms. But the work (mostly nightmarishly tormented paintings and drawings: twisted, scary, unholy) is from one brain, that of a San Francisco artist named R.S. Connett. 'Though I may seem untroubled and serene my brain is a cauldron boiling over,' Connett explains. 'In my mind there seem to be no absolutes, no ultimate truths, no black and white, just massive areas of grey.'

Offensiveness itself is a grey area which plenty of other sites come into, some of them showing that tastelessness can blur from the confronting to the funny. **A Tasteless Place** offers O.J. Simpson trial sounds, a gallery of killers and cannibals, 'disgusting profane blasphemy' (a section dealing with religious

WORLD WIRED WEIRD

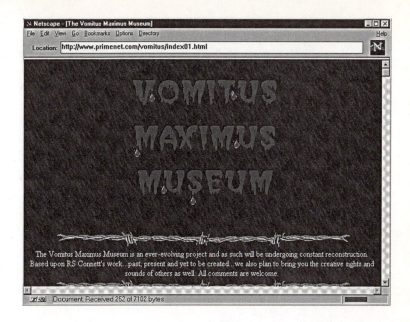

misdemeanours), a number of photos of people dying or about to die unexpectedly, and links to the best/worst newsgroups.

Future Space has a quite extraordinary set of links:

> 'The Terrorist Web—In honour of all the great men and women who have thrown bombs into crowded shopping malls; Mutilations Inc—A what-not-to-eat-guide for the online vegetarian; Virtual Bulimia—An online vomit fest with an interactive purge-binge cycle for those who are trying to get their metabolism under control; The Interactive Tooth Extractor—Here it is, straight from dental school, digitised tooth extraction made easy, painless and fun; The Serial Killer Hit List—Look for your favourite serial killer, rate him or her against the best of their peers.

And many more.

My personal favourite sites are, oddly enough, both pet-related. **Roadkill Quarterly**, which welcomes you with a cheerful visiting statistic ('You are sick bastard #843'), is a

Webzine dedicated to 'those unique, furry critters who lay down their lives every year in the ultimate battle between nature and machine'. As its title hints, it's devoted to one of the under-discussed joys of travel. A recent issue carried an article from Australia by a couple of amateur dead cane toad photographers, who captured the toadkill on the Bruce Highway in Northern Queensland.

Another source of perverse amusement is a HotWired article by Josh Quittner about **The War Between rec.pet.cats and alt.tasteless**, two Usenet groups. When one bored group of tasteless people decided to invade the prettiest, nicest group it could think of, the results were almost as funny as anything Monty Python or *The Young Ones* ever came up with.

Addresses

Dan's Gallery of the Grotesque
http://www.grotesque.com

The Vomitus Maximus Museum
http://www.primenet.com/vomitus/

A Tasteless Place
http://www.iceworld.org/~bent/

Future Space
http://www.mayhem.net/coming.html

Roadkill Quarterly
http://www.isisnet.com/empire/rkq

The War Between rec.pet.cats and alt.tastless
http://vip.hotwired.com/wired/2.05/departments/electrosphere/alt.tasteless.html

See also...

Squashed Bug Zoo
http://squashed.roach.org/zoo.html

A gallery of photos of the smallest roadkill.

Sick Links
http://www.igc.net/~nsurf/sick.htm

One guy's tour through the Net underbelly.

Pets on the Net

HI! I'm an American short-hair black and white neutered male, and I weigh in at a hefty 17lbs. I am approximately four years old, but we're not sure because I was a stray for a while.

Hi, my name is Noddy. My favourite pastime is catching things. You throw it—I catch it. I'm not a complicated dog.

Bandit has been Brian's companion animal (read 'cat') since September of 1989 . . . Bandit has learned how to turn on his human's computer and how to surf the Internet (but his human wishes he could keep the cat hair out of the Microsoft Mouse!). Here are some sites on the Net Bandit likes.

Hook into the Net, they told me. It's a great way to meet people. So far, I'm meeting a lot of their pets.

What strange urge drives someone to put up a Web page for Rex or Fluffy? People who would not be seen dead putting vainglorious tributes to themselves on the Web seem to think nothing of presenting us with the intimate details of their furry, feathered and finny friends. Even weirder, they have developed the unnerving habit of trying to make us believe that Spot, or Bandit, or Noddy, did it himself. Yep, he just did that UNIX course at college and hey presto! You wanna know why cats sleep all day? It's because they're up all night crunching computer code.

Now I loved Arnold Ziffel on *Green Acres*. I thought he was a pretty smart pig. Mr Ed had a few brains. And I'm prepared to believe that if Skippy could fix the radio and drive the speedboat, she could also handle simple stuff like HyperText Mark-up Language. But I still have my doubts about **Mr Puddy**. His real name is Mukta Augustus, of Ann Arbor. Mukta is apparently Sanskrit for 'liberation' and 'freedom from

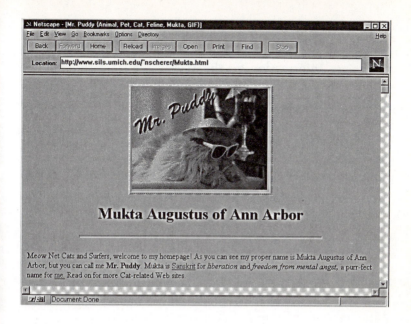

mental angst'. He's a three-year-old Persian cat who has his own Web page and photo gallery and runs an advice column for other virtual felines: Ask Mr Puddy (xenopus@umich.edu).

> Mr Puddy, why do I constantly have the urge to jump into the kitchen sink, especially when the water is running—is it normal? Sincerely, Alfredo.
>
> Dear Alfredo, I feel that your urge to jump into the kitchen sink when the water is running is actually an act of undoing in response to excessive exogenous grooming. Undoing is an unconscious psychological defence mechanism by which one symbolically annuls something unacceptable that has already been done. Love, Mr Puddy.

The World Wide Web is bulging with digital dogs and cyber-cats. You can find links to whole packs of them at

InterPet. The site also keeps tabs on dozens of Web pages and Web-based pet organisations.

Doggy Information on the Web has a similarly large list of links to places of canine cyberculture. Get a screen saver. Check out the guide dog sites. Read *Travels with Samantha*, by Philip Greenspun, a Web-based dog novel.

Golden Retrievers in Cyberspace has stories, too, of successful rehabilitations of injured and abandoned dogs. If you're heading here, be warned: it gets pretty weepy. There is also an **Australian Dogs Page**, which links to canine clubs, controlling bodies and media as well as general doggy WWW sites. **PetNet**, another local, is a comprehensive Net resource directory for proud pet parents around the country.

Then there's **Adopt a Greyhound**, a service which finds homes for retired racing greyhounds. This (actually, pretty cool) site has a section on famous greyhounds through history, from 6000 BC Turkish temple drawings to Santa's Little Helper in *The Simpsons*. It also offers—or perhaps that should be 'fails to stop people from offering'—greyhound poetry:

> The eager face, the waggly tail
> express the purest thought
> Without condition or restraint
> A love that can't be bought

I have nothing against animals. Heck, some of my best friends have had facial hair problems. It's just a little odd to stumble across these global communities of fans and fanatics. The Internet allows you to listen in on other people's worlds. This can be fascinating. It can be dull. And it can also, like most eavesdropping, leave you feeling vaguely unclean. Any faith, no matter how benign, can look weird to a non-believer.

Anyway, if you bat for the other team, so to speak, you'll find more to your liking at **Cats on the Internet**, which, of course, has sections on other people's cats and a list of feline links. If you're willing to suspend disbelief, you can even chat to a moggy at **Talk to my Cat**, a Web document which uses speech synthesis to make your words audible to the animal near the owner's computer. Play with its mind. NB: If it starts talking back, seek medical help.

Or maybe that's too spooky and **The House Rabbit Society** site will be more up your cuddly path.

If not, there are alternatives to the overly cute and adorable. **Brian Lee's Rat Page** has links to rat info and images, various rat home pages and organisations such as **The Swedish Rat Society** and **The Rat and Mouse Club of America.** Brian also rabbits on about his rats, discussing rearing techniques and rat psyches and idiosyncrasies.

Unsurprisingly, when the little friends go off to frolic in that Great Backyard in the Sky, there's even a Net way of dealing with that. **The Virtual Pet Cemetery** is 'the world's first on-line pet burial ground. If you wish to immortalise your beloved pet in the tombs of cyberspace for eternity, now is your chance.' All you have to do is e-mail them an epitaph (photo optional).

All cynicism aside, this is a two-boxes-of-Kleenex site. A typical example:

> Misty was a brown mutt. She was very loved. My parents had saved her from being killed by some people who didn't want her any more. My parents had her a couple of years before I was born. She passed away when I was 8 years old. Misty and I were very attached. I would not be alive today if it wasn't for her. I lay choking in my crib when she awoke my parents. We had our bad times when I was bugging her and she bit me, but I always forgave her. We also had our fun times like when we played Tug Of War with her sock. We soon found out she was blind when she got lost in the woods. We found her though. She was then diagnosed with kidney failure. She passed away at the vet's office. I will never forget that dog. I cried for 3 days straight and still get choked up when I think

of all the fun we had together. We used to do everything together. I am now 14 years old and miss Misty very dearly.

Me, I think I'll avoid the emotional investment and stick with virtual pets like **The Amazing Fish Cam** and the **Amazing Parrot Cam**. Both of these sites focus a camera, on an aquarium and a birdcage respectively, and update the photo every minute or so. No cleaning. No food costs. And you can go away for the weekend without worrying about who will look after them.

Addresses

Ask Mr Puddy
http://www.sils.umich.edu/~nscherer/Mukta.html

InterPet
http://vanbc.wimsey.com/~dmtaylor/InterPet/ip_pages.html

Doggy Information on the Web
http://www.bulldog.org/dogs/

Golden Retrievers in Cyberspace
http://www.rahul.net/hredlus/golden.html

Australian Dogs Page
http://www.pcug.org.au/~sbaker/dogs.htm

PetNet
http://www.petnet.com.au/

Adopt a Greyhound
http://delta1.org/~greyhound

WORLD WIRED WEIRD

Cats on the Internet
http://http2.sils.umich.edu/~dtorres/cats/cats.html

Talk to My Cat
http://queer.slip.cs.cmu.edu/cgi-bin/talktocat

The House Rabbit Society
http://www.rabbit.org

Brian Lee's Rat Page
http://www-personal.umich.edu/~bclee/rats.html

Swedish Rat Society
http://www.mds.mdh.se/~ltd92fsk/srs_main.html

Rat and Mouse Club of America
http://www.rmca.org/

Virtual Pet Cemetery
http://www.lavamind.com/pet.html

The Amazing Fish Cam
http://www.netscape.com/fishcam

Amazing Parrot Cam
http://www.can.net/parrotcam.html

Weird Science

WAY BACK there in the 1980s, teen culture guru John Hughes made a film (later spun off into a godawful TV series) called *Weird Science*. In this flick, a pair of teenage computer nerds come up with a software program that creates, in a cyclone of smoke and sparks, a real, live, flesh and blood lustbucket of a woman, entirely at their command. A digital *I Dream of Jeannie* in a bikini instead of harem pants.

And what was the obvious thing for these hormonally-charged, sex-deprived geeks to do with this suppliant vision of loveliness? That's right—run off a few million copies of the software and make themselves instant billionaires. Of course, they didn't. And they didn't lay a hand on her either. They just asked her for advice on how to get girls.

Whether it's teen boffins, Baron Frankenstein or the wild-haired, bug-eyed Christopher Lloyd in the *Back to the Future* series, the mad scientist remains a potent figure in contemporary mythology.

The **First International Virtual Conference on Mad Science**, held through 1996 on the Net, has been a tongue-in-cheek celebration of 'a much maligned domain of human knowledge' whose 'practitioners have for too long been relegated to B-movies and remote ancestral estates'. Dozens of people presented fictional research papers at the ongoing conference, dealing with such weighty topics as 'Fly Breeding for Health and Happiness', 'Hand Painting Cockroaches As a Therapeutic Exercise for Mad Scientists', 'The Production of Greenhouse Gases in Academic Seminars' and 'The Practicalities of Photosynthesis in Humans' Its site explains:

> The purpose of the conference is to promote a general understanding of mad topics within the broader scientific community, to encourage new

WORLD WIRED WEIRD

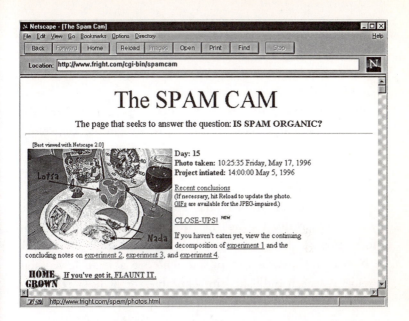

researchers to dabble with things best left alone, to attract commercial sponsors to the potential benefits of mad science in the business world, and to replace the old drooling maniac stereotype of the mad scientist with a new drooling maniac image which is more appropriate to the modern era.

Topics of interest include, but are not limited to: creating life to satisfy egocentric motives, unleashing entities beyond human control and comprehension, tampering with the life-sustaining forces of the Universe, exceeding the limitations of the human body via grotesque metamorphoses, new applications for old technologies (alchemy, necromancy, etc), ill-advised collaboration with alien and/or supernatural intelligences, lifelong devotion to researching the pointless and inane, callous disregard for human experimental subjects, and exacting bizarre revenge on contemptuous and derisive peers.

The Swedish **Anders' Mad Scientist Page** brings together a lot of resources for the would-be laboratory lurker, with links to events, a range of mad scientists and evil geniuses on the Net ('They laughed at me! But I will show them. One day it will be I who laughs at them instead!'), and organisations and businesses devoted to mad science.

But as always, no matter how cute the play actors are, the real thing is madder. Sites relating to odd scientific endeavour abound on the Web, partly because they let off steam for Web-literate academies, and partly because the Web is the perfect forum for nonsense.

The Annals of Improbable Research maintains a Web presence to spruik for its *HotAIR* magazine, but also keeps information on the site about the Ig Nobel Prize winners. The Ig Nobels are awarded to people who are able to have their obscure research published in reputable (or at least recognisable) journals, but 'whose achievement cannot or should not be reproduced'. Last year's winners included a pair of English food researchers, who succeeded with their report on soggy cereal entitled 'A Study of the Effects of Water Content on the Compaction Behaviour of Breakfast Cereal Flakes'; a trio of American medicos for a study called 'The Effects of Unilateral Forced Nostril Breathing on Cognition'; four Japanese academics 'for their success in training pigeons to discriminate between the paintings of Picasso and those of Monet'; and an American dentist for research into 'Patient Preference for Waxed or Unwaxed Dental Floss'.

Weird Science is more serious than the name implies, and catalogues unconventional research and 'anomalous physics', as well as serving as a home base for Seattle's monthly weird-science hobbyists' meetings and the Society for Unusual/Non-conventional Science's mailing lists. In many ways, its For Sale page is the most left-field part—this is the place to come when you're looking for 40 giant pulse-discharge capacitors or a crystal (boule) of pure germanium which came from a neutron detector at Los Alamos.

Though the service is limited online, **The Fortean Times** has become one of the UK's most popular sites. Subtitled 'The Journal of Strange Phenomena', it's a monthly magazine of 'news, reviews and research on all manner of strange phenomena and experiences, curiosities, prodigies and portents'. The magazine was started in 1973 to continue the work of the 'iconoclastic philosopher' Charles Fort. 'Fort was sceptical about scientific explanations, observing how scientists argued for and against various theories and phenomena according to their own beliefs, rather than the rules of evidence. He was appalled that data not fitting the collective paradigm was ignored, suppressed, discredited or explained.' The site does a lot of selling, but finds room to squeeze in a few articles to get your teeth into, as well as a clickable World Weird Map—find out what's odd in your area.

Strange Science: The Last Word is part of the *New Scientist* site, a large question-and-answer billboard where people answer each other's queries. All sorts of questions arise, from whether mussels are capable of producing pearls (yes) to why crunchy foods affect your vision (the shock waves apparently cause rapid movement of the eyes, which distorts what you see) to why men have nipples. ('Male and female human embryos are identical in the early stages of their development. If the foetus receives a Y chromosome from its father, a hormonal signal is produced: the labia fuse to form a scrotum, the gonads develop as testicles and a male results. Otherwise the "default" female remains. Various structures in the adult reflect the symmetry of male and female and their common embryonic source. Men have nipples because they have already begun to develop when the "switch to male" signal is received.')

Probably the most fun you can have as a fringe science

lover is on the individual sites of the experiment-obsessed. Canadian Pete Hickey felt the need to do a little **Beard Research** after he got sick of people telling him that a beard keeps you warmer in winter. Hickey shaved half his beard off (picture on site) and subjected himself to a series of tests. 'I ran, cycled, and skied. Yes, it does feel warmer with a beard. Also more comfortable. The side without the beard felt colder.'

Mark Frank and Patrick Michaud see themselves as pioneers of the science of culinary entertainment. Their **Fun With Grapes** site details their attempts to 'create a spectacular lightshow' using ordinary grapes and a microwave oven. 'Properly prepared, the common seedless grape can be made to combust spectacularly when subjected to a short (5–10 second) duration of microwaves.'

And then there's **George Goble**, a man who doesn't have time to muck around with firestarters. The Indiana electrical engineer has a worrying tendency to light his barbecues with a few handy litres of liquid oxygen. You can see the movies on his site. But do yourself a favour. Don't try it at home.

Addresses

First International Virtual Conference on Mad Science
http://www.ftech.net/~madsite/

Anders Mad Scientist Page
http://www.nada.kth.se/~nv91-asa/mad.html

The Annals of Improbable Research
http://www.improb.com/

Weird Science
http://www.eskimo.com/~billb/weird.html

Fortean Times
http://alpha.mic.dundee.ac.uk/ft/ft.html

Strange Science: The Last Word
http://www.newscientist.com/ps/strange/index.html

Beard Research
http://mudhead.uottawa.ca/~pete/beard.html

Fun With Grapes
http://www.cbi.tamucc.edu/~pmichaud/grape/

George Goble
http://ghg.ecn.purdue.edu/

See also...

Weird But True
http://munshi.sonoma.edu/jamal/weird.html

A huge list of surprising 'facts': 'Cut off the head of an attacking rattlesnake and it will continue to attack with its headless stump which can apparently see. If you move the stump will follow and will actually attempt to bite.' 'In many, many statistical tests it has been found that we humans prefer one rectangle to all others; that whose sides are in the ratio of 1 to 1.618.' 'Wire a rubber tree plant to a lie detector and burn one of its leaves with a cigarette lighter. You will get an agitated electrical response.'

Bad Science
http://www.ems.psu.edu/~fraser/BadScience.html

A site dedicated to righting frequent mistakes made by teachers, journalists and all those who circulate false 'scientific' ideas.

Random Research Question Page
http://www.coedu.usf.edu/behavior/research/research.html

'Scientists needing grants, professors up for tenure, 8th grade science fair contestants—Rejoice! Your days of worry are over! This page is capable of generating countless valuable research questions to aid you in your careers!' A random question generator, it offers gems like 'What are the effects of insulin levels on chipmunk refuse?'

The Spamcam
http://www.fright.com/cgi-bin/spamcam

'The page that seeks to answer the question: Is Spam organic?' You'd best hope you catch one of this series of experiments in its early days. If you drop into the site during advanced decomposition, you might not eat for a day or two.

Science Jokes Archive
http://www.princeton.edu/~pemayer/ScienceJokes.html

A great site. Broken down into the various categories. Find out what mathematicians and theoretical physicists laugh about. I have no idea whether any of them are funny.

The Studmuffins of Science Calendar
http://www.studmuffins.com/

Normally I wouldn't recommend a commercial site, but the Studmuffins of Science calendar seems worthy. Science can be fun . . . even sexy. Real scientists aren't poorly dressed geeks who repair their eyeglasses with masking tape and paper clips. And the Studmuffins of Science calendar presents definitive proof. Designed to show PhDs at work and at play, the calendar features a dozen handsome, fun-loving, accomplished scientists, swimming, biking, skating, and enjoying some time away from the lab. Even in the work shots, not a single slide rule is in evidence.

Beer Lovers

I AM having one of those Homer Simpson moments. I know I should be thinking of something witty and erudite to keep your mind ticking over for the rest of this chapter. I know I should be thinking of something profound, something challenging. But I'm not. I'm thinking: 'Mmm, beer . . .'

I'm hanging out in the **alt.beer** newsgroup, reading posts from hopheads on the merits of brews I have never seen and probably never will, boutique beers with unpronounceable names from Eastern European republics and African military strongholds. One guy, way ahead of me in these matters, brags that he can order a large beer in four different languages. German: 'Eine gross Bier, bitte.' Spanish: 'Uno grande cervesa, por favor.' Polish: 'Yedno dooja peevo perprochun.' English: 'One big beer, please.'

Is there anything the Internet can't teach you?

The Web is bustling with beer lovers. Hundreds of sites are dedicated to the amber fluid. **The Great Aussie Beer Page** is 'for those who thought that Aussie beer was just Fosters and XXXX'. Maintained by Dr Bradley Collins of Sydney University's School of Chemistry, it is a self-appointed ambassador for Australian brewing, preaching the merits of the local drop to the online world.

Tony Laughton's **What's Brewing Home Page** is also Australian, a database for home brewers, with tips and recipes. **Beer Alcohol and Calories** is a comparative test of the brain-cell killing, waistline-expanding capacities of more than 200 beers.

Malt of the Earth is a club which allows you to have a specialist beer, from a microbrewery, shipped to your home. Its service only extends to the USA at the moment, but we can live in hope.

Beer Links is a comprehensive guide to breweries, festivals, tastings, events, publications, home pages, newsgroups and Web miscellanea. Similarly, the **WWW Virtual Library's Beer & Brewing Index** contains links to hundreds of specialist sites: breweries, pubs, regional listings, publications, organisations, festivals and personal beer home pages. Sadly, its Beer Related Software section does not offer you the chance to download a version of *Doom* or *Quake* that is best played under the weather. The programs on offer are spreadsheets for home brewers.

Collectors are not left out of the picture. The **Beer Cap Page**, **Beer Mat Collectors Page** and **Stein Collectors Haven** ('How many of you know the history of lidded drinking vessels?') offer people the chance to share and compare their collections. And buyers peddle their hop-soaked wares through the **Beer Classifieds**.

And those who want to explore the arcane can get their fill on the **Medieval/Renaissance Brewing Homepage**, where they can find answers to important questions such as: 'Medieval wines—how sweet were they?' Learn to make a good mead and a knockout raspberry cordial (I kid you not).

When you're done there, head to the **WWW Beer Survey**, a site which lets you vote for your favourite beer, no matter where in the world it comes from. You choose a continent, lodge your votes on a form, then check the results so far. Last time I looked at the local poll, Fosters had edged ahead of Steinlager, with VB, Redback and XXXX rounding out the top five.

Odds are, however, that wherever you start, you'll end up at **The Real Beer Page**, whose Virtual Brewery Tours section plans your boutique-beer crawl. Type in a postcode (US only, but there are expansion plans) and it lists all the local makers. The site also links to online 'brewspapers and brewzines' and has an incredibly comprehensive games section, which takes in board, card, dice, coin, endurance and TV-related contests. But

WORLD WIRED WEIRD

the site's star feature is the fabulous 'Burp Me' contest. Here, people send in sound files of themselves belching, which can be downloaded and replayed. One guy, with a little technological help, has sent a recording of himself burping 'Yankee Doodle Dandy'. Homer Simpson would be proud.

Addresses

The Great Aussie Beer Page
http://www.usyd.edu.au/~bcollins/OZBEER.HTML

What's Brewing Home Page
http://beer.apana.org.au

Beer Alcohol and Calories
http://alpha.rollanet.org/library/AlClbinger.html

Malt of the Earth
http://www.matlbev.com/

Beer Links
http://www.avbc.com/avbc/beerlinks.html

WWW Virtual Library's Beer & Brewing Index
http://www.mindspring.com/~jlock/wwwbeer.html

Beer Cap Page
http://www.cam.org/~kibi/beercaps.html

Beer Mat Collectors Page
http://www.breworld.com/breworld/beermats.html

Stein Collectors Haven
http://gramercy.ios.com/~gpaul/

Beer Classifieds
http://www.mindspring.com/~jlock/beerads6.html

Medieval/Renaissance Brewing Homepage
http://www.pbm.com/~lindahl/brewing.html

WWW Beer Survey
http://www.vpdesign.com/beer/beerquiz.htm

The Real Beer Page
http://realbeer.com

Virtual Vampires

NOW DON'T go rushing to your stereotypical conclusions. This is the '90s. They're not vampires—they're the orthodontically gifted. And they're out there colonising the dark corners of the Vorld Vide Veb. I'm hanging about (upside down, naturally) in the **alt.vampyres** newsgroup. They spell it that way because it's ye olde spelling and therefore a lot sexier and *très gothique*. It also makes the group that little bit harder for dopey Net tourists to find.

If you can get around all the Bible thumpers telling the poor residents of the group what surely awaits them on The Other Side, this is the place to find people who wear black and don't do a lot of cooking with garlic. Though most of the postings are flippant, there is also a serious strain winding through, which manifests itself in some pretty tragic poetry (*'The Coffin, I Found Peace Within'*) and regular requests for contact with real, 'living' Nosferati.

'I am mortal and I want to be one of the undying,' a typical one writes. 'If you are a real vampyre with real powers that really exist in the physical, real world, please call or write me. You know, powers such as super human strength and speed, flying, shapeshifting, psychic abilities, etc.' The place for this person to go is **The Net.Vampiric**, which breaks its work into three categories: social, literary/artistic, and informational. The social section includes information on mailing lists for vampfans and has a collection of what it says are e-mail addresses of vampires (just the kind of pen pal you're looking for). The information section includes, among other things, the updated FAQ for *alt.vampyres*, which explains not just what the newsgroup is for, but how you should behave if you visit, and why others behave as they do:

> The people who pose as vampires do so for a very good reason: they enjoy it. They have a perfectly good grip on reality; some people watch movies for fun, some people read fiction, and some choose to impersonate vampires. That may seem like a strange way to act, but if you don't like it you don't have to do it. Nobody will think any the worse of you if you don't act as a vampire—provided you're polite to those who do.

The Web is absolutely clotted with Vampire sites. The undead are obviously spending a lot of their free time during the day getting vired. You can read thousands of words of history, trace the development of the vampire as a silver-screen character, find out how to take advantage of Dracula tourism. If you're into DIY, you can even get the lowdown on how to make realistic fangs. A handy place to start is **Vampyres Only**, a very happening site which has its own library (whole texts of books are available, including that of Bram Stoker's *Dracula*). There are also chat rooms where you can go to discuss your love of darkness, galleries or art, and which offer sound and video footage, directions to related Web sites and even some undead humour.

Creatures of the Night has a lot of general info, but better value, despite the awful name and the fact that it looks a little thin at first, is **The Ooga Booga Page Vampires Section**. Bursting with haemoglobin, the site offers bibliographies of vamp lit and a huge archive of vampire lore. It insists, for example, that:

- Vampires who go undetected for seven years can go to another country or place where a different language is spoken and become human again. They can never remarry but when they die, the whole family become vampires.
- Among other ways, you can become a vampire by being the seventh son of a seventh son (obviously there are a lot of Catholic vampires), if a cat jumps over your corpse, if you

are bitten by a vampire, if you are excommunicated from the Greek Orthodox Church, if there is a knot of any kind (on a tie or a piece of rope) in your coffin, or if you have eaten the meat of a sheep that was killed by a wolf.

- There are vampire legends around the world. The bloodlusters go by various names: Ekimmu (Assyria), Lilitu (Babylonia), Jaracaca (Brazil), Obour (Bulgaria), Ch'Iang Shih (China), Katalkanas (Crete), Mara (Denmark), Vrukalakos (Greece), Alp (Germany), Pamgri (Hungary), Dearg-Duls (Ireland), Baitol (India), Languitis (Malaysia), Bruxsa (Portugal), Nosferat (Romania), Viesczy (Russia) and Baobham (Scotland).

The Vampire WWW Server is another sizeable archive of material, mainly concerned with role-playing games, but also including sections devoted to fiction, graphics and mood music

(Gorecki, Philip Glass, Graeme Revell's soundtrack of *The Crow*) that make a visit worthwhile.

The one that really kills me (and I suppose that is the point) is **Romantic Notions — Vampire Romances** — Mills and Boon with a little throat puncturing tossed in. Vein poppers rather than bodice rippers, these are serious novels that you can send away for. Potted plot summaries are offered on site: 'She never imagined that such creatures could exist: vampires who travel through time and the night to hunt the darkened streets of London, vampire children in ruffles and lace who appear innocent but are older and more powerful than any mortal. She never dreamed that she could be so deeply in love.' Sounds like a two boxes of tissues job to me.

To be fair, the virtual vampires do have a sense of humour. Gregg Henry's **Vampire Duck Page** offers 'horrorscopes', links to 'neat vampire sites' (neat?), and three yes/no tests. The Vampire Probability Test lets you know whether you have a little of the undead in you. The Vampire Vulnerability Test lets you know whether you might get a little of the undead in you if you don't stop hanging around dark places in open-necked shirts. And the Human/Vampire Compatibility Test lets you know if you are likely to get a specific bit of the undead in you. If you know what I mean. And all of them are done with an appropriate mix of sincerity and self-parody: 'Do you prefer the night? Were you personal friends with Napoleon or Genghis Kahn? Do you leave horror films frequently starving? Have you outlived your great, great-grandchildren? Do you dislike getting burned to death?'

All in good fun. I think I'll go out tonight. Speaking of which, before I forget, **Road to Selene: The Vampire Page** will tell you how to make the fangs.

Addresses

The Net.Vampiric
http://ucsu.Colorado.EDU/~whitneym/vamp2.html

Vampyres Only
http://www.vampyre.wis.net/vampyre/index.html

Creatures of the Night
http://www.awpi.com/Combs/CotN/

The Ooga Booga Page Vampires section
http://star06.atklab.Yorku.ca/~peterpan/vamp1.html

The Vampire WWW Server
http://vampireweb.com/vampire/index.html

Romantic Notions—Vampire Romances
http://wwide.com/rn7.html

Vampire Duck Page
http://www.cs.utk.edu/~ghenry/vampired.html

Road to Selene: The Vampire Page
http://www.gsu.edu/~lawjdp/vampire/index.html

See also...

Dracula Tours
http://www.redshift.com/~talisman/Dracula.html

A travel agency offering to help you follow in the footsteps: 'We'll move from the ruins of Dracula's Palace in Bucharest to the Monastery of Snagov where he was buried. We'll see Bran Castle which dates back to the 14th Century, and witness a re-enactment of the famous WITCH TRIALS very common in Transylvania during the 18th century. Follow in Jonathan Harker's famous footsteps as we dine on the same meal Harker enjoyed with Stoker's famous character. Sit 'round a camp fire as the REAL descendants of Dracula's knights tell of stories inherited from their ancestors about the dreaded prince.'

Dracula's Home Page
http://www.ucs.mun.ca/~emiller/

Elizabeth Miller is a professor of English at Memorial University in Newfoundland. She specialises in nineteenth-century British Gothic fiction, 'with particular emphasis on Mary Shelley's *Frankenstein* and Bram Stoker's *Dracula*'. She claims to be 'very active in Dracula Studies'—I obviously went to the wrong university—and is president of the Canadian chapter of the Transylvanian Society of Dracula. Read her work here, a site which mixes photos with the journals she kept during her travels to Romania.

The Vampirism Research Institute
http://users.aol.com/lirielmc/private/vri.htm

An organisation devoted to understanding vampirism and the 'enactment of vampiric tendencies: blood drinking, psychic or emotional draining, a preference for living at night or in the dark, vampiric relationships with others, etc'.

Suggested Reading For alt.vampyres
http://radon.eecs.berkeley.edu/~mudie/vampfic.html

A long and detailed list of vamp-lit recommendations from the denizens of the newsgroup.

The Vampire Movie List
http://www.netaxs.com/~elmo/vamp-mov.html

If it had a cape and fangs and it was on the silver screen, it's here. A comprehensive, worldwide list of bite flicks.

Vampire Junction
http://www.afn.org/~vampires/vj.html

An online vampire zine. Not much in the way of layout or graphics, but plenty of poetry and stories from bloodlusters.

Vampirella
http://scorpion.si.edu/vampi/

Mostly of interest to comic collectors, this is a site dedicated to the 2-D queen, a character who managed to combine every fanboy's dreams. Not only is she one of the undead, but she has outsized breasts!

Forever Knight
http://www.hu.mtu.edu/~gjwalli/fktoc.html

The wonders of high-concept Hollywood never cease. This is a vampire cop show. 'He was brought across in 1228. Preyed on humans for their blood. Now he wants to be mortal again. To repay society for his sins. To emerge from his world of darkness. From his endless, forever night...'

Abandon Hope All Ye Who Enter Here
http://www.public.iastate.edu/~vampyre/

I did, because it was taking so long to download.

Yes, There Is a Hell

JEAN-PAUL SARTRE reckoned hell was other people. His misanthropy is not exactly a surprise. After all, he was surrounded by 50 million French people when he said it. If he'd lived to see the digital age, of course, he would have recanted. Other people might be a pain in the *derrière*, but hell is something else. Hell is where you go when you're downloading.

When I die and go *downstairs* — and I know I will, because I have been to the **Decapitate An Angel** site and chopped away at something with wings — Satan will be there standing in front of a bank of a million computers, every one of them trying to download a video viewing program. And it will be my job to watch them doing it. For eternity.

But heck, that's my problem. The question I want to deal with here is slightly more universal. If cyberspace is its own universe, does it have a hell? Cyber-heaven I've experienced — it's one of those days when your modem behaves like a river in flood rather than an artery in a body that has seen too many cheeseburgers and chocolate milkshakes. But cyber-hell? The prospect seemed worth checking out. The sniffing search engines returned with messages about the Hell Blues Club, Matt (*The Simpsons*) Groening's *Life in Hell* comic strip, *Hell* — the CD-ROM featuring Dennis Hopper, and a couple of Joseph Heller home pages.

They also found some guy in **Canada** who's convinced he lives in hell (and having not been there, I'm not about to argue with him) before finally alighting on **Hell** itself, a full-speed, fundamental religious site with a pretty flaming background, which warned me that not only does hell exist, but Satan is alive and well and still a bastard of a landlord. 'Some people don't believe in him either,' the site says. 'Guess what? If you don't believe in Satan, then one of his little demons is

WORLD WIRED WEIRD

whispering in your ear right now [and I thought I'd left the television on]. Behind you! No, you can't see it. But believe me it's there.'

This seriously spooky site, which goes on to explain, just in case you hadn't worked it out, why the biblical hell isn't 'party time', features sound files of an interview with a 'denizen of hell' and a young woman who has apparently been there. Unfortunately, my machine didn't want to play them. Satan's little wizards were obviously mucking around with my Pentium chip. But things improved when I found the fun hell questionnaire at the bottom of the screen . . . though maybe I wasn't taking it in the right spirit.

A second site, also called **Hell**, proved more satisfying. 'Even in cyberspace there is a hell,' the home page proclaims, with a map of Europe and an arrow pointing suspiciously towards Norway (Yeah right, Old Cloven Hoof is a cold climate kind of guy—if you buy that, I've got an Opera House and a Bridge you might be interested in). On closer inspection, it turns out to be a bit of Web tourist touting. Hell does exist. It's in the cold country and it has a population of 352, one of whom, Mona Grudt, was Miss Universe in 1990. The site explains:

> Hell has a rich historical background and had its first known settlement around the year 4000 BC. From that time we find the first known runic characters. Hellir, which was the original name of the town, dates back to the year 2000 BC. Hell is the heart of communications between northern and southern Norway. Back in the old days, you had to cross the river on a ferry to go further north. The first bridge across the river was built in 1856, and is now the main thoroughfare of the European Highway No. 6.

The Highway to Hell. Boom tish! For the life of me, I can't understand why it's not more famous as a travel destination, if only because postcards would look great with a hell postmark. Thankfully, this site offers a postcard service. You send them the name, address and message, and for $US5, they'll send the card to a person of your choice. Frighten your family! 'Hi, Mum, I seem to have died somewhere back there. Can't remember how exactly, but at least I'm rugged up and warm now.' Hell's postcode, by the way, is 7570.

Last, but by no means least, **Hell—The Online Guide to Satanism** is a very nice looking site (not only does the Devil have the best tunes, he apparently has the best Web designers) which seeks to explain that we've got it all wrong. Its message is that Satanists are not entrail-reading, baby-sacrificing, blood-gulping loonies, but are generally benign and basically a jolly nice bunch of chaps. Rent payers. Babysitters. People who bring their library books back on time.

The site explains that in 1966 Anton Szandor LaVey

'declared the dawning of a new age. One in which strength and pleasures of the flesh were to be celebrated, not despised. The Church of Satan was born. Three years later Dr LaVey released his magnum opus, *The Satanic Bible*, which for the first time in history defined the philosophies of Satanism. Today almost thirty years later the Church of Satan remains alive and well.' The site explains those philosophies, as well as connecting with other groups, offering Satanic news and links (some of which are actually pretty dodgy, like the White Supremacists). As for that old rumour about the worshipping of the Christian Devil, well, we apparently don't know what we're talking about. Satan, in the Church's view, is a purely symbolic figure. Satanists don't believe in Gods or Devils. They do believe, however, in the Nine Satanic Statements:

1. Satan represents indulgence, instead of abstinence!
2. Satan represents vital existence, instead of spiritual pipedreams!
3. Satan represents undefiled wisdom, instead of hypocritical self-deceit!
4. Satan represents kindness to those who deserve it, instead of love wasted on ingrates!
5. Satan represents vengeance, instead of turning the other cheek!
6. Satan represents responsibility to the responsible, instead of concern for psychic vampires!
7. Satan represents man as just another animal, sometimes better, more often worse than those that walk on all fours, who, because of his 'divine spiritual and intellectual development' has become the most vicious animal of all!
8. Satan represents all the so-called sins, as they all lead to physical, mental, or emotional gratification!
9. Satan has been the best friend of the church as he has kept it in business all of these years!

Now stop me if I'm barking up the wrong tree here, but, with the exception of Statements 3, 6 and 9, which are kind of wishy-washy anyway, Satan appears to represent getting drunk, getting laid and falling over. Satanists believe in pretty much the same things that engineering students and football clubs on holiday in Fiji do. So much for the alternative vision.

Addresses

Decapitate an Angel
http://www.halcyon.com/maelstrm/angel.html

Home of the Jigger From Hell (The Canadian Guy)
http://alf.usask.ca/homepages/undergrads/jdj099/index.html

Hell
http://www.primenet.com/netdt/hell.html

Hell (Norway)
http://www.imsworld.com/hell/

Hell — The Online Guide to Satanism
http://webpages.marshall.edu/~allen12/index.html

See also . . .

Mike's Personal Hell
http://www.cs.cmu.edu/afs/andrew/usr/mk7v/www/

A Web artist building his own graphic version of hell online.

Satan's Playground
http://www.spacestar.com/users/baalack/

Another set of links and documents, much like The Online Guide to Satanism.

RESOURCE FILES

Finding Your Way Around

IT'S THE basic problem of the Information Age. Too much is never enough, but on the other hand, it's too much. We have so many options that we become paralysed and unable to make decisions. What we need are people to cut and shape all this input for us, so we don't have to wade through the info-swamp to get to what we're looking for.

On the Net, you often feel like you've been let loose in the world's biggest library, with every book out of order. And you're blindfolded. And as if that weren't enough, by the time you work your way through one shelf, finding out what things are, all the books have changed.

How to get around? Well, the whole thing is pretty badly signposted, really. But gradually, the Net is developing filtering systems to help you make sense of what is going on. Some very insightful people have realised that this is where the money is going to be. It's one thing having a cool Website. It's quite another working out how to direct people to it. And if everyone has to go through your site to get to anyone else's, well, hello advertising dollars and stratospheric hit rate.

So here's a bunch of launchpads I've found really useful:

Yahoo
http://www.yahoo.com

The vortex. First in and best dressed, Yahoo set itself up as the Net's Big Bang—everything radiates from here. All Net info seems to tumble through this vast, sprawling set of directories. If you're willing to dig, you'll almost certainly find what you're looking for. Access via subject, through its carefully kept set of lists, or by a word search of the whole site.

Alta Vista
http://www.altavista.digital.com

The fastest growing search engine on the Net. Lets you search both the Web and newsgroup. It's

'TOTO, I DON'T THINK WE'RE IN KANSAS ANYMORE'

neatly laid out and, if you can stand the info overload, will help you find things the other engines miss.

Point Communications
http://www.pointcom/com

My four cents' worth (inflation) is that this has been the best and most useful place to start your Web wanderings. The New and Noteworthy section reviews about twenty fresh sites a day. All of these are then tucked away into various easy-to-follow sections, forming a library that may not be as big as Yahoo's, but has more detail and a greater sense of the value of each item. The paragraph-long site reviews give you a much better idea of whether you'd like to visit each one or not, which can save a lot of time you would otherwise have wasted watching irrelevant home pages download.

Clearinghouse
http://www.clearinghouse.net

An alphabetised, subject-oriented index, run through the University of Michigan, of online resources. As its name implies, it's like a gigantic warehouse of ideas and Websites covering more themes and ideas than you could wade through in a lifetime. Rather than linking to sites, it links to the best lists of sites, crediting each list's curator.

Addicted to Stuff
http://www.morestuff.com

This site starts with the argument that one needs only two tools in life: WD-40 to make things go and duct tape to make them stop. All the links here, and there are hundreds, possibly thousands, are divided into these two categories. This is a truly marvellous place which concentrates on the stuff that seeps through the cracks of others and presents them in a bright, snappy, eminently readable way. If you can't blow at least a day checking out some of its recommendations, you're brain dead.

Cool Site of the Day
http://cool.infi.net/

The oldest and arguably the best of the single-siters. And if not the best, then the oldest. Originator Glenn Davis has handed over the reins and moved on to other things, but the modus operandi

RESOURCE FILES

continues. Every day, Cool Site nominates a new site it considers worthy of your attention. Sometimes you'll agree. Sometimes you won't. It also has a Categorically Cool section, in which it makes weekly nominations in five categories: knowledge, art, home page, bizarre, and commercial.

Project Cool
http://www.projectcool.com

Where Davis went next. Comes in four sections: Sightings, Coolest on the Web, Developer Zone and Future Focus. A site of the day, an archive of coolness, reference tools and a series of articles about Net culture. Effortlessly groovy.

Spider's Pick of the Day
http://gagme.wwa.com/~boba/pick.html

Spider's pick of the Web. Get it? Much like Cool Site of the Day, but concentrates on links that are a little more out there, a little more surprising. Or at least in my experience it does. All the past picks are catalogued and easily accessible on site, so you can check in once a month and stay reasonably up to date.

Australian Cool Sites of the Day
http://www.com.au/aaa/Cool_Site.html

'AAA Cool Sites of the Day are selected for their education and entertainment value, graphic design and originality and also for continuing revisit value. These Top 40 sites are released at 10 pm Sydney time each Sunday night (AEST) and are selected from nominations and the Top 100 listings on our home page, which was designed to give fast recognition to new sites serving a fast growing industry.'

Crappy Site of the Day
http://www.winternet.com/~crappy/

Quality is overrated. This place may be yet another '... of the Day' site, but at least it's devoted to the less luminous parts of the Net.

Same Site of the Day
http://pnx.com/falken/samesite.htm

Ah, stasis. Are you bored with having to know every fashionable place to hang out? Too cool to keep up? Well, The Same Site of the Day is for you. 'Soak it up! Yes, for your browsing enjoyment, it's the link to the same place it was yesterday!'

All-in-One Cool Sites Page
http://www.webcom.com/~tbrown/coolsite.html

A collection of collectors. This site brings a lot of the more interesting bookmarkers together under one umbrella. From Hawaiian Site of the Day to Short Attention Span Site of the Week (which seems like a contradiction in terms to me).

Beyond the Black Stump Cool Sites
http://werple.mira.net.au/~lions/secret.htm

A fabulous and comprehensive Australian source of What's Cool and What's New sites. From the meta-sites like the All-in-One Cool Sites Page to specific concerns like Castle of the Week and

Today's Calendar and Clock Page, this one has 'em all. More than 200 links to overview lists of all kinds. If you can't find somewhere to go from here, sell your modem.

Web Soup
http://sctest.cse.ucsc.edu/roth/WebSoup/

A handy time saver for the impatient—and on the Net, aren't we all? It polls more than 100 of the What's Cool sites and catalogues the information, which can be searched in a number of different ways. Tabular format is probably best. This site is waaaaay cool.

WWW.AU Web Directory
http://www.sofcom.com.au/WWW.AU/SubjectIndex.html

How many Australian sites are out there? Sometimes the American influence is so strong that it seems like there must be very few. But that's not true. We were bitten by the Net bug a little later, but Australians have been just as enthusiastic about getting their own sites up to tout for the attentions of global passers-by. This site provides a subject-driven catalogue of what's available out there, collecting and sorting everything with .au at the end of it into dozens of categories. A one-stop culture shop.

Weird Places on the Net
http://www.euronet.nl/users/deiman/

Half the fun of the Internet is being taken off in odd and surprising directions, following your nose and ending up somewhere completely different than you intended, but just as interesting. This place warns you that some of the hundreds of sites it links to are so bizarre that you surf there at your own risk, but really, most of them will only elicit a smile or a shake of the head at their addle-pated idiosyncrasies. It's a small-'c' catholic archive of all kinds of fringe behaviours and ideas. And for that alone, is an essential bookmark.

Useless WWW Pages
http://www.chaco.com/useless/index.html

So shoot me. I love a dumb gag. Or a cheap one. Or even better, both at once. Some of my favourite sites have been found through this amazing compendium of thousands of silly, pointless, boneheaded outings. Sit back and enjoy other people's pratfalls.

Infoseek Net Search
http://home.netscape.com/home/internet-search.html

The simplest of the search engines. Just type in a word and off it goes, finding usually at least 100 things it can tie to your request. Or, as with Yahoo, you can search it by subject index. Most importantly, it also links to a bunch of other search engines.

Lycos
http://www.lycos.com

OK, so there are a bunch of search engines around. And they're probably not greatly different from each other. I like Lycos. Why? Because it always seems to work for me. You plug in a couple of words and it comes back with all the items it can find that use those words, rating them on their closeness to your request.

The Green Eggs Report
http://www.ar.com/ger/

This is a device which lists all the Web addresses mentioned by people in various newsgroups, so you can find references you think you've lost, or just see what people are talking about. It picks up around 1500 every day and sorts them into groups.

URouLette
http://www.uroulette.com:8000/

The only way to travel ... blind. Click on the roulette wheel and find yourself hurtling out to somewhere unknown.

Warhol's Famous for 15 Minutes
http://www.grapevine.com/warhol/warhol.htm

Similarly, this site sends you to an almost random Web page—the selection changes every quarter hour.

Film

General Sites

The Internet Movie Database
http://ballet.cit.gu.edu.au/Movies/blurb.html

Don't be frightened by the scale of it. I was, but you've been warned. The Internet Movie Database is an exhaustive and exhausting volunteer effort. There are more than 75 000 filmography entries in the database. More than 200 000 people are covered. There are details on just about every filmmaker you've never heard of, as well as those you have. There are sections for actors, actresses, directors, writers, composers, cinematographers, editors, production designers, costume designers, producers and those not covered in the main areas. There are credits for more than 60 000 films, from contemporary blockbusters to silent classics to animated shorts. There are lists of links, alternative titles, trivia, goofs, literary sources, plot summaries, quotes, release dates and ratings. You can get info on soundtracks, the technical details of filming, video availability ... are you getting the picture?

CineMedia
http://www.gu.edu.au/gwis/cinemedia/CineMedia.home.html

Along with the database, this is the Internet's largest film and media directory. Its cinema section features extensive round-ups of Websites devoted to the movies, actors, studios, schools, organisations, directors, festivals and events, production details, histories, video and laser discs. If it's there to be found, you'll find it here.

Film.com
http://www.film.com/

Another seriously large site. It keeps a database of reviews, usually with multiple viewpoints on each film. You'll also find a store selling laser discs, videos, soundtracks, and other fetishisable items, as well as a set of screening rooms, where you can find out about the latest movies, stars and filmmakers, with downloadable video, audio and stills. There's an industry section, to keep you up to date with the behind-the-scenes shenanigans. And a number of places you can have your own two cents' worth.

The Film Zone
http://www.filmzone.com/

A huge and very useful American film site. It looks at all types of film with a slightly jaundiced, mercifully unglossy eye. Independent movies, foreign films and 'the garbage-belching monster that is Hollywood' all get fair play here. There are interviews, a sizeable reviews section, an obscurities corner, an archive and links to important sites. Well worth a visit.

The Academy of Motion Picture Arts and Sciences
http://www.ampas.org/ampas/

Oodles of info about Oscar or, as Jim Carrey described it, 'the lord of all knick-knacks!' There's also plenty of background material on the Academy, its various events, programs, fellowships and lesser-known awards.

The Envelope Please: An Interactive Guide to the Academy Awards
http://oscars.guide.com/

This site gets active around Oscars time, featuring biographies of all the nominees, plus short grabs from the films.

The Film Festivals Server
http://filmfestivals.com/index.htm

Keep up with what's going on around the world as every city that ever was rushes to be included on the festival circuit. It doesn't matter that there just aren't that many films to go around. A newsletter, interviews and extensive festival coverage.

Australian Resources

Sydney Film Festival
http://www.sydfilm-fest.com.au/

News section, background material and an archive of the festival's awards. Get a program of the films in the next season, with special screening details. Lots of booking info and invitations to

RESOURCE FILES

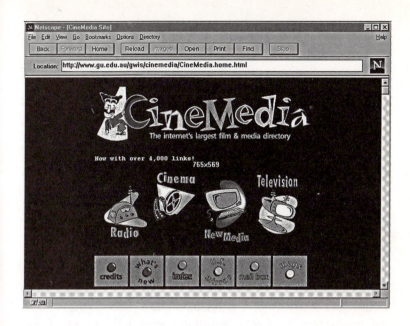

become a friend of the festival. Not really useful till festival season rolls around though—the rest of the time it's pretty quiet.

Melbourne International Film Festival
http://www.cinemedia.net/MIFF/miffhome.htm

Ditto for MIFF, a site which explodes around festival time, but can be a slow visit at other times. The same kind of information as Sydney, and it lets you download its trailer.

Flickerfest
http://www.merlin.com.au/flickerfest/

The Sydney International Outdoor Short Film Festival began in the playground of an inner-city high school five years ago. A terrific idea, it continues to grow, and after setting up successful national tours has established a European base in Amsterdam. The site has been promising short films and videos to download.

Australian Film Commission
http://www.afc.gov.au/

The AFC is 'the primary development agency for the film industry in Australia. With revenue earned mostly from film investments and interest on deposits, and an annual Federal Government appropriation, the AFC provides financial assistance and support for the development of new talent, as well as the production of film and television programs. Under its charter the AFC can only invest in Australian creative personnel and projects.' *AFC News*, its monthly newsletter, is offered online, as well as a wealth of resources and downloadable publications dealing with various parts of the industry.

Australian Film Institute
http://cinemedia.net/AFI/

'The Australian Film Institute is Australia's national film culture organisation, promoting knowledge, appreciation and enjoyment of the art of Australian film in particular. The Institute is involved through its range of programs with filmmakers, screen educators, students, historians and film lovers throughout the country.' Given that blurb, the site is only OK, but it has skeleton info about the institute, its yearly awards, its exhibitions and a catalogue and research material.

Australian Film, Television and Radio School
http://www.aftrs.edu.au/

The national home of education and training for the industry. 'The aim of AFTRS is to recognise and develop new and emerging talent and to provide industry professionals with opportunities to gain additional skills and assist them in their creative and professional development.' The site houses the course handbook, short courses brochures, media resources, issues of its film and television technology newsletter and professional contacts.

The Cinema Connection
http://socialchange.com.au/TCC/

A sprawling resources site which offers news, reviews, and interviews. It also has information on awards, new releases, box office and ratings, organisations, directors, actors, and all types of film (short, classic, art, cult). There is a history section, and directions to archives, libraries, museums and film preservation bodies. As well as a list as long as your arm of behind-the-scenes links.

Greater Union
http://www.greaterunion.com.au/

Curent movie info. What's playing in the various complexes, at what times. Cheap movie deals. An excellent collection of movie links. A feedback/review section, online articles from *Movie* magazine, and a quiz.

Hoyts Australia
http://www.sofcom.com.au/Hoyts/index.html

A daily listing of what's on in its various cinemas around the country.

The Village
http://www.village.com.au/

The most expensive and lavish of local distributor sites, this one not only spruiks for Village's content, but offers a Net home for *Who* magazine, some interactive games and a lot of tricks to hold your attention longer than it probably should. Craftily blurs the line between advertising and content.

Nine Cool Film Sites

The Making of *Citizen Kane*
http://www.voyagerco.com/CC/gh/welles/p.makingkane.html

This site offers the background on the casting, writing, makeup, cinematography, music and direction of Orson Welles's classic. It can get so arcane that it becomes curious: '*Citizen Kane* presented a formidable challenge for makeup artist Maurice Seiderman ... [Welles's] nose was unusually shaped for his type of face—the bridge was under-developed and the nostrils were unusually large—which caused his face to photograph abnormally flat. Seiderman made Welles's nose more photogenic by designing an addition which gave it a long and narrow bridge.'

Blade Runner Page
http://www.uq.oz.au/~csmchapm/bladerunner/

Info on the different versions of the film, a background briefing on the plot, photos, sound files and video clips, memorable quotes, collectables resources, trivia, sequel debate and more.

2001: A Space Odyssey
http://www.lehigh.edu/~pjl2/films/2001.html

Like the film, this site is a collection of images, open to interpretation, with a collection of links at the end to sound files and other sources of information.

Bloodlust
http://www.ozemail.com.au/~jswjon/

Included mainly for its shameless self-promotion, this is a Z-Grade Melbourne shocker. It describes itself as 'a stylish and macabre action thriller, with a strong vein of dark humour, about three modern-day vampires who rip off the mob and find themselves pursued into a living hell by a psychotic rabble of syndicate hitmen, redneck cops and religious fanatics'. It was banned in England a couple of years back and therefore has some notoriety.

Eraserhead
http://users.aol.com/RayWolf1/eraser.htm

Hands up those who really think they knew what the hell David Lynch was on about in this movie. American journalist and reviewer Ray Wolfe thinks he does and presents an online guide to possible interpretations of this cryptic creation.

Fast Times at Ridgemont High
http://www.columbia.edu/~gan3/fast.html

The film Sean Penn will never live down (or up to). His Jeff Spicoli is forever etched into the memory of cinema fans. No matter how serious and grown-up he pretends to be, many will always remember him as the archetypal stoner. Preserving the evidence, this site is chockablock with sound and video clips from the movie.

Forbidden Planet
http://www.tizeta.it/home/duo/fbhome.htm

The unofficial home of Robbie the Robot, the first and coolest screen automaton. This 1956 film was about the closest '50s sci-fi got to A-grade. Based on Shakespeare's *The Tempest*, it actually had something in the way of a budget and special effects that were not entirely cheesy.

Heathers
http://www.best.com/~sirlou/heathers.html

'The *Heathers* home page ... how very!' This film pretty much summed up the way a lot of people, myself included, felt about high school, i.e. it would have been a much nicer place if you could have killed a few people and been allowed to get away with it. *Heathers* was Winona Ryder's first biggie and also brought us the charms of Shannen Doherty. 'It's a modern re-telling of the timeless tale of boy meets girl, boy and girl fall in love, boy and girl kill girl's friends, boy tries to kill girl, boy commits suicide.'

The Kingdom
http://www.octoberfilms.com/kingdom/index.html

A hysterically funny, surreal outing from Danish director Lars Von Trier *(Zentropa)*. The four-hour film about a hospital, pieced together from a TV mini-series, is a 'bizarre excursion through a medical institution that is meant to embody the height of reason, but where nothing reasonable ever happens'. *ER* meets *Twin Peaks* in a very ugly grudge match.

Things to Read

Drew's Scripts-O-Rama
http://home.fish.net.au/~drew/scripts.htm

A gigantic Web-wide catalogue of film scripts. Hundreds of scripts are available here, ready to be downloaded for free and studied by would-be scribes and cinema buffs. If Joe Eszterhas can make $3 million a script, why can't you? Anyway, the site allows you to pick the format its information appears in: '1) Marlon Brando Style (with table): The best, be patient. 2) Kathleen Turner Style (no table): Meaty, but can still move. 3) Kate Moss Style (bare bones): Everything you need, but nothin' extra.' There are even scripts here for films that weren't made, such as *Alien vs Predator*. Gee, I wonder what was wrong with that idea?

Cinema Muerto
http://users.aol.com/Cinemam/muerto.htm

An e-zine devoted to bad cinema. Its editor, Dirk Stern, boasts that they have not found 'one reviewer on our staff who has ever comfortably sat through an entire film', but adds that the benefits almost always outweigh the drawbacks. 'Bad movies are just that—BAD. It is both normal and natural to want to leave a theater or turn off a VCR when the acting starts insulting your intelligence. But remember this, if you leave in the middle of the movie you will miss all the pearls of wisdom which make all bad movies so much fun. Once the film is over, all of the horrible memories of boredom and poor taste are replaced with fond remembrances of plot flaws and laughably cheap special effects.'

Premiere
http://www.premieremag.com/home.html

The highly successful American magazine, which has made its name by finding more ways to brown-nose movie stars than even *Vanity Fair*, publishes a Web version. Useful for its previews.

Entertainment Weekly
http://pathfinder.com/@@k6nM1sMiGQEAQACx/ew/

Arguably even more downmarket. And that can't be a bad thing.

Mr Cranky Rates the Movies
http://internet-plaza.net/zone/mrcranky/

At least this guy has a scale that is believable. It goes from 'Almost tolerable' through 'Consistently annoying' and up, all the way to 'So godawful that it ruptured the very fabric of space and time with the sheer overpowering force of its mediocrity'. His reviews, of films and videos, are short and sharp. '*Sense & Sensibility*: Two-and-a-half hours in a theatre waiting for these English twits to express an iota of human feeling.' And the site has a great disclaimer: 'Mr. Cranky frequently engages in vicious personal attacks on actors, directors and other filmmaking personnel. Being the amazingly introspective, self-analysing personality that he is, Mr. Cranky realises that this type of behaviour is only a childish defence mechanism that allows him to repress his own intellectual and physical inadequacies.'

Teen Movie Critic
http://www.dreamagic.com/roger/teencritic.html

It's a shtick that won't last, but while he can get away with it, the Teen Movie Critic is milking it for all it's worth. The youngest of fifteen children, this seventeen (probably eighteen by now)-year-old

American has had a lot of time to sit in dark rooms watching films, and if you want the latest flick reviewed from the adolescent, hormonal point of view, here's the place to come. 'I give reviews and give my own personal criticism on what is bad, okay, good or excellent. I give this review mainly for teenagers who are not sure what's cool and what's not. Now, listen up. These are my criticisms. If you don't like them, then you don't have to continue reading this page.'

Odds and Ends

Six Degrees of Kevin Bacon
http://www.primenet.com/~fnargle/erisson/bacon/

A site dedicated to the idea that Kevin Bacon, in acting terms, is the centre of the universe. This theory is proven by a game which allows you to connect any major actor with Kev within six short steps of acquaintance (a familiar idea to anyone who has seen *Six Degrees of Separation*). It's spooky how well it works.

Hong Kong Movies
http://www.mdstud.chalmers.se/hkmovie/

The thriving Hong Kong film industry makes some of the funniest, fastest, most action-packed films you could ever see. This site has filmographies, film lists, interviews, reviews, an FAQ and more. There's a searchable database of HK movies and actors, and links to other HK sites—find out what last week's box office was like!

The Hitchcock Page
http://www.primenet.com/~mwc

Hitch, of course, has a big site devoted to him. You can find a thorough biography, a comprehensive filmography, and a catalogue of all his TV work. Trivia buffs will get their jollies reading the list of all the director's cameos. And if you're a serious fan, you can download an animated version of the shower scene from *Psycho*.

James Bond Movie Page
http://www.dur.ac.uk/~dcs3pjb/jb/jbhome.html

'It was estimated recently that half the world's population has seen a James Bond movie'—Albert R. Broccoli. This sprawling tribute to everything stirred, not shaken, has separate galleries for Her

Majesty's Secret Service, the movies, the cars, the girls, the villains and the gadgets, as well as links to other Bondian Web sites.

The Movie Cliches List
http://www.like.it/vertigo/cliches.html

A five-star site which makes its living out of Hollywood's never ending love affair with the same handful of ideas. Indeed, the cliché business is so huge and sophisticated that its study has to be broken up into more than 70 categories, from Airplanes to Wood. By way of example, Shopping: 'When bringing home bags of groceries in a film, it's required that you spill at least one bagful on the kitchen floor. Bags of groceries are never heavy. Whenever anyone in a movie goes shopping, they always come back with stuff sticking out of the top of the shopping bag, usually carrot tops and French bread. Corollary: every shopping bag contains at least one baguette.'

The Movie Sounds Page
http://www.moviesounds.com/

Sound grabs from dozens of famous films. Just in case. You never know when you might need to hear a bit of *Gone With the Wind* or *Terminator 2*.

CyberCinema
http://www.cyber-cinema.com/

A movie poster store from which you can order online. From the classics to this year's blockbusters, you'll find your wall covering of choice here.

The Godfather Trilogy
http://www.exit109.com/~jgeoff/godfathr.html

A Website you can't refuse, as some bright spark described it. Trivia, quotes and sounds. Background on the movies. Statistics and gossip. The novel. The chances of a Part IV.

Mark's Godzilla Page
http://www.ama.caltech.edu/users/mrm/godzilla.html

One of a handful of sites dedicated to the real Lizard King. It has acres of info on Godzilla's past and present adventures (the movie series has recently been revived), with many, many pictures.

Check out all the other cool monsters Godzilla has fought, lovingly catalogued with their own handsome pics. Plus a batch of 'Zilla links.

Troma
http://www.troma.com

The production house that brought you *The Toxic Avenger, Rabid Grannies, Stuff Stephanie in the Incinerator* and *Blondes Have More Guns*. 'Troma is the brand name for movie theatre adventure of a calibre Hollywood can't match. It is the brand name for films that have gestated at the bottom of the toxic swamp, then bubbled up to improve our imperfect world. You may love them or you may hate them, but you'll never forget a movie hatched at Troma Studios.' Tromazine, Trombabilia, Tromatic links, 'Sex Advice for the Truly Desperate', video clips and a scriptwriting contest. Plus much, much more. A very fine site.

The Bagpipes Go to the Movies
http://www.ems.psu.edu/~fraser/PipesMovies.html

Ah, more loony Web. Scott Williams and Alistair B. Fraser have taken it upon themselves to list alphabetically every use or appearance of the pipes in film and television. Pick a letter, any letter. How about K? '*Kidnapped*—1960 (97 minutes) Directed by Robert Stevenson and starring Peter Finch, James MacArthur and Peter O'Toole, this is the story of an 18th century Scottish boy cheated out of his inheritance by a conniving uncle. The film contains a scene where Allan Breck Stewart and another Highlander duel with bagpipes instead of swords. The pipes are single tenor-drone types. The tunes played are simple, but well played.'

Quentin Tarantino, a God Among Men
http://www.mind.net/nikko11/QT.html

Sigh. If we must...

TV

NB: *Star Trek* and *X-Files* sites breed like rabbits in cyberspace, so I have corralled a few of them off at the end of this section, to keep them from infecting the others.

General Resources

TV Net
http://www.tvnet.com/TVnet.html

Can be completely overwhelming at first, but if you stick around and learn the ropes, this turns out to be probably the most comprehensive collection of Web-related televisiana there is. Its Ultimate TV List contains, at last count, more than 4000 links to hundreds and hundreds of individual programs. It runs reviews, has a search engine to help you find what you're looking for, and monitors TV schedules around the world. Find out on what night of the week your favourite show is playing in Belgium. There are also sections on ads, polls, hot lists, industry watchers and … oh, forget it. Just go there.

CineMedia/Television
http://ptd15.afionline.org/CineMedia/cmframe.html

Has a list to rival TV Net's. Also sections on media regulation, the history of the broadcast media, actors, schools, organisations, sound and images, and a very good miscellanea file of unclassifiable, but interesting, related sites.

The Australian TV Guide
http://www.sofcom.com.au/TV/index.html

The guide lets you browse the TV schedules by timeslot or channel. You can search for a favourite program or just wander and see what you find. The site also includes Tony Lammens' pick o' the day column and a list of links.

BBC TV
http://www.bbcnc.org.uk/tv/index.html

Home of the Beeb. Some would say the home of television. Here you will find schedules and

RESOURCE FILES

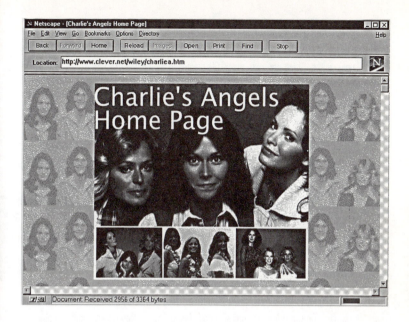

material on the current output of the various departments: news, drama, current affairs, children's, natural history, music and arts, science and technology. There's also an archive and BBC training and service information. And you can find out what the weather's like in England today (dismal).

Tardis WWW TV Database
http://www.tardis.ed.ac.uk/~dave/guides/index.html

'This database contains episode guides, complete with full guest star, writer and director credits, for many TV series. You can search for an actor's name, and will be given a list of all the TV shows (in this database) that she/he had appeared in.' Pretty much text only, but a mine of info on a huge number of shows, with an emphasis on British ones but also more American programs than it would be sane for me to try and list.

TV Bytes: WWW TV Themes Homepage
http://tvtrecords.com/themes/

Finally, someone puts together a site which allows you to answer all those niggling questions that hit you at 3 a.m., such as 'What were the words to the *Green Acres* theme song?' This site has about 1000 (I wasn't going to count) themes archived for you to download. But you have to register and you can't have more than five a day. It's a service for the serious collector as well as the simply curious. There are more than 200 themes in the Comedy section alone—this is the place to go if you want the theme song only used in the *pilot* of *Gilligan's Island*.

Columbia Tristar Television Home Page
http://www.spe.sony.com/Pictures/tv/cttv.html

The jump-off site for all the shows made at Sony's huge studio lot in LA. The official home pages of *Hudson Street, Ned and Stacey, Mad About You, Married . . . With Children, Seinfeld, The Nanny, Party of Five, Forever Knight, Days of Our Lives, The Young and the Restless, Jeopardy* and *Wheel of Fortune*.

Sitcoms Web Page
http://pmwww.cs.vu.nl/service/sitcoms/

Links and nothing else. *All in the Family, Bewitched, Blossom, Cheers, Family Ties, Full House, Grace Under Fire, Growing Pains, Herman's Head, Home Improvement, Larry Sanders Show, My Two Dads, Married with Children, Murphy Brown, The Nanny, Roseanne, Saved by the Bell, Seinfeld, Step by Step*.

Soap Links
http://members.aol.com/soaplinks/index.html

Jumpoff site, with links to *All My Children, Another World, As the World Turns, The Bold and the Beautiful, Days of Our Lives, General Hospital, Guiding Light, The City, One Life to Live, The Young and the Restless, Central Park West* and *Melrose Place*, plus directions to many, many other pages concerned with non-US soaps, soap actors and cyber-soaps.

The Game Show Page
http://silver.ucs.indiana.edu/~wlambert/GameShows.html

Come on down! Game show quizzes and links. An exhaustive list of board games, Emmy Awards, birthdays of game-show personalities, and the rules for more than 70 past and present programs. All in a bright and bubbly package—though it could do with a little bad organ music in the background.

RESOURCE FILES

The UK Game Show Page
http://users.ox.ac.uk/~kebl0110/GS/gs.html

It takes all kinds. I haven't heard of most of the shows linked to this page, but you might have. And if not, it's a curious look at the fast food TV diet of another country.

TVplex
http://www.directnet.com/wow/tv/index.htm

The TV arm of the huge Gigaplex site, this has a weekly news sections which follows the industry and a bunch of interviews with the stars of various shows.

Community Broadcasting Association of Australia
http://www.scu.edu.au/cbaa/tvlist.html

Lists all community channels and their links.

The Jihad to Destroy Barney on the World Wide Web
http://deeptht.armory.com/~deadslug/Jihad/jihad.html

Every so often, a good cause just seems to come along. Anyone who has ever seen the hideous purple dinosaur kiddie favourite will know that fifteen minutes of exposure makes you homicidal. 'You are sick and tired of that purple felt demon, and you want to make his head explode. That's why we're here. This is the Jihad to Destroy Barney on the World Wide Web, the Web page that says, without hesitation, that Barney Must Die, All Else is Irrelevant.' It has an FAQ, artwork and a lot of fantasising about ripping someone's stuffing out.

Mr T
http://www.l0pht.com/~veggie/MrT.html

There haven't been many stars bigger and more charismatic than Mr T, stalwart of that fabulous '80s drama, *The A-Team*. Boggle in wonder at the episode guide, look away in fear from the Mr T photo archives, be surprised by Mr T's vital stats (he likes milk, he likes playing Go, he's not circumcised), learn from his biography ('Any man who don't love his momma can't be no friend of mine').

Now Showing

ER
http://www.seas.gwu.edu/student/danny/er/

As usual, there's an official site too, but the fan site is better. This tribute archives an FAQ and a wealth of information about hospital staff. There are episode summaries, the theme tune as a sound file and some great odds and ends, including a quote collection, drinking games, and a list of the dubbing cast for the Italian version.

Friends Home Page
http://www.dartmouth.edu/~andyjw/friends/

Not the most beautiful of sites, but crammed with info on this twentysomething phenomenon. The usual guide to the episodes, but also drinking games, a sprawling favourite quotes section (is there any line they don't like?) with sound accompaniment, a photo gallery and links to the many other *Friends* Websites, newsgroups and magazine articles. Oh, and there's plenty of info on *Friends* merchandise.

Lois and Clark
http://www.webcom.com/~lnc/

For underwear-as-outerwear obsessives, *Lois and Clark* has info, soundbites, interviews, episode listings, etc. Download your very own man of steel.

Melrose Place: The Basement
http://melroseplace.com/basement.html

'The source for all the inside info on the sexiest, most tumultuous apartment building in Southern California, if not the world!' It's the place to get all the latest Melrose Place gossip, keep abreast of the news, check upcoming plotlines and chat live about the show with other hopeless fans. 'You get the best vantage from down here,' it promises. 'After all, down below is where all the DIRT lands.'

Gladiators
http://dspace.dial.pipex.com/town/square/fm71/index.htm

Oof! Thud!! Kapow!! No, it's not *Batman*. This is the multi-continental cyberhome of one of the stupidest shows of our time, television at its purest and most idiotic. Don't get me wrong. I love watching a couple of pumped-up muscle machines bopping each other with outsized cotton buds. I just wish they'd do it in a bear pit. Anyway, the show is huge all around the world. Which creates an excuse for this site.

The Lurker's Guide to Babylon 5
http://www.hyperion.com/lurk/lurker.html

Cyberspace being a bold new frontier and all that, sci-fi shows have dominated the scene so far, though the gradual normalisation of the Net is ironing that kink out. Which is not to say that this site isn't a goody. It examines the universe of *Babylon 5,* its settings, characters and philosophy and takes you backstage to see how the show is made. Hidden away on the site is an excellent list of resources at **http://www.hyperion.com/b5/**.

The Official Baywatch Web Site
http://baywatch.compuserve.com/

Proof that you can surf the Net one-handed.

Some Golden Oldies

The Cult TV Episode Guide
http://www.ee.ed.ac.uk/~jmd/CultTV/

An English database for obscure and not-so-obscure small-screen outings, from *The A-Team* to *The X-Files*. Everything you always wanted to know about *The Sweeney, The Good Life*, or the incredibly short-lived *The Girl From U.N.C.L.E.*

Prisoner: Cell Block H
http://www.dcs.ed.ac.uk/~ncs/pcbh.html

It's an English site, hence the English name. It has fan club info, a mailing list, episode guides, bios, a rogue's gallery of photos, details of the prison, the lyrics of the theme song. And a plug for *PCBH: The Musical*.

The Echo Point Homepage
http://yoyo.cc.monash.edu.au/~pilgrim/

'Why is there a homepage devoted to the least successful in a long line of less than exceptional Aussie soaps? A show so roundly lambasted by critics and ignored by the public that it was shorter lived than even *Paradise Beach*? Why not? Some, myself included, feel that *Echo Point*'s complete and utter failure makes it worthy of the honour of its own homepage ... So what if it's crap, derivative and unsuccessful?'

Aunty Jack
http://pcug.org.au/~stmcdona/auntyjac.html

Sound files from one of the greatest Australian programs ever. Who can hear the theme song often enough? What we wouldn't give to have our bloody arms ripped off again...

The Gumby Chronicles
http://www.atlantic.net/~exene/Gumby/index.html

Not exactly about the show. This site tells the behind-the-scenes story of the last of the famous international clayboys, Gumby. According to the site's historians and biographers, Gumby is a chain-smoking, hard drinking, womanising, casually violent sonofabitch. Nothing at all like his plasticine television persona.

Hey Hey It's the Monkees Homepage
http://www.primenet.com/~flex/monkees.html

It's quite fitting that a band which was all about hype and packaging should have such a well-kept, swish Website. Mountains of info on the show and the music. You can play and sing along to sound files, check out the photo gallery, read the bios, do the trivia quiz and find out exactly how the Monkees influenced *Star Trek*. (No, I'm not going to tell you.)

The Encyclopedia Brady
http://www.primenet.com/~dbrady/

It's early days for the ambitious site, but pretty soon, every last bit of Brady ephemera will be lovingly alphabetised here. 'Albuquerque: City where Mike's aunt lives. Alden, John: Pilgrim who sailed from England on the *Mayflower* and helped found Plymouth Colony in 1620. He later married Pilgrim Priscilla Mullens. Alden is portrayed by Peter in Greg's short film, *Our Pilgrim Fathers.*'

The Lost in Space Page
http://www.access.digex.net/~ragjr/lostspac.html

Was, is, and I think always will be one of my favourite shows. This fan site has loads of sound samples, an episode ranking and a huge list of the insults that the sanctimonious Dr Smith came up with for TV's greatest robot: 'Addlepated Amateur, Aluminium Canary, Animated Weather Station, Arrogant Automaton, Automated Oaf, Babbling Birdbrain, Babbling Bumpkin, Blithering Blatherskite, Bloated Blimp, Blundering Bag of Bolts, Broken-down Has Been, Brutish Product of the Mineral World, Bubble-headed Booby . . .' And so on.

Gilligan's Island
http://www.epix.net/~jabcpudr/gilligan.html

Info on the pilot, the 98 televised episodes, the two animated series (1974's *The New Adventures of Gilligan* and 1982's *Gilligan's Planet*), the three telemovies (1978's *Rescue From Gilligan's Island*, 1979's *The Castaways on Gilligan's Island* and, losing the plot completely, 1981's *The Harlem Globetrotters on Gilligan's Island*). We are soon to be graced with *Gilligan's Island: The Movie.*

The Avengers Home Page
http://www.ee.ualberta.ca/~dawe/avengers.html

'The Avengers was a slightly tongue-in-cheek spy/action/adventure series produced in England during the 1960s.' If the photos of Diana Rigg aren't enough, there are histories, filmographies and biographies, sound files, book, video and trading card information, and a news section keeping tabs on rumours of a new Avengers movie.

Dr Who Home Page
http://nitro9.earth.uni.edu/doctor/homepage.html

Reverse the polarity of the neutron drive! The Time Lord lives! This is where you'll find info about the Doctor's past, or pasts. There's a list of Who Web resources, an FAQ, an information archive, lost and missing episode details, a bloopers list and directions to various fan clubs, as well as actor bios and birthdays.

Monty Python WWW Homepage
http://www.iia.org/~rosenr1/python/python.html

An extensive archive of the before, during and after of the Pythons. Sketches, songs, films, records, sound files from various sites around the Net, a list of books, biographies of the culprits, updates on their current projects and more.

Are You Being Served? Homepage!
http://www.webcom.com/~jrice/aybs.html

No kidding. Trivia tests, a chance to vote for your favourite characters, cast and episode lists, photos, interviews with Mr Humphries, sound clips and more pussies than you could feed with a tonne of Whiskettes.

The Charlie's Angels Home Page
http://www.clever.net/wiley/charliea.htm

Hubba Hubba. A shrine to Kate Jackson, Jaclyn Smith, Farrah Fawcett, Cheryl Ladd, Shelley Hack and Tanya Roberts. It features episode guides, reader responses and Angel Trap, a zine with its own Angel photo gallery.

M*A*S*H Archives
http://www2.best.com/~dijon/tv/mash/index.html

Many of these sites have a remarkably similar makeup: a sound file of the opening theme, photos of the cast and show, an FAQ, an episode guide, a character list, and a few other bits and pieces. But if you're a M*A*S*H fan, it'll still be bliss.

The Bionic Page
http://www.scifi.com/bionics/

Here's the place to slip back into the past and 'review data on bionically enhanced agents' AKA Bionic Replacement Catalogue #87310/SAB Steve Austin and Bionic Replacement catalogue #87312/JSB Jamie Sommers. Hang out at OSI Headquarters and view the mission list of the operatives.

Battlestar Galactica Home Page
http://mcmfh.acns.carleton.edu/BG//

God, I miss those bad-guy Cylons, with the little red lights flipping back and forth across their dials. This site takes the show totally seriously. It has the usual FAQ, program guides, images from the series, dialogue and sound effects, '*Galactica*-related fonts and software for PC and Macintosh' (let me at it), and 'information about the future of *Galactica* and the *BG* revival campaign'.

Blake's 7
http://www.ee.surrey.ac.uk/Contrib/SciFi/Blakes7/

Blake's 7 was an example of the ability of English science fiction dramas to combine good actors (Paul Darrow as Avon) with polystyrene sets and hilarious visual effects. And for that, we love it.

The Young Ones
http://www.best.com/hammers/comedy/youngone/youngone.htm

The complete scripts for both series, air dates. And, not to be missed, the complete works of Rick, the People's Poet.

The Pee-Wee Herman Worship Page
http://www.seanet.com/Users/weazel/peewee.html

Sound file of his greatest sayings: 'I know you are, but what am I?', 'Why don't you take a picture? It'll last longer!', 'That's my name, don't wear it out!' You can hang out at Pee-Wee's Playhouse with all his friends, read the episode list or sashay off to linked Pee-Wee sites.

Anders' Twin Peaks Page
http://www.stud.unit.no/~anpa/twinpeaks/twinpeaks.html

It makes perfect sense that this *Twin Peaks* site should be from Norway. Where else would it be from? It's OK, and has a few picture galleries, some quotes, an FAQ and a list of links, but it doesn't exactly reflect the flavour of the show.

The Moose's Guide to Northern Exposure
http://www.netspace.org/~moose/moose.html

The end of *Northern* in early 1996 was a sad day for all lovers of classy, subtle television. The

Moose's Guide has everything you'd expect about the show, the episodes and the characters, as well as archives of the music, and the scripts, essays and comments from fans. And there's a random quote generator.

Absolutely Fabulous
http://online.anu.edu.au/nceph/Tor/

'Sweetie darling' and 'Lacroix!' abound. Separate home pages for Eddie, Patsy, Saffy, Bubble and Mum. Break out the virtual Bolly and swill your way in. Play the theme, check the links, spill the booze on the carpet.

The Truth Is Out There

The X-Files
http://www.thex-files.com/

The official site for the program, it includes 'an extensive episode guide complete with pictures from the episodes; downloadable items such as video promos, audio promos and advertisements; information about the show and its creator; cast biographies and photos; and thorough character biographies including pictures of your favourite—and not-so-favourite—characters'. There's also a fan forum, a strong merchandise section and breaking news of the show's various activities. Of course, you shouldn't trust any of it.

The X-Files (another)
http://www.rutgers.edu/x-files.html

Less well organised but arguably more value than the official site, this one has sound files of the theme music, promos, FAQs, episode guides and links to a myriad other sites. The oldest *X-Files* fan club is based here too.

X-Rate
http://www.iinet.net.au/~brianp/xfiles/

In cyberspace, The *X-Files* spread like the flu virus. Any show that has more than 100 sites in its honour must be considered an epidemic. This Australian site is a good place to start, with links to almost every related subject, including *The X-Files* drinking game.

X-Files: Trust No One
http://www.neosoft.com/sbanks/xfiles/xfiles.html

Excellent site with episode guides, FAQ, links, background readings, sound and picture files. Everything the X-Phile could want. The best of the lot, I think.

Trekking

Star Trek WWW Pages
http://www.vol.it/luca/startrek/index.html

A comprehensive list of fan-run sites from all around the globe, including a bunch of Australian ones. You can be pretty sure that everything you will want or need is here.

Australian Star Trek Page
http://yoyo.cc.monash.edu.au/~vivek/startrek.html

Local goodie, with information about all the TV manifestations of *Trek*, a bunch of related documents, pictures, sound files and stories written by fans.

The Captain James T Kirk Sing-a-long Page
http://www.ama.caltech.edu/users/mrm/kirk.html

'Little known to the civilised world, the great William Shatner [Kirk on the original *Star Trek* TV series] recorded a masterpiece of an album—*The Transformed Man*—back in 1968.' And just so none of us will be able to forget, the site includes downloadable chunks of the record in question. It also links to pages about albums by Spock, Data and Uhuru.

The Klingon Language Institute
http://www.kli.org/

Klingon was invented by Marc Okrand for use in some of the *Star Trek* movies. He invented not just a few words to make the Klingons sound alien, but a complete language, with its own vocabulary, grammar, and usage. The institute's aims are 'first, to promote, foster, and develop the Klingon language, and second to bring together Klingon language enthusiasts from around the world and provide them with a common forum for the discussion and the exchange of ideas.' There is also a ...

Vulcan Language Page
http://web.apertus.com/~joela/vulcan/index.html

Not to be outdone ...

Music

Ten Important Sites

Yahoo Music List
http://www.yahoo.com/Entertainment/Music/

The mother of 'em all. Last time I looked, there were more than 10 000 sites listed in its Artists section alone and more than 170 links to Marching Bands sites! You'll find directions to everything and everyone, from sheet music to karaoke bars, from chart histories to music videos to songwriting tips to trivia contests.

The Ultimate Band List
http://american.recordings.com/wwwofmusic/ubl/ubl.shtml

If Yahoo doesn't kill you, the UBL certainly will. Browse the bands alphabetically, by genre, or view the complete listings. You'll find bands of all kinds, Websites, newsgroups, mailing lists, FAQ files, lyrics and chord charts, and digitised songs.

iMusic
http://www.imusic.com/

The best all-in-one music site on the Web. Daily news features (with occasionally reliable Real Audio live performances), hundreds of bulletin boards to chat about your favourite bands, acres of chart info, polls, contests, games, record reviews. The writing isn't always great, but the energy and vibe of the site will keep you coming back.

Internet Underground Music Archive
http://www.iuma.com/

A site which has been responsible for converting thousands of young people to the Net, this library of lesser-known acts has been growing like Topsy since, oh, the dawn of Web time (1993). Its archive covers new bands and keeps tabs on the old ones that have made it. Beyond the links to bands, many of which have sound files, there are also links to various important record labels and magazines.

Addicted to Noise
http://www.addict.com/ATN/

Net-only primo music mag with columnists of the calibre of Dave Marsh and Greil Marcus. Interviews with musicians, daily news, album, film and TV reviews with sound grabs, music and technology columns, and plenty of links. And its own Real Audio radio station.

Aussie Music Monolith
http://www.odyssey.com.au/wtc/monolith/directry.html

'The Monolith is dedicated to bringing you the very best of Music on the Web with a particular emphasis on Australian Music.' It links to artsists, charts from around the world, places you can download music software, lesson sources, instrument references, music media, video and audio clips, industry contacts and professional services. It also includes *The Top 10 Australian Music Websites,* a vote-based list of the ten most popular music sites, published each week.

Australian Music World Wide Web Site
http://www.amws.com.au/

More than 300 links to local acts, playlists for radio stations and music-TV programs, links to the various venue and gig guides for Australian cities, and general info on Australia.

Aussie Music Online
http://www.aussiemusic.com.au/

'AMO aims to take Aussie Music to the world and to bring the world to Aussie music.' The Magazine has regular info and columns on the various scenes, while the Shop allows you to order some good local sounds. There are plenty of links and contacts, as well as directions to where to hear Aussie music around the world.

Hyperreal
http://www.hyperreal.com

The place to go for rave culture and dance music resources. This enormous, sprawling site is fastidiously maintained and exceptionally neat, given that it is probably run by people who spend their lives in a state of sleep deprivation, constantly dancing and pushing the boundaries of substance

RESOURCE FILES

abuse. Anyway, whatever you want to know about raves is here. Its drugs section alone is worth the effort.

The Australian Music Industry Directory
http://www.immedia.com.au/

Contains links to every Australian band on the Web and also has the names and phone numbers of the movers and shakers of the music industry. This could be your big break. Track them down, play them your demos. Start letter-writing campaigns. Agitate!

CD Now
http://www.cdnow.com/

A number of music stores have opened huge and impressive mail-order Websites. This is the biggest and has more than 165 000 discs in its catalogue. It will airfreight your choice to your door in less than a week, at around two-thirds of the retail price (freight included), with bigger discounts if you buy in bulk. Don't break the $200 mark, though, or you can be taxed on the savings.

Musical Travels

The Blue Highway
http://www.vivanet.com/~blues/tbh.html

A Hall of Fame for the blues. Separate homepages for: Robert Johnson, Mississippi John Hurt, Bessie Smith, Muddy Waters, B.B. King, Buddy Guy, W.C. Handy, Charley Patton, Blind Lemon Jefferson, Leadbelly, Son House, Bukka White, T-Bone Walker, Willie Dixon, Howlin' Wolf, Sonny Boy Williamson, Lightnin' Hopkins, Albert King, Elmore James and John Lee Hooker. There are also cyber-tours of the American blues terrain and a batch of essays on the genre's history and culture.

The Turkish Music Home Page
http://vizlab.rutgers.edu/~jaray/sounds/turkish/turkish.html

An archive of Turkish music, with links to pages dealing with specific regional sounds. There are essays on history and influences and information on how to get cassettes of the material.

The Encyclopaedia of African Music
http://matisse.net/~jplanet/afmx/ahome.htm

Subtitled 'Music from Africa and the African Diaspora', this site allows you to search its database by country or wander through its alphabetical artist list, its African links and music resources.

Chinese Music Page
http://vizlab.rutgers.edu/~jaray/sounds/chinese_music/chinese_music.html

An archive of Chinese music which has plenty of sound files. It traces the development from traditional instrumental styles through various brands of folk and ceremonial music to the tumultuous changes of the twentieth century, and culminates in an exploration of the influence of the West.

Hindi Movie Songs
http://www.cs.wisc.edu/~navin/india/songs/index.html

Anyone who has ever been to India or seen Indian MTV equivalents will know that movie songs are a vast and lively genre unto themselves. This site contains info on many of them, with lyrics and indexes of singers, music directors, lyricists, films, and actors.

Bali & Beyond Home Page
http://www.kaiwan.com/~gamelan/balihome.html

A site for lovers of gamelan, Indonesian orchestral music characterised by gongs, chimes and percussion. Has info on Balinese and Javanese gamelan, music terms and structures as well as a history of the form, with details of instrument making and regular features on musicians.

Peruvian Music
http://www.rcp.net.pe/snd/snd_ingles.html

This small site contains nothing but a handful of sound files of Andean flute music from Peru.

TuneWeb
http://www.ece.ucdavis.edu/~darsie/tunebook.html

A huge archive of traditional Celtic tunes (Irish, Scottish, or Breton in origin), with a few others (American songs, English country dances, and various misfits). Reels, jigs, slip jigs, slides, hornpipes, polkas, slow airs and more.

Indian Classical Music
http://www.aoe.vt.edu/~boppe/MUSIC

From ragas to riches. Here you'll find a general introduction to the classical music of north and south India, lists of ragas, biographies of master musicians and vocalists, a tabla bibliography and online catalogues, should you wish to place orders.

Samba in Sweden
http://www.algonet.se/~johanw/

A site dedicated to the samba scene in swinging Sweden. Need I say more?

Ten Sites Dedicated to Acts I Happen to Like

Tom Waits Digest
http://www.nwu.edu/waits/

An online journal following Waits's peregrinations, with loads of news and happenings, as well as a collection of stories about the man, comments on his work, an index of band members, lyrics and guitar chord charts, and a guided tour through a back catalogue of official albums, rare recordings, guest appearances, compilations and tributes.

Dead Can Dance
http://www.nets.com/dcd/

DCD put together ideas and sounds from the last five centuries of European music, from traditional Irish ballads to middle eastern wails, adding their own flourishes to the recipe. Fittingly, this is a simple and elegant site, with sections for general information, news, biographies, a discography and links to other sites.

Sonic Youth
http://mmm.mbhs.edu/~wdeng/sy.html

They may be settling into middle age, but they're still the best live rock act on the planet. This site has a discography, lyrics and journal entries from band members.

Kraftwerk
http://www.cs.umu.se/tsdf/KRAFTWERK/

The site honouring these vacky Chermans has all the usual info, sound and video clips, as well as an archive of appearances and interviews.

Everything But the Girl
http://www.ebtg.com/

You take a pass from the collection on the home page and use it to get access to all kinds of information about the duo, who had a hand in the site themselves. It's very graphics-intensive, but the information is all there, and if you have time on your hands it's more than worth exploring.

Miles Davis
http://www.wam.umd.edu/~losinp/music/md-list.html

An 'evolving hypertext discography' of Miles Davis. Entries are arranged chronologically by recording date or dates. Each links to more information about that record. Might not sound like much, but Miles was *busy*.

RESOURCE FILES

Björk's Web Sense
http://www.bjork.co.uk/bjork/

Subtitled 'the Website of the six senses' because of its cute little map of the senses. Click on Sight, Hearing, Smell, Taste, Touch, and Intuition and you will be transported to a site somehow related to that theme. There are also discographies, photos, videos and sounds, and something called The Quote, which has its own file: 'If I want to think about having sex with 87 peacocks I can and it's not a crime, but in reality they might not be up for it, you know!' (Björk in *The Guardian*, 2 June 1995). Oh, and you can mail her at *websense@bjork.co.uk*

KLF
http://www.york.ac.uk/~ph100/HTML.Mike/KLF.html

A couple of years ago, on a remote island off the coast of Scotland, KLF burned £1 million of the royalties from their records. No-one is quite sure why, least of all the band themselves.

Elvis Costello
http://east.isx.com/~schnitzi/elvis.html

Ignore the crappy sound file which welcomes you. Unlike many fan sites, this one is crammed with information, often of the kind that is unavailable elsewhere: previews of forthcoming albums, up-to-the-minute news. Plus loads of interviews, sound files, pictures and the guitar chords for just about every song the prolific artist has ever written. One of the best.

Esquivel
http://www.users.interport.net/~joholmes/esquivel/esquivel.html

The creator of Space Age Bachelor Pad Music, a groovy sound in which everything is just slightly wrong. 'Who'd have thought that out of a genre as debased as "easy listening" would come something so mind-curdlingly bizarre and beautiful?' asked *Simpsons* creator Matt Groening.

Ten Miscellaneous Cool Sites

The Similarities Engine
http://www.ari.net/se/

You type in the name of a band you're fond of (I went for Portishead) and this Swedish site shoots back a bunch of other acts it thinks you might like, which it recommends with different levels of confidence.

The Canonical List of Weird Band Names
http://204.254.248.7/~chelle/bandname.html

Here are some of those listed under the letter P: 'Paisley Brain Cells, Pansy Division, Part Time Christians, Peace Love and Pitbulls, Pee, Phallus Dei, Phenobarbidols, Pieces of Lisa, Pimps of Venus, Poultry in Motion, Pounded Clown.' Of course, being American, the site missed Australia's best ever band name, belonging to Melbourne act, People With Chairs Up Their Noses.

Kilroy Moot's Devotronic Bandbox
http://www.ict.org/~kanis/band/index.shtml

Having trouble finding a name for your folk quartet or beat combo? Pick a genre and let the computer randomly select a couple of words from its collection of well-worn phrases. I tried alternative, heavy metal and folk, and came up with Talking Golfers, Turgid Scrym and Craggy Horizons.

DiscoWeb
http://www.msci.memphis.edu/~ryburnp/discoweb.html

In cyberspace, no-one can hear your polyester trousers rustling to the beat. I'm of the opinion that disco was bad enough the first time, but ... this is such a good site! It has a virtual mirror ball, a top 101 disco songs list (almost all duds), a history, its own jukebox and the latest on KC and the Sunshine Band. There's also a link to the International Leisure Suit Convention site.

Cyberspace Opera
http://www.en.utexas.edu/~slatin/opera/

This is a worldwide effort to write a cyberspace opera. '*Honoria in Ciberspazio* is a romantic, comic, collaborative opera. We invite everyone who visits these pages to send in rhymed couplets of poetry based on concepts or quotes from the opera's plot which tells of five humans routinely connecting to the Internet from their separate computers, searching for significant romances, but encountering unreal cyborg-generated ''clone'' personae portrayed by dancers. Eventually the humans turn away from their clones and frolic together in a romantic fleshmeet (real life meeting) during which the promise of bonding in cyberspace is revealed to them through the character Honoria's insight.' So far, dozens of people have taken part.

Gregorian Chant Home Page
http://www.music.princeton.edu/chant_html/

Its motto is 'In omnem terram exivit sonus eorum, et in fines orbis terrae verba eorum', whatever that means. 'The main purpose of the Gregorian Chant Home Page is to support advanced research on Gregorian chant.' A history and heaps of links to related sites.

The Rolf Harris Web Page
http://http2.brunel.ac.uk:8080/~me93jrb/RH/

To all those skeptics who have been waiting for a reason to go out and blow thousands of dollars on a computer and a modem, here it is: The Rolf Harris Web Page. The stylophone goes digital, with links to other Rolf material, much of it taken from the **alt.fan.rolf.harris** newsgroup.

Air Guitar
http://www.digitalrag.com/mirror/air/air.html

A site devoted to the fineries of lounge room strumming. The visitor is welcomed by R. Bud Philson, president of the Philson Air Guitar Company. 'By acquiring this Philson Stratoblaster Air Guitar, you've already proven you have what it takes to rock and roll in the big leagues. All you need is a little polish, and you can take your Philson on the road' etc etc.

The Muzak Corporation
http://www.muzak.com/muzak.html

What downloading possibilities!

Rocktropolis
http://rocktropolis.com/

'The city that cannot sleep.' A giant virtual rock and roll theme park, recently rebuilt from the ground up to make it even more impressive. This is a real Keeping up With the Joneses site, packed with the latest tricks and techniques. You can browse news mags, check out recent releases, vote for up and coming bands, throw televisions out of hotel windows, drive your Rolls Royce into the pool, get thrown into jail with other recalcitrant rock stars, confess your sins to the King, sack out at the local motel, go to the movies or visit the worldwide musicians' bulletin board, among many, many other options.

Books and Literature

Some General Resources

Book Lovers: Fine Books and Literature
http://www.xs4all.nl/~pwessel/

The Web has plenty of bibliophiles. This site has links to others dealing with writers and poets, libraries, publishers and booksellers (of both new and second hand/antiquarian books). It suggests general places to start, then leads you off on travels through book history, rare books, global literature and even typography. You can almost smell the ink.

Project Gutenberg
http://www.vuw.ac.nz/non-local/gutenberg/

It has a very simple purpose: it wants to bring as much literature to the World Wide Web as is humanly possible. Project Gutenberg has thousands of public-domain works in their electronic form. It's an unparalleled electronic library, with a monthly update of new titles.

OzLit
http://www.vicnet.net.au/~ozlit/

A seriously large collection of Australian literary resources, compiled by Peter & Mareya Schmidt. It points the way to all the relevant Australian sites for authors of prose and poetry, their works, and various types of literary research. Its news section lets you find out what's on the best-seller lists, and when and where literary festivals and events are being held. It also offers directions to the publishing companies and booksellers online.

Oz Kidz Literature
http://www.gil.com.au/ozkidz/ozlit.html

Queensland-based site which has its own agony aunt/librarian, Ms Lit, and links to sites such as the Children's Book Council of Australia and various authors. It invites submissions and reviews from kids and teachers, and offers an excellent launchpad to other kids' lit sites.

Weblit
http://www.rust.net/~rothfder/nfweblit.html

The short guide to literature on the Web. What's new, authors and poets, downloadable texts, author FAQs and links to other sites.

Writers' Resources on the Web
http://www.interlog.com/~ohi/www/writesource.html

The place to start, and the place to finish unless you have a lot of stamina. There are so many resources here that they are broken down into genres: business, children's writing, horror, journalism (an offshoot of horror), mystery, poetry, romance, screen/stage, science fiction and fantasy, technical and scientific, travel writing, and other areas. You'll find dozens of links on the craft of writing, advice on everything from how to make the most of your historical research to how to overcome writer's block. Oh, and how to sell.

Poet's Corner
http://www.lexmark.com/data/poem/poem.html

'An extensive collection of poems provided for you to peruse and contemplate. You will find many things here, both obscure and familiar, from well and lesser known poets, from medieval ballads in middle English to poems of the early 20th century. This site is named for a corner of Westminster Abbey where a number of famous English poets are buried.' Has more than 500 poems from almost 200 poets.

Banned Books Online
http://www.cs.cmu.edu/Web/People/spok/banned-books.html

This site houses a group of texts that have, at one time or another, been banned in the US or elsewhere, although what's naughty about them is usually anyone's guess. From Joyce's *Ulysses* and Voltaire's *Candide* to John Cleland's *Fanny Hill*.

Hyperizons: The Hypertext Fiction Homepage
http://www.duke.edu/~mshumate/hyperfic.html

The ramifications of hypertext for literature are many and curious. What happens when authors and readers are no longer bound by linear narrative, for example? This site links to a seriously

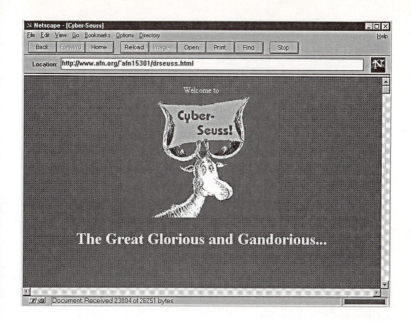

large number of sites dealing with similar concerns, including novels such as *The Hypertext Hotel*. Find also info on the history and structural rules of hypertext fiction.

Delirium
http://pathfinder.com/@@jSiJwXMJswAAQLCz/twep/Features/Delirium/DelTitle.html

The first serialised novel on the Web, written by Douglas Cooper, well known twisted novelist. Updated every two weeks. Tells the story of a kooky architect out to murder his biographer, among many other things. A hypertext work, it has a very loose structure and encourages you to drift around its graphics-heavy entries.

Gleebooks
http://www.merlin.com.au/gleebooks/

You can order online from this Sydney institution, but the best reason to visit the site is to read its zine, *The Gleaner*, which offers reviews of current releases, occasional author interviews and discussions of the latest news in the world of books and writing. It also has links to best-seller sites and allows you to submit your own reviews.

PolyEster Records & Books
http://www.polyester.com.au/PolyEster//

'Polyester is two shops located in inner city Melbourne. One sells music. Hey, if it's available in the world, and especially Australia, we can get it for you. The other sells books. We carry all Melbourne zines, plus most from out of state. Plus, we specialise in weird books. My particular bent is the world conspiracy, and the paranoid notion that there is indeed a group of Mr Bigs out there. UFOs, the Rothschilds, Howard Hughes—well, you explain it.' The site has a fully searchable catalogue of off-Broadway goodies. Definitely worth checking out if you're into cultural esoterica.

Ten Classic Books Available in Their Entirety Online

Alice's Adventures in Wonderland
http://www.cs.cmu.edu/Web/People/rgs/alice-table.html

Lewis Carroll's fantasy, with Tenniel's illustrations.

Crime and Punishment
gopher://ftp.std.com:70/00/obi/book/Fyodor.Dostoevsky/CrimeAndPunishment.txt

The story of Raskolnikov's descent, written by Fyodor Dostoevsky in 1866, may well be the greatest novel ever penned.

The Tell-Tale Heart
http://www.hti.umich.edu/bin/pd-idx?type=header&idno=PoeEAHeart

Edgar Allan Poe's spine tingler.

Don Quixote
gopher://gopher.vt.edu:10010/02/62/1

An essential resource for anyone writing a book about the Net. Miguel de Cervantes's story of fixation, written in 1615.

Lady Chatterley's Lover
http://www.datatext.co.uk/library/dhl/chat/chapters.htm

D.H. Lawrence said about *Lady Chatterley's Lover*: 'I always labour at the same thing, to make the sex relation valid and precious, instead of shameful. And this novel is the furthest I've gone. To me it is beautiful and tender and frail as the naked self is.' To the rest of us, it's just literary smut. But we can respect that.

War and Peace
gopher://gopher.vt.edu:10010/02/151/2

You want epics? Here's Leo Tolstoy's most famous one.

The War of the Worlds
http://www.fourmilab.ch/etexts/www/warworlds/warw.html

They're coming, they're coming. An H.G. Wells classic.

The Wind in the Willows
http://etext.lib.virginia.edu/cgibin/toccer?id=GraWind&tag=public&images=images/modeng&data=/lv1/Archive/eng-parsed&part=0

Kenneth Grahame's eternally charming tales of the riverbank.

Antigone
http://the-tech.mit.edu/Classics/Sophocles/antigone.sum.html

Sophocles's play about the deeds of Oedipus's daughter.

The Art of War
http://timpwrmac.clh.icnet.uk/Docs/suntzu/szcontents.html

Sun Tzu's classic text on the laws of confrontation and battle.

Books Online: Titles
http://www-cgi.cs.cmu.edu/cgi-bin/book/maketitlepage

There are hundreds of books available online. This is the best index for them, with easy hyperlinks to help you along your way.

Ten Author Sites

Jane Austen Info Page
http://uts.cc.utexas.edu/~churchh/janeinfo.html#janetoc

This huge site has an extraordinary amount of information on Austen and her writings, perhaps because she has been so fashionable of late. You will find her writings, all available online, most with annotations, and even fragments of unfinished works. There are satires of her work, and a section devoted to Austen jokes: the Jane Austen Top 10 song list, the Jane Austen punishments list, and some failed pick-up lines from Jane Austen. Also a biography, quotes from her letters, bibliography and links to online academic work.

Raymond Carver Page
http://world.std.com/~ptc/

I don't know what goes on in your head, but in mine, there is a shrine to Raymond Carver. Among his perfectly polished short stories are gems so flawless that it's hard for me to imagine reading their equal. This site offers a bio, a list of published fiction and poetry, references to books and documentaries about Carver, and photos of his grave and some of the places he wrote about.

Milan Kundera
http://www.du.edu:80/~staylor/kundera.html

Czech please! Here you'll find a biography of Kundera, as well as lists of his poetry, fiction and essays.

Douglas Coupland
http://www.coupland.com/index.html

It was inevitable someone would come up with a really good site about an author. So far, most have been pretty simple. Douglas Coupland's, put together by the author and a couple of film/Web friends, pushes the envelope a long way. It not only has articles and short pieces you won't have seen, it has downloadable film and TV samples, audio clips of the author reading, Coupland's collection of favourite book covers and enough little bits of weirdness to make the trip more than worthwhile.

Dr Seuss
http://www.afn.org/~afn15301/drseuss.html

'The Great, Glorious and Gandorious . . . Dr. Seuss!' CyberSeuss is way too good for kids to have it to themselves. It has many of his stories online, background information on Ted Geisel (the real Dr), some of his early works, and links to all the other places on the Web that traffic in Seuss material, like GrinchNet.

William Gibson Information
http://ee.oulu.fi/~thefinn/gibson/gibson.html

Gibson is often referred to as the father of cyberspace because he was the first to use the term, in his novel *Neuromancer*—which he wrote on a typewriter. This site has rundowns on all his novels, and links to other sites.

The Castle: Joseph K's Franz Kafka Homepage
http://www.cowland.com/josephk/josephk.htm

Ah, Mr Cheery himself. There's quite a lot of material about Franz available on the Web, pretty much all of it funnelled through this destination. There's a short bio of the existential groover, then links to homepages, larger bios and bibliographies. Many of his works and letters are available online (read *The Trial* in Russian), and there are links to sites about movies adapted from the novels. There's even some humour.

Cormac McCarthy
http://pages.prodigy.com/cormac/index.htm

A suitably bare-bones Web tribute to the least public author this side of J.D. Salinger. McCarthy has given one interview in 30 years of writing, and that one reluctantly, as a favour to a new publisher. The site is the official home of the Cormac McCarthy Society, which I imagine is a bunch of people who sit around saying: 'Heard any more about what McCarthy's up to?' 'Nope, you?' 'Uh-uh.' There is a sketchy biography, a list of his books and some slightly uncertain info on upcoming projects.

Herman Melville
http://www.melville.org/

Thar she blows! The usual background info, book lists, and connections to other Melvillean sites. Plus links to whales, sailing and other literature.

Ernest Hemingway
http://www.ee.mcgill.ca/~nverever/hem/cover.html

The Papa Page rivals Jane Austen's for size and input. It 'is not an extensive archive nor a detailed scholastic study of Hemingway. It simply contains an outline of his life experiences, his tastes, and his works.' There's a picture album ('hunter, soldier, writer'), a long and winding biography, a bibliography, a series of quotes, some of his paintings, and a collection of related links. There are photo tours of places Hemingway lived in and travelled to, and essays by others on his work.

Author Author
http://www.li.net/~scharf/author.html

An excellent one-stop source for material on authors, literary Websites and resources, online libraries and more.

Author's Pen
http://www.books.com/scripts/authors.exe

From an online book store called Book Stacks, this service has links to its own pages on more than 200 authors.

Miscellanea—The Other Bookshelf

The Elements of Style
http://www.columbia.edu/acis/bartleby/strunk

The gospel according to William Strunk and E.B. White. This little book has probably saved more writers than any other.

Salon
http://www.salon1999.com/

A smart, hip, funny, interactive journal of 'books, arts and ideas'.

The Collected Works of Shakespeare
http://www.gh.cs.usyd.edu.au/~matty/Shakespeare/

Sydney University's Matty Farrow has put together this site, which includes all the plays and the poetry of the Bard. 'Please note,' he asks, 'that I am in no way an expert on Shakespeare or his works. I am unable to answer the many (often thinly disguised) requests for help with homework, school essays or reports.' If you do need help, he has a list of other sites about Will.

City of Bits
http://www-mitpress.mit.edu:80/City_of_Bits/

William Mitchell, an Australian professor at the Massachusetts Institute of Technology, has made *City of Bits*, his book on the implications of the Internet for architecture and the citizens of our emerging 'virtual cities', available online. Every word is here, but more than that, many of them are hypertext links to further discussion or source material. Takes the concept of electronic text a little further than most.

The Beat Generation
http://www.charm.net:80/~brooklyn/Topics/BeatGen.html

'The Beat writers were a small group of close friends first, and a movement later. The Beat Generation in literature comprised a relatively small number of writers, of which Jack Kerouac, Allen Ginsberg and William S. Burroughs are the best known today.' A large and jazzy site with pages devoted to all those who sailed in the good ship Beat.

The Dickens Project
http://hum.ucsc.edu/dickens/index.html

More than a dozen universities in the USA and Israel have banded together to create this academic resource for teachers and students of 'the great Victorian novelist'. 'This page explains the project, but doesn't offer much information on Dickens himself; because it is geared toward graduate students and researchers, the Project's Website presupposes a knowledge of Dickens' work.' There are, mercifully, links for Dickensian lay people.

Nancy Drew: Girl Sleuth, Girl Wonder
http://sunsite.unc.edu/cheryb/nancy.drew/ktitle.html

A site that is equal parts tribute and critique. Appears at first to be a celebration of Nancy Drew's general wonderfulness, but as you drive further and further in, it begins to question the Drew mythology, and her role in supporting the male-dominated status quo.

The Book of Bitterness
http://www.webfeats.com/sealander/Bitter_Book.html

An anthology of the best writings in alt.bitterness, that place where people go to rid themselves of bile. If you've got even a hint of *schadenfreude* in you, this is the place to hang out. After a while, they just seem to get funnier and funnier. Other people's misery—is there anything like it to cheer you up?

The Jean Paul Sartre Cookbook
http://www.cs.berkeley.edu/~hodes/sartre-cookbook.html

By Alastair Sutherland: 'October 3: Spoke with Camus today about my cookbook. Though he has never actually eaten, he gave me much encouragement. I rushed home immediately to begin work. How excited I am! I have begun my formula for a Denver omelette. October 4: Still working on the omelette. There have been stumbling blocks. I keep creating omelettes one after another, like soldiers marching into the sea, but each one seems empty, hollow, like stone. I want to create an omelette that expresses the meaninglessness of existence, and instead they taste like cheese. I look at them on the plate, but they do not look back. Tried eating them with the lights off. It did not help. Malraux suggested paprika.'

Cartoons and Comics

Toon Resources

The Ultimate TV List Cartoon *Anime Manga*
http://www.tvnet.com/UTVL/car_list.html

Best place to start. Lists dozens and dozens of programs. Under each program are the hypertext links to the site, or sites, about them.

Cartoon World
http://www.cet.com/~rascal

This place has video clips, pictures and sound files of a bunch of cartoons and characters, from *Daffy Duck* to *Speed Buggy* to *Underdog*. Check out the archive of theme songs or the classic quotes. There are colouring book pages you can print out for kids, and plenty of links to other sites.

Animation Nerd's Paradise
http://www.cowherd.net/catseye/anp/

Home page for Michelle Klein-Häss, a staff writer for *Anvil Anthology Magazine*, an industry journal. Has animation news and feature stories, and an ongoing animation issues poll. There are also reviews of animated movies and TV shows, an art gallery, and a tour of animation-related Websites. Oh, and it also has the meaning of life.

fps: The Magazine of Animation on Film and Video
http://www.cam.org/~pawn/fps.html

Only parts of this magazine are made available on the Web, but beyond the handful of animation articles, there is a hip list of fan favourites and a truly excellent list of animation resources on the Net.

The Non-Stick Looney Page
http://www.tncnet.com:80/~jmccarthy/

For lovers of Looney Tunes. This site takes you inside Termite Terrace, the affectionate name the

Warner Bros animators had for their workplace. There are also graphics, sounds, links to other sites, a character list, an FAQ, a list of Academy Awards, and bios of the greats: Tex Avery, Mel Blanc, Bob Clampett, Friz Freleng, Chuck Jones, Robert McKimson, Carl Stalling, Frank Tashlin and others.

Spumco
http://www.spumco.com

Net home of the company that brought us the wonderful *Ren and Stimpy, Jimmy the Idiot Boy* and *George Liquor, American.* 'You've probably heard about all of those Websites with snapshots of naked girls from porno movies, and juicy stories about sex, drugs, beer and heavy metal rock music. You know what I'm talking about. Your hotlist is probably chock full of them! Well, I hate to disappoint you, but the Spumco Homepage isn't anything like that. But, if you like cartoons, you've struck pay-dirt! This site is stuffed to the gills with raw, uncensored, glorious cartoon excitement!' John Kricfalusi's characters populate the site, which offers background info on their creation, essays and interviews to do with the history and practice of cartooning, and a store where you can buy cels and other Spumco products.

The Cartoon Factory
http://www.cartoon-factory.com/index.html

The best online cel gallery, with many of your favourites: Disney, Warner Bros, Hanna-Barbera, Chuck Jones, *The Simpsons, Ren and Stimpy, Peanuts* and other shows. It not only sells cels, but offers info on how to care for them.

Shows

The Simpsons Archive
http://www.snpp.com/index.html

For me at least, this site is a Holy Grail, one of the best things that have happened to the Web. It has: Did You Miss? Lists of little asides and flourishes; interviews with cast, staff and others associated with the show; a trivia quiz; a list of the prank calls made by Bart; a drinking game; a list of things Homer has said 'Mmmmm' about; trading card information; info on the colours used to draw the characters; info on how to get the Simpsons Chess Set; lyrics from 'The Softball Song'; an essay on Homer and Archie Bunker; a list of Homer's ten favourite pastimes; an overview

RESOURCE FILES

of 'The Stellar Acting Career of Troy McClure'; images and sounds, and much more. What are you waiting for?

Duckman
http://bluejay.creighton.edu/~jduche/duckman.html

'What the hell you starin' at?' I'm also a sucker for the permanently persnicketty Duckman. This site has an info file, cast biographies and episode synopses. It also links to all the other important Duckman sites, including the official one (http://www.duckman.com/), which, for once, doesn't taste like a bowl of three-week-old cereal.

Felix the Cat
http://www.felixthecat.com/index.html

I always wanted one of those bags of tricks, but I could never find out where you buy them. This excellent site has everything you could want to know about the kitty, with a history, a guide to Felix's TV adventures, a trivia section and much more. This site pays tribute to Felix through the ages. Now if only its online store (the Cat-o-Log) sold the bags…

The Flintstones
http://www.chickasaw.com/~cchamber/flint.html

Fan Cassie Chamberlain searched the Web for a Flintstones site, but couldn't find one. So she built it, from bedrock up, herself. And did a great job. Find news, series info, sounds, a for-sale section, books, TV scheduling times, links, pictures, trivia, a mailing list service, and guides to favourite episodes. Did you know that since 1966, there have been nineteen movies and spinoff series? They're all listed here, *from The Man Called Flintstone* (a 1966 movie) through *Fred and Barney Meet the Thing* (a 1979 special) to *The Flintstones Family Christmas* (a 1993 movie).

Frostbite Falls
http://mindlink.net/charles_ulrich/frostbite.html

'Hey, Rocky! Watch me pull a rabbit out of my hat!' This is the Net home of *Rocky and Bullwinkle*, an unofficial Website dedicated to the cartoons produced by Jay Ward. It includes think pieces, news of recent events (could there be a revival?), answers to frequently asked questions about the show, answers to seldom-asked questions, and lists of episodes and personnel.

The Scooby Doo Home Page
http://hubcap.clemson.edu/~jsikes/scooby.html

Offers sound grabs, pictures, Scooby snack recipes and a load of kooky theories and questions about the cartoon dog and his friends.

The Wile E. Coyote Page
http://www.eskimo.com/~wecoyote/wile_e

Can be hard to get to, but it's worth finding this tribute to the aspiring Everyman figure of cartoons, Wile E. Coyote. I hate to make generalisations, but there are two types of people in this world: those who barracked for the road runner and those whose hearts were with the coyote. If you're in the first category, you should know that the rest of us hate you. This tribute site features a gallery of images and sounds taken from Looney Tunes cartoons. Director Chuck Jones provides a list of the sacred Ten Rules of Road Runner. There is also a filmography and a handful of sound files (there wasn't a lot of dialogue to choose from).

ReBoot Home Page
http://uts.cc.utexas.edu/~ifex534/main.html

ReBoot is the first TV series ever produced entirely with computer graphics. The slick, stylish, Canadian-produced animated kids' show is shown around the world and dubbed into several languages. The action takes place inside a computer, as sprites Bob, Dot and Enzo battle villains Megabyte and Hexadecimal. In the middle of this action, the User will input a game, and the show's characters will 'reboot' into characters in the game. This cool prog site has all the usual FAQs and guides, with links to other *ReBoot* sources and a Did You Miss? section covering the multitude of in-jokes.

Plymptoons
http://found.cs.nyu.edu/plympton/index.html

Bill Plympton's short, strange and often attractively violent animations are hits wherever short-film lovers congregate. This site offers all the latest info on Bill's animation, live-action films, and upcoming projects. There's a biography of Bill, tips on how to survive in the dog-eat-dog-eat-Sherman tank world of animation, and a shop where you can buy your very own *Plymptoons* video.

A History of Walking
http://hepworth.cfa.unsw.edu.au/gallery/Hist.walk/walk.html

QuickTime animated movies and 'picture stories of walking from alien cultures', the work of artist/animator John E. Hughes.

Manga/Anime

Anime and *Manga* Resource List
http://www.csclub.uwaterloo.ca/u/mlvanbie/anime-list/

Not a lot in the way of graphic accompaniment, but this site is a warehouse of links. From this comprehensive library, you can find subject-classified links to all kinds of *manga* sites. Movies, TV series, clubs, image galleries, fan art galleries, *anime*-related home pages, fan fiction, newsgroups, commercial sites, convention listings and more.

The Akira Homepage
http://www.informatik.tu-muenchen.de/cgi-bin/nph-gateway/hphalle8/~rehrl/Akira.html

The most popular and best-known example of *manga* is *Akira*, by Katsuhiro Otomo, the story of a boy and his friends in post-apocalyptic Tokyo. Released in stages as a comic, it was also a highly successful animated movie. The site has details and pics from the 2000-page printed work, and dozens of screen grabs from the movie, background info on the author, an *Akira* club artbook, an FAQ, a CD guide and some recommendations for *Akira* addicts.

Anime Graphics Centre
http://www.mcp.com/people/nemesis/

A gallery of images for *anime* addicts, with hundreds of pics taken from more than twenty films, with a few video clips and some site links tacked on.

Comics Resources

Comics 'n' Stuff
http://www.phlab.missouri.edu/~c617145/comix.html

Though it's updated too infrequently, this is widely viewed as the most comprehensive list of comics on the Web. If you're serious about checking stuff out, bring a packed lunch—you're in for a stay. This enormous repository also has a news section, chat rooms, and an FAQ file.

WebComics
http://www.webcomics.com

An index of all the free daily strips on the Web.

Alternative Comics: A WWW Guide
http://copper.ucs.indiana.edu/~mfragass/altcom.html

A 'one-stop hotlist for alternative/underground/non-mainstream comics', this amazing site is the best overall guide to cool, left-of-centre comics on the Web. It has sections for books and longer works, weekly and daily strips, and publishing companies. You can also find information on creating comics, various reviews and essays, interviews, and Web addresses of magazines, journals, clubs and societies.

Comic Book Depot
http://www.insv.com/comxdepo/

What's new in comics, as well as other news, a search facility for various publications and a set of links both to comics and publishers. Find out what the big companies are planning to release this year.

Comics World
http://www.farrsite.com/cw/index.html

'Visit ComicsWorld every week for the latest in news and information from the worlds of comics, gaming, films, and television.' News, reviews, trivia, and interviews.

Comic Sites
http://www.smartlink.net/~olcapss/links.html

Simple, clear links list to dozens on interesting sites.

The Comics Page
http://www.oznet.com/comicspage/contents.htm

A monthly Web zine featuring news, articles and reviews as well as its own ongoing superhero comic ('Captain Purple: A Hero in His Own Mind!'). There's a merchandise section, a calendar of events, classified ads, dealer listings and a few links to other comics sites.

The Comic Book Legal Defense Fund
http://www.insv.com/cbldf/

A non-profit, charitable organisation incorporated in 1990 to help comic book professionals keep the US censors at bay. 'As a new wave of conservatism floods the publishing industry, the CBLDF continues to raise the money and awareness needed to fight the censors every step of the way.' Interesting both because it deals with the comics we are able to buy and because it details the history of comic censorship.

The Hype! Comic Café
http://www.hype.com/comics/cafe/comicafe.htm

Updated once a week, this is a hangout for comic-related gossip and news. There's a weekly release list and discussions of various character actions and events.

The Comics Journal
http://www.halcyon.com/fgraphic/home.html

'The Comics Journal is the comic book industry's leading magazine of news and criticism. Each month, the Journal brings to its audience lengthy, in-depth interviews that probe the inner workings of the spotlighted creators' frame, body of work, and craft. The Journal also features exacting and comprehensive reviews of many past and current comics works; it recently expanded its review section to enable it to more fully cover the wide diversity of the comic book field. As if all this weren't enough, The Comics Journal is also the only source of hard-hitting, investigative journalism that covers (and often uncovers) business and trade news related directly or indirectly to the comics industry.' No, really, for once the spruiking is pretty accurate.

The Superhighway of Superheroes
http://www.io.org/~ericben/super/

A self-proclaimed marketplace and forum for comics and collectable card games (*Magic: The Gathering* and the like). Comics and games for sale and auction, as well as a Wanted to Buy section.

Comix World
http://www.comix-world.com/

'Comix World exists to provide a home base to enthusiasts, dealers, and those who are just interested in comix. Our objective is to bring together a complete set of resources for existing collectors, and to introduce the enjoyment of comix to a whole new universe.' It has a dictionary of comics, links to information about upcoming shows and conventions, and comics Website addresses.

New Comic Book Releases
http://www.mnsinc.com/hyworth/comics/new.html

The title says it all. Weekly updates.

Comics

The Coconino County Home Page
http://www.krazy.com/

My favourite comic strip of all time is George Herriman's *Krazy Kat*. For the first three decades of this century, the love-drunk kitty endured the brick throwing of Ignatz, believing them to be messages of love. This charming, innovative, philosophical strip is celebrated at this site. There is a gallery of drawings, along with plenty of background information for those who have never made the acquaintance.

Disney Comics
http://www.update.uu.se/~starback/disney-comics/

A worldwide survey of Disney-comic availability, creator and character databases, links to other sources, info on books, fanzines and clubs and directions to all sorts of related material. If you need the Duck Universe explained to you, if you want to find out what they call Donald Duck in Finland (Aku Ankka) or China (Tang Lao Ya), this is the place for you.

Tank Girl
http://www.cs.ucl.ac.uk/staff/b.rosenberg

The movie bit the big saveloy (though Naomi Watts was kind of cute), but the comic from which it was so rudely and crudely extracted remains a testament to how good comics can get (right up there with Evan Dorkin's *Milk And Cheese*). This site tells the story from Tank Girl's original appearances in *Deadline* magazine to her move onto the world stage as the role model *du jour* for teenage girls for about six minutes somewhere back in 1995.

Calvin and Hobbes Comic Gallery
http://infolabwww.kub.nl:2080/calvin_hobbes/

The retirement of this strip by author Bill Watterson was a sad event for fans. There are a handful of cyber-tributes that will keep the flame burning as the strip goes into endless repeats and book sales. This site includes a book list, info on the author and strip, directions to other sites and newsgroups, a doorbell to press, various Calvin and Hobbes items and a character popularity poll.

The Doonesbury Electronic Town Hall
http://www.doonesbury.com/

Much more than just a strip archive. And in some ways, much less. 'So what's doing here? Think Participatory Democracy. Think Cyber Citizenship. Think Conventional Wisdom. Finished? Good, because we're none of those things.' This site has daily news from the political front (yes, real news), five chat spaces to discuss issues, a Today in Doonesbury Archive that goes back twenty years, in four-year jumps. And of course, it has places where you can buy things. Proceeds go to listed charities.

The Dreaming: The Neil Gaiman Page
http://www.holycow.com/dreaming/

'Neil is a (fabulous, magical, wonderful) writer,' this site insists. Picking up from where Alan Moore left off at the start of the decade, Gaiman has taken the comic book to new heights—or depths, if you prefer. There is real writing, real thought and nuance in his works, which include *The Sandman, Death: The High Cost of Living,* and the wonderful, unnerving *Mr Punch*. This site keeps track of Gaiman's public appearances and offers news, reviews and interviews.

The Amazing Spiderman
http://minuteman.com/spiderman/

Spidey has his own page, and a fairly sizeable one it is too, with regular updates of what is going on in the Marvel comic, an archive of past stories, an FAQ, and listings of major events, strange stories, villains and vigilantes, Spidey's equipment and his allies. There are images, sounds, fan fiction, a library of reviews, quizzes and competitions, discussion groups, feedback forums and the chance to vote for your favourite stories.

Dilbert Zone
http://www.unitedmedia.com/comics/dilbert/

Netheads love Dilbert. This comic strip site is linked by sites all around the Web, perhaps because the artist, Scott Adams, is a Net lover himself. On it you'll find a store, an archive of the strips, an interview with the author, some 'shameless self-promotion', a newsletter, character descriptions and a photo tour of the creation of one of the strips.

Red Meat
http://www.desert.net/tw/current/meat.htm

A black-and-white strip from a guy called Max Cannon, whose shtick is the use of the same picture in every frame of each strip. Only the dialogue changes. What he arrives at is a humour that is oddly, unsettlingly funny. There's also an unofficial Website, at **http://www.emerald.net/soren/redmeat/**

Migraine Boy
http://www.visualradio.com/migraineboy/

Migraine Boy, a guy who knows his way around a headache, is one of the darlings of the US alternative scene. The strip/cartoon doesn't always make perfect sense, in that self-consciously wacky, '90s obscurantist way, but who cares? Greg Fiering's creation here undergoes a few simple animations, with Real Audio.

The Narrative Corpse
http://www.voyagerco.com/books/corpse/corpse.html

In January 1996, the Voyager Company, arguably America's smartest multimedia publishers, launched *The Narrative Corpse*, an online experiment in serial comic publishing. On each day, for 69 days, a different artist contributed three panels to an unfolding story.

Superguy
http://www.halcyon.com/superguy/index.html

So what do you make of a comic book that is bigger than most novels, incredibly complex, and boasts fewer pictures than most phone books? *Superguy*, from the foetid minds of a collective of writers, gives us a universe, sorry, altiverse, populated by dozens of superheroes and supervillains, all with dumb names.

Zines

NB: The World Wide Web is home to hundreds of magazines, many of which are no more than electronic versions of the mags you'll see on newsagency shelves. The best guide to the mainstream can be found at The Electronic Newsstand. In this resources file, I have decided to concentrate on zines, which are smaller, usually independently published magazines with more attitude and less to lose. They are usually labours of love, often devoted to interesting minutiae that other media ignore. With a few exceptions, what you will find here is either not available at all off the Web, or is hard to find in print form.

General Resources

The Electronic Newsstand
http://www.enews.com/

The catch-all library for magazines on the Web. Includes links to more than 2000 mag sites, from the professional operations to zines, from *Architronic* to *Zug*.

Factsheet Five Electric
http://www.well.com/conf/f5/f5index2.html

Factsheet Five is the zine world's hub. A zine which reviews other zines, it provides a guide to 'parallel culture', defined as 'weird stuff that you may stumble across, but can't find through the usual channels'. In this case it's DIY media. The electronic site is not as dynamic as the paper one, but has a page dedicated to e-zines, as well as zine-making tips.

John Labovitz's List of All Known E-zines
http://www.meer.net/~johnl/e-zine-list/

Here's the mother lode. Just about every zine you'll find on the Web is linked alphabetically here. There are short explanations of the tone, content and frequency of each, with contact e-mail addresses. The best index.

RESOURCE FILES

My Personal Top Ten, in No Order

Suck
http://www.suck.com

Subtitle: 'the last word on the Net'. A smart, cynical Webzine which sends up online culture, among other things. Operated by two guys out of a back room at *Wired*. Updated every weekday, it's probably a little acerbic for mainstream tastes, but I like a little bile with my cornflakes. Though its contents list is long and lateral (it's more an essay), it's worth digging about for the goodies. Oh, and it also has a groovy disappearing masthead.

Virtual City Magazine
http://www.virtcitnow.com/

A cool cyberculture hangout with online articles, annotated links to good sites (including the 66 Cyber Stars of the Year) and cute, cute cartoon sci-fi graphics. It even has a sense of humour.

Word
http://www.word.com/index.html

'Issues. Culture. Pffft!' Word is the closest thing the Web has to a coffee-table magazine. It's as much an experiment in art as in publishing. Ambiguous, amorphous section headings lead you off to feature articles that are a marriage of design and content. Fact and fiction arrive with a New York state of mind. Web sites don't get more elegant or fashionable than this.

Disgruntled
http://www.disgruntled.com/

Subtitle: 'The Business Magazine for People Who Work for a Living'. Combines news, feature articles, satire and commentary from the perspective of those for whom 'work is a four letter word'. If you are disgruntled about your job, this mag wants to hear from you. One of the handiest things about the site is that every page has a 'Boss' button at the bottom of it. Should you be wasting time reading when the boss approaches, hit the button and it brings up an impressive looking table of figures headed 'Our Mission Is to Increase Shareholder Value'.

SonicNet
http://www.sonicnet.com/

Alternative-music zine with gorgeous design, from New York. Has its own chat rooms, a good links section, reviews, rants and info on upcoming shows (as well as reader verdicts) in the NY region. Features have included things like the ongoing Losers' Guide to New York and Losers' Guide to Boston, as well as The Indie Rock Guide to Dating. Chat rooms regularly host the famous and funky.

bOING bOING
http://www.well.com/user/mark/

A cool journal which explores the nexus of technology and pop culture. Ceased to be a paper zine in early 1996 so that housekeepers Carla Sinclair and Mark Frauenfelder could concentrate on bigger projects, but there are archives here and *bOING bOING* will be back in some form.

Click
http://www.click.com.au

Web-only Australian mag for lovers and designers of multimedia. All the tools and lots of good thought, not just about the form, but also, importantly, about the meaning.

Interesting Ideas
http://www.mcs.com/~billsw/home.html

Started as a photocopied newsletter, this mag is now a fab Web presence, 'a chilling example of the Internet's transparency to marginal ideas'. It's really one guy's take on the world, from roadside art to his hatred of sport to his love of *Sesame Street*'s Bert.' What the site offers most of is perspective. It's not trying to please everybody, so it works.

Spiv
http://www.spiv.com

Actually a collection of Web zines, all at one site. Or maybe it's just one big zine with different departments. Who cares? Has a bunch of sections dealing with music, fashion, attitude and much more. Nrrd is an excellent cyberculture site, with some of the best names in the business (RU Sirius, Douglas Rushkoff, Mark Frauenfelder, Jude St Milhon and more) on its credits page. A bookmark must.

Eight Track Heaven
http://www.bway.net/~abbot/8track/

A zine dedicated to that obsolescent wonder and '70s icon, the Eight-Track Cartridge. Even better, it has a What's New section, a delicious non sequitur. Find out all about the history of this invention, how it works, where to get one, what was and is available, and where to find its hardcore community of fans. Subscribe to the 8-Track Mind newsletter. Learn The 8 Noble Truths of the 8-Track Mind, including 'State of the art is in the eye of the beholder.'

Some Vocal Locals

Evolution
http://www.highway1.com.au/arts/evolution/

The online version of *REVelation*, an eclectic culture mag. Perth, a hotbed of weirdness and alternative viewpoints, is the home of this venture, which covers issues such as indigenous rights, smart drugs, cyberspace and the views of contemporary luminaries, marginalised groups, cultural issues and just about anybody with a good story. 'Our motto has always been Drink Local, Act Global.' As funny as it is serious. Or should that be the other way around?

Planet Byron Webzine
http://www.om.com.au/planet_byron/

'Planet Byron will highlight the diversity and creativity found in the Byron (Bay, northern NSW) area, home of many leading-edge writers, artists, entrepreneurs, and innovators in many fields. Planet Byron will also highlight a state of mind, a way of being, a level of consciousness that encompasses all races, religions, colours, creeds and politics.' Believe it or not after that rave, the zine is really good. It does tend to waffle a bit, but there's plenty to keep you interested. Jump straight to the fast lane to find the goodies.

the i magazine
http://www.thei.aust.com

One of the most heavy of the local pop culture sites, *the* i is more than worth bookmaking for its range of serious, well-written pieces on various sound and screen luminaries. Its journos, who work for various off-line publications, have the pull to get access to people other Net ventures can't.

Electric Dreams
http://www.phys.unsw.edu.au/~mettw/edreams/

A journal dedicated to collecting and sharing nocturnal creativity. It was started as an e-mail newsletter in 1994, by people unhappy with the amount of crap floating about in the **alt.dreams** newsgroup. The large text-only letter has transcripts of loads of dreams, with commentaries. It can be very serious and analytical, and it can also be funny.

Spunk
http://www.usyd.edu.au/~mwoodman/spunk.html

A resolutely low-fi music mag with a slick, hi-fi Web presence. Dedicated to the more attractive end of the indie band spectrum. Interviews from current and back issues, 'a friendly chat page where like-minded music lovers can mingle, a vast range of links to other recommended zine sites on the Net and the opportunity to become a cherished member of the Spunk Rat frat'.

Underworld
http://www.aussiemusic.com.au/underworld/

'G'day, glad you could make it. Grab yourself a Chiko Roll off the barbie. You're at an Australian site now, so read a bit slower and fer God's sake, get another lager. UnderWorld is an alternative (whatever that means) music and culture zine. The print version comes out quarterly through Melbourne's Shock Records and includes a CD compilation (*Medium Rare*) of rare/unreleased/new indie-style music.' There are short articles on music trends, interviews with bands, reviews and reviews of reviews, and more.

Burst
http://www.real.net.au/

Web mag dealing with many areas of the arts, pop culture and lifestyle. Film, music, theatre, games, cafes and galleries. Interviews and reviews aplenty. As with most such sites, the concept is great but the writing uneven. Stick around while they find their feet.

A Bunch of the Rest

CakeTimes
http://www.caketimes.com//

A left-field pop culture mag that never fails to surprise. It's arty, curious and deals with a range of stuff: literary, artistic, cultural, stupid ... I've been back regularly, and I'm still not sure exactly what it's trying to do, but I enjoy the attempt.

Intrrr Nrrrd
http://nervecore.com/e-zine/

Underground rock as the new religion. This extensive zine contains rants, chat rooms, audio files and recommendations, plus tools for site builders.

Feed
http://www.feedmag.com/

Feed believes in the promises of the new media, but isn't getting carried away. It's one of the better places to visit when you're feeling overhyped and oversold. Pop culture, politics, navel and crystal ball gazing. All from a smart and critical perspective.

Tripod
http://www.tripod.com/

Subtitle: 'Tools for Life'. This is an excellent idea, one of those that seem bone-jarringly obvious when you see them. A bunch of soon-to-be university graduates realised they had no real idea what awaited them out in the world or how to cope with it, so they set up a zine devoted to helping people like themselves. It comes in three sections: work & money, politics & community, living & travel, and has everything from an online résumé doctor to a home page builder.

Urban Desires
http://desires.com/

Calls itself 'an interactive magazine of metropolitan passions'. There are departments for the written word, art, tech-toys, sex, music, performance, food, style and travel. You can search its library or hang out in one of the chat rooms.

The Netly News
http://pathfinder.com/@@gVeMXwcAPwRourrf/Netly/

'There are 35 million stories in cyberspace,' the site proclaims. 'We give you a new one every day.' If a site has its own theme song, it's OK by me. This groovy mag, exquisitely designed and effortlessly navigable, is a kind of Web watcher. 'Every day, we'll take you to a new place or introduce you to people we think are worth hearing about. And we'll do it quickly. We want to be the first thing you browse when you pop online. Along the way, we plan to take risks, try new stuff and use the medium's best tools. Some of what we do will work. Some of it probably won't. We get paid either way. For now.'

Foxy
http://www.tumyeto.com/tydo/foxy/foxy.html

What would we have done without postmodernism? This site is a simultaneous send-up and celebration of the culture of girls' teen mags. Boy kisses! Yuk!

Crash Site
http://www.crashsite.com

'Where chaos, horsepower and madness unite.' They left out sheer effort, something that's gone into this site in abundance. Video clips, articles on left-of-centre bands, fiction, political activism, digital art exhibitions, sports excursions and oddities ('Disease Central—A Young Person's Guide to Rare, Incurable, and Disfiguring Diseases', 'War as Entertainment: What's your favourite war? Come see if it made our top ten!').

Tum Yeto Digiverse
http://www.tumyeto.com/

I think these over-sugared, Nintendo-generation, fluoro geeks tell it best themselves: 'Tum Yeto Digiverse is the archiving culmination of particular subcultures available on the Internet. . . . It is a focusing point for semi-related physical activities such as skateboarding (Skateboard.com), surfing (Surfers.com) and snowboarding (Snowboard.com). Plus the extracurricular interests such as music (Earfood.com) and literature (InkLinks). Each of these departments is an editorial base for archiving and featuring interviews, articles, reports, currents, tips, directories and real time IRC personality features all reflecting the individual department.'

Blair
http://www.blairmag.com/

Trashy, kitschy, campy pop culture never tasted so good. 'Blair is a Web-only superzine for kooks and retards such as yrself! come on in! viva la yoplait!'

The Nostalgic Wave
http://www.hype.com/public.htm

Canadian web publishers Hype! have a site chock full of zines, including movie, comic, video game and music rags. The Nostalgic Wave is the best of them. It asks visitors to cast their mind back to the pop culture of their youth, and, thus aided, is slowly putting together a database on everything from TV shows like Space 1999 and video games like Donkey Kong to Rubik's Cube, Mr Potato Head and cultural landmarks like the Hong Kong Phooey Chop.

Epicurious
http://www.epicurious.com/epicurious/home.html

A funky little food mag, courtesy of CondéNet. It takes a humorous approach to serious dining and features, among other items, a hole gauge for circular foodstuffs, a recipe swap, and a virtual book on table manners and kitchen hints.

Rant
http://home.erols.com/rant/rant/

A magazine about everyday frustrations, about letting off steam at the little things that get up your nose. 'We will point to the idiocies and the abuse thrust upon the people of earth and contribute to further the competence of society,' it promises, before launching into a series of unconnected spleen ventings on everything from politicians to people who appear in ads.

Cyber Culture Magazine
http://www.cvp.com/cyber/

'Cyber Culture is about Cyberspace and Netizens all around the world. We seek out strange new pages and digital civilisations . . . to boldly go where no one has gone before! Actually, it's a magazine about—nothing. We have no focus, nor do we want one.' The magazine has irregular articles, settled alongside regulars such as a daily humour column and questions of the week. Not all of it works, but enough does to make stopping by worthwhile.

Retro
http://www.retroactive.com/

A bimonthly magazine of twentieth-century entertainment, lifestyles and design. It promises that anything that was ever cool will end up here. When I dropped in, it had a batch of Real Audio clips of Hawaiian music from the 1930s. Retro 'can help you to enjoy life more in the present by grooving on some of the finest of the past'. It focuses on the first two-thirds of the century, 'with an occasional dip into the newly retro 1970s'.

JetPack
http://www.jetpack.com/index.html

Jetpack is a funky pop culture mag which replaced the hugely popular BuzzNet in early 1996. From ground zero in San Francisco, it covers underground music, sports and hobbies (from cooking to hot-rodding), and movements in the technological and art worlds. It also offers its own fiction.

Nuke
http://www.nuke.com/

'The NUKE InterNETWORK brings you the most up-to-date information on your favourite entertainment activities; namely video games, computer games, movies, television, comics and cards. You'll also find links to the sites you never thought you'd see, downloadable demos from top game developers, and exclusive interviews.' In short, heaven for teenage boys.

Electronic Gourmet Guide
http://www.2way.com/food/egg/index.html

American Webzine devoted to food and cooking. Major articles, news, interviews. recipes, tips, trivia games, competitions, letters to the editor and links. Well put together, if a little upmarket.

Ooze
http://www.io.com/~ooze/

'Journal of Substance, Wit, and Dangerous Masturbatory Habits'. OK, so the taste quotient is pretty low. So their T-shirts feature a design of a baby with a fork in its head. There's nothing wrong with a bit of angry humour here and there. It'll be too irreverent for some, but if you don't mind that, it's more than worth a dip into this bitter font: 'Poems I Wrote in First Grade, Deathstyles of the Rich & Famous, Journal Entries of the Insane, Excerpt from Green Eggs and Hamlet.'

dEPARTURE fROM nORMAL
http://www.xwinds.com/dfn/dfn.html

dfn 'publishes original photos, drawings, paintings, stories, poems, music, animation, and any other form of art submitted that can be digitised; we are particularly interested in work created by artists, authors, and musicians who are non-corporately sponsored. Our mission statement could be this: we do everything because we want to. We accept everything, as long as we like it. We offer everything we accept, and nothing we do not accept.'

Ad Nauseam
http://www.crl.com/~jnelson/nauseam/

'A running commentary on the information society. Rantings and blatherings on the Internet and its tremendous growth.' A much-needed sceptical, skewed look at the info revolution.

Ben Is Dead
http://benisdead.com/

Online version of one of the most famous paper zines, every issue of which deals with a different theme, from boys to childhood memories to comics. Includes updated info, news breaks and calls for contributions.

The Overflow

Institutes

The Museum of Dirt
http://www.planet.com/dirtweb/dirt.html

This place is awe-inspiring. It's a showcase of jars of dirt sent in from sites of significance around the world: the graves of Gertrude Stein, Jim Morrison and Oscar Wilde; the backyard of film director John Waters; Robert Redford's ranch; the Betty Ford Clinic; Bob Hope's home; the Menendez house; the site of Yitzhak Rabin's assassination; the *Simpsons* writers' bungalow; the Alfred P. Murrah federal building in Oklahoma City; and the place on Sunset Boulevard where Hugh Grant picked up Divine Brown. Wonders of the world are covered, too, from the Great Wall of China to Ayers Rock.

The Bureau of Missing Socks
http://www.jagat.com/joel/socks.html

'The first organisation solely devoted to solving the question of what happens to missing single socks. It explores all aspects of the phenomenon, including the occult, conspiracy theories, and extra-terrestrials. We offer support for the matching-sock deprived, and, catalogue, research, index and document all extant material related to socks since the dawn of the shoe.' OK, sounds dumb, but this site is actually really interesting, with an enormous range of sections: Sock News, a Round Table where missing sock theorists can ruminate, Great Sock Mysteries, the Missing Socks Search (a database which offers you the opportunity to search the world for yours), the Missing Socks Singles Club (add yours to the list), sock histories and a worldwide survey.

The International Paperweight Society
http://www.armory.com/~larry/ips.html

'The IPS is dedicated to furthering awareness of the art of the glass paperweight. A library donation program is available. Members may have paperweight related books donated in their name to their local library. Travelling exhibits are sponsored with input from members. Museums are encouraged to put their paperweights on display rather than keeping them in storage.' It really does take all kinds.

Centre for the Easily Amused
http://www.amused.com/

'Our hard-working experts have been exploring the Internet since long before it was trendy in their search for the Ultimate Guide to Wasting Time.' Payload! Cathie Walker and Brian Leslie have compiled a handy guide to at least a thousand sites guaranteed to entertain you for a minimum of five seconds each. An incredible effort. Actually, despite its self-deprecating (or is it insulting?) title, it's a fabulous, fascinating resource. Covers random silliness, sites that do things, music and mags, movies and TV, sports, and has its own Short Attention Span Site of the Day.

Oddities

The Kooks Museum
http://www.teleport.com/~dkossy/

Donny Kossy has spent years researching fringe thought, interviewing people who seriously believe all the kinds of things that the rest of us just laugh at. Jimmy Carter is Bill Clinton's father. The world is flat. Greg Norman is not a choker. The virtual museum has a lobby, gift shop and several galleries, including the Schizophrenic Wing, Conspiracy Corridor, Hall of Hate, Solution to the World's Problem Exhibit, Hall of Quackery, and The Wider Wonderful World of Kooks. Learn about goat gland science, the demons of rock music, salvation by spaceship, and even scientific proof that Satan created dinosaurs just to irk God.

Rude Things in My Fridge
http://www.wbm.ca/users/kgreggai/html/fridge.html

'How can anything that used to taste so good smell so bad?' One man's attempt to come to terms with the Dantesque circles of hell that inhabit his whitegoods. In glorious colour.

The World Wide Web Fights Grudge Match
http://www.cheme.cornell.edu/~slevine

Ever wondered what would happen if the cast of *Neighbours* had to wrestle the cast of *Home And Away* on a giant plastic sheet covered in pig fat? No? Then this site isn't for you. It puts up speculative scenarios—Microsoft vs Disney, Gary Coleman vs Webster, Khan vs Lex Luthor, *Terminator* vs *Predator*—and lets the user vote. Example: 'This week we bring you a battle for

RESOURCE FILES

ocean supremacy: Flipper and Jaws in a battle to the death . . . Both contestants are highly motivated. Jaws is hungry. He hasn't eaten for days, and the chum in the water isn't helping. Flipper has been hypnotised by a leading dolphin hypnotist with a one-word phrase: "kill". The two are simultaneously released in close proximity. Only one will survive.'

Pasta Designed by Architects
http://www.archiweb.com/gallery/pasta/index.html

Why not? What I'd like to see is pasta makers turning their hand to designing skyscrapers.

Hobbies

Sock Puppets
http://Blue-Skies.taligent.com:2000/Sock.html

I don't know why, but I've always had a thing for sock-puppets. John McKee's sock puppet photos are few, but you have to give him credit for imagination: most of them are taken while skydiving. Hard to get an audience for your puppeteering when you're plummeting towards the Earth, but that doesn't stop him trying. Don't forget to check out the sock puppet X-ray—these things have weird skeletons.

Internet Anagram Server
http://lrdc5.lrdc.pitt.edu/awad-cgibin/anagram

Also known as 'I, rearrangement servant' and 'inert Net grave near Mars'. Parliament, it tells us, is an anagram of 'partial men'. Clint Eastwood is an anagram of 'old west action'. Type in a word and let the computer rearrange its letters for you. Fabulous for help if you want to cheat on those newspaper brain teasers.

Drop Squad
http://www.dropsquad.com/

A bunch of American college dudes whose self-appointed mission in life is to drop things from great heights, electronically recording the falls and their consequences. They are nothing if not catholic in their missile choices: from hamburgers to fruit to Christmas trees. With splatter movies and photos.

Computer Karaoke
http://www.teleport.com/~labrat/karaoke.shtml

Save your embarrassing singing for the comfort of your own home or workspace. This site offers an archive of karaoke files in midi format, with lists of hot spots and a master index of songs to help you find the tune you're looking for.

Splat That Rat
http://bakmes.colorado.edu/~bicanic/nph-coolest.cgi?309,15

An excellently stupid idea. A little animation of a rat running for a hole across the other side of the screen. Point and squash.

How to Keep an Idiot Busy for Hours
http://www-csag.cs.uiuc.edu/individual/pakin/idiot/chapter1.html

You kind of know, of course, who the idiot is before you even click on it, but that doesn't stop you...

RESOURCE FILES

Human Frailties

The Big Black Hole of Pain
http://tribble.com/bighole.html

Need to get it all off your chest? The Big Black Hole of Pain is the place to go to leave your troubles. For the rest of us permanently cheery souls, it's a chance to wallow in vicarious misery, from the flip and angry ('Lately, it seems that the assholes of the world are outnumbering the rest of us') to the moving and heartfelt: 'Sigh. Dad, it's been over five and a half years since I've seen you. I'm sorry you and Mom couldn't work it out. I'm sorry that I was never terribly fond of that woman who became your second wife. I'm sorry I never felt much of anything for your fourth child, my first half-sister, who was less than 6 months old when you died. But most of all I'm sorry that we somehow drifted apart over the years . . . I'm sorry that you couldn't struggle free of the death grip that alcohol had on you. When I was a kid, you were a great Dad. Sometimes I wonder what the hell I did wrong, why our relationship got weak over the years . . . I really miss you, Dad. I just hope I can be as good a Dad to my little guy as you were to me.'

The Interactive Patient
http://medicus.marshall.edu/medicus.htm

A program which allows you to simulate a patient encounter. Meant as a teaching tool for physicians, residents and medical students, it offers a case to the user, who has to interact with the virtual patient, requesting more information, performing a physical exam and checking lab data and X-rays.

Rectal Foreign Bodies
http://www.well.com/user/cynsa/newbutt.html

The site has X-rays, real and bogus. Yeah, right, you slipped in the shower.

Dave's Web of Lies
http://www.cs.man.ac.uk/~hancockd/

Is it a clever-dick statement about the nature of cyber-information or just fun and flummery? This site has more than 425 000 lies to peruse and use, on topics from artichokes to zebras. 'Ultra-fast query handling is provided by our leading edge Search-o-Matic (c) software which can scan up to 10 000 lies per second.' Beginning at the beginning, I typed in 'artichokes'. It works! 'Many common skin complaints can be readily cured by the liberal application of a paste of Cheddar cheese, Dolphin dripping and artichokes.'

Laws of Love
http://www.hials.no/~ga/love/laws.html

Gard, a Norwegian, is obviously not having the best time of it lately. His rules *d'amour* suggest a man who would find Leonard Cohen albums upbeat. 'If you hope that you have found love, you'll get very disappointed. If you think that you have found love, you're wrong. If you know that you have found love, you have been misinformed. If you have found love, you won't know about it before it is lost. There's always someone who is happy for his/her entire life, and it isn't you.' And it certainly isn't him either.

Joe's Amazing Relationship Problem Saver
http://studsys.mscs.mu.edu./~carpent1/probsolv/rltprob0.html

A one-on-one cyber-therapy session. It asks you yes/no (maybe/not for long) questions and you just click until the two of you find the heart of your problem. Or should that be the problem of your heart? Joe Carpenter claims no qualifications to give advice, but maybe the button-clicking will cheer you up anyway.

The Foolproof Guide to Making Any Woman Your Platonic Friend
http://www.phantom.com/~joelogon/platonic.html

'You meet a girl who is everything you ever wanted in a life-partner: attractive, funny, smart, great personality, laughs at your jokes, understands who you are as a human being, etc. You talk to her briefly, and find out that she is even more attractive now that you've spoken to her. You ask her out. She says to you: "I just want to be friends." Shudder. The real F word, the one men just don't want to hear. "I like you as a friend"—Hitler invaded Poland for less than that.' Commiserate with Joe as he works through his misery online.

The Dream Archive
http://www.tbyte.com/people/joe/dreams/welcome.htm

'Warning: this gallery contains the unexpurgated dreams of healthy human individuals which, needless to say, means it contains graphic writings and images not suitable for small children, the easily offended, fundamentalists, and the otherwise experientially impaired'—J. Allan Tucker, curator. Cars, guns, nurses, school, beasts, bodies, water, parties, homes and a catch-all category for anything that doesn't fit. If you want to see what other people are up to while they're asleep, this is the place. Do your own analysis for free. At least it's proof that others are capable of conjuring images just as bizarre as you are.

The Farting Page
http://www.nbn.com/youcan/fart/fart.html

Why we do it. Prediction: sooner or later some geek will come up with downloadable smell files. And this will be the first use someone makes for them.

Other

Hutt River Province
http://www.net-quest.OntheNet.com.au/Hutt/

The sovereign state in the west of Australia has ventured into the digital ether. Prince Kevin invites you to obtain membership of HRP. 'After a suitable time, a person holding a Membership Certificate will be able to obtain a Drivers Licence, a Valid Passport and Lifelong Citizenship to the Principality. Enquiries are also welcome for Knighthoods in the Honorable Order of the Unicorn. You May Be Eligible—Enquire Now!'

The Wall o' Shame
http://www.milk.com/wall-o-shame/

An attempt to 'characterise the erosion of our world by displaying true stories and tidbits that are just too nonlinear'. One guy's collection of sad and tragic things, from Internet postings about body odour to bizarre advertisements—'Only the Polytron reduces an entire mouse to a soup-like homogenate in 30 seconds.'

Things to Do When You're Bored
http://www.pixi.com/~owens/bored/bored.html

This site from a Hawaiian teenager comes in three parts: things you can do with absolutely nothing, things you can do with very little and things you can do with another person. A couple of examples:

'Push your eyes for interesting light show. (Amusement Potential: 1–5 minutes) See a variety of blobs, stars and flashes. Try to make out things—is your subconscious trying to send you a message? Can you control what you see by pressing different areas with different forces? Would it be possible to somehow see the same effects on TV?' or 'Watch TV, repeat everything said in Italian accent. (Amusement Potential: 5–10 minutes) Sort of entertaining. Fun to pretend the people on the screen are actually talking that way.'

Roadkill Trophies (TM)
http://www.avana.net/pages/personal/jwhcpg/roadkill.htm

World War I and II fighter planes painted little pictures next to the cockpit, keeping tally of the planes shot down. This site offers 'magnetic sticker novelties' for you to display on your car after you've taken out one of God's creatures on the highway. For a few dollars, you can choose from armadillo, raccoon, possum, frog, squirrel, turtle, snake, bird, rabbit, skunk, purple dinosaur and pink elephant.

The Advertising Graveyard
http://www.inch.com/~jeffz/ad.html

Believe it or not, some ads are just too funny, too rude or too risky to make it to the screen. This site presents commercials that were stopped by frightened clients, focus groups or nervous agencies. The guy who set it up had a few bus posters plugging the 1995 Beatles TV special knocked back and thought, Heck, why throw them away? One look at the one on the home page will tell you why.

The World Birthday Web
http://www.boutell.com/birthday.cgi

Exactly what it sounds like, a place to register your anniversary. See the names of hundreds of strangers sharing your special day. Feel really small and pointless.

The Pratt Knot
http://www.charm.net/~jakec/PrattKnot.html

A 1980s innovation, the knot obviously came into being because Mr Jerry Pratt thought a better mousetrap was too easy a challenge. It hasn't so much gone out of style as taken a long time to catch on. 'It's not often that a new necktie knot comes out. The Pratt knot that's illustrated here was first officially mentioned right at the end of the eighties. It was the first new knot reported to the Neckwear Association of America in fifty years. They are momentous events, these comings of new knots.' With diagrams.

Sumo
http://www.hal.com/~nathan/Sumo/

OK, so the pay-TV networks are going on about their sports channels, but which of them are promising us coverage of sumo, the finest *mano a mano* contest man has yet devised? This site contains all the latest results and links to a tonne (and that is the word) of other sumo pages, including reports from the *Yomiuri Shimbun* newspaper. Go the big fellas!

APPENDICES

A Declaration of the
Independence of Cyberspace

by John Perry Barlow (barlow@eff.org)

February 8, 1996

Davos, Switzerland

Governments of the Industrial World, you weary giants of flesh and steel, I come from Cyberspace, the new home of Mind. On behalf of the future, I ask you of the past to leave us alone. You are not welcome among us. You have no sovereignty where we gather.

We have no elected government, nor are we likely to have one, so I address you with no greater authority than that with which liberty itself always speaks. I declare the global social space we are building to be naturally independent of the tyrannies you seek to impose on us. You have no moral right to rule us nor do you possess any methods of enforcement we have true reason to fear.

Governments derive their just powers from the consent of the governed. You have neither solicited nor received ours. We did not invite you. You do not know us, nor do you know our world. Cyberspace does not lie within your borders. Do not think that you can build it, as though it were a public construction project. You cannot. It is an act of nature and it grows itself through our collective actions.

You have not engaged in our great and gathering conversation, nor did you create the wealth of our marketplaces. You do not know our culture, our ethics, or the unwritten codes that already provide our society more order than could be obtained by any of your impositions.

You claim there are problems among us that you need to solve. You use this claim as an excuse to invade our precincts. Many of these problems don't exist. Where there are real conflicts, where there are wrongs, we will identify them and address them by our means. We are forming our own Social Contract. This governance will arise according to the conditions of our world, not yours. Our world is different.

Cyberspace consists of transactions, relationships, and thought itself, arrayed like a standing wave in the web of our communications. Ours is a world that is both everywhere and nowhere, but it is not where bodies live.

We are creating a world that all may enter without privilege or prejudice accorded by race, economic power, military force, or station of birth. We are creating a world where anyone, anywhere may express his or her beliefs, no matter how singular, without fear of being coerced into silence or conformity. Your legal concepts of property, expression, identity, movement, and context do not apply to us. They are based on matter. There is no matter here. Our identities have no bodies, so, unlike you, we cannot obtain order by physical coercion. We believe that from ethics, enlightened self-interest, and the commonweal, our governance will emerge. Our identities may be distributed across many of your jurisdictions. The only law that all our constituent cultures would generally recognize is the Golden Rule. We hope we will be able to build our particular solutions on that basis. But we cannot accept the solutions you are attempting to impose.

In the United States, you have today created a law, the Telecommunications Reform Act, which repudiates your own Constitution and insults the dreams of Jefferson, Washington, Mill, Madison, DeTocqueville, and Brandeis. These dreams must now be born anew in us.

You are terrified of your own children, since they are natives in a world where you will always be immigrants. Because you fear them, you entrust your bureaucracies with the parental responsibilities you are too cowardly to confront yourselves. In our world, all the sentiments and expressions of humanity, from the debasing to the angelic, are parts of a seamless whole, the global conversation of bits. We cannot separate the air that chokes from the air upon which wings beat.

In China, Germany, France, Russia, Singapore, Italy and the United

APPENDICES

States, you are trying to ward off the virus of liberty by erecting guard posts at the frontiers of Cyberspace. These may keep out the contagion for a small time, but they will not work in a world that will soon be blanketed in bit-bearing media.

Your increasingly obsolete information industries would perpetuate themselves by proposing laws, in America and elsewhere, that claim to own speech itself throughout the world. These laws would declare ideas to be another industrial product, no more noble than pig iron. In our world, whatever the human mind may create can be reproduced and distributed infinitely at no cost. The global conveyance of thought no longer requires your factories to accomplish.

These increasingly hostile and colonial measures place us in the same position as those previous lovers of freedom and self-determination who had to reject the authorities of distant, uninformed powers. We must declare our virtual selves immune to your sovereignty, even as we continue to consent to your rule over our bodies. We will spread ourselves across the Planet so that no one can arrest our thoughts.

We will create a civilization of the Mind in Cyberspace. May it be more humane and fair than the world your governments have made before.

Books That Might Be Helpful

World Wide Web Top 1000, ed. R.F. Holznagel (New Riders)
Annotated site guide from Point Communications.
http://www.pointcom.com

New Riders's World Wide Web Directory (New Riders)
Huge, phone book-like directory.
http://www.mcp.com/newriders

The Virtual Community, Howard Rheingold (Secker and Warburg)
Landmark exploration of exactly what it is that draws us to the online culture, what it can give us, and what we can give it.
http://www.well.com/user/hlr/index.html

Cyberia, Douglas Rushkoff (HarperCollins)
One of the earliest attempts to pin down exactly what cyberculture is. Rushkoff is definitely in the optimist camp, but his book makes fascinating reading.
http://www.users.interport.net/~rushkoff/

Being Digital, Nicholas Negroponte (Knopf)
The word from the Net prophet. Negroponte, *Wired*'s back-page guru and clairvoyant, gives us a view of life based on bits rather than atoms.
http://nicholas.www.media.mit.edu/people/nicholas/

Escape Velocity, Mark Dery (Hodder & Stoughton)
Something of an antidote to the evangelists. Dery's view is more pragmatic, more grounded than the flights of the other authors, without being as pointlessly negative and baiting as Clifford Stoll was in *Silicon Snake Oil*. A must.
http://www.well.com/user/markdery/

alt.culture, Steven Daly and Nathaniel Wice (4th Estate)
An a-z guide to contemporary Americana, with a lot of Web and newsgroup links.
http://www.altculture.com

Net Chick, Carla Sinclair (Henry Holt)
Fast, funny guide to oestrogen online. Places for women to hang out.
http://www.cyborganic.com/People/carla/

The Happy Mutant Handbook, ed. Mark Frauenfelder, Carla Sinclair, Gareth Branwyn, Will Kreth (Riverhead Books, New York)
Mischievous Fun For Higher Primates. A zippy trip through the bubbling subcultures of the digital, and not-so-digital age.
http://www.putnam.com/putnam/Happy_Mutant/

Chaos and Cyberculture, Timothy Leary (Ronin Books)
Out there? Of course. The late, lamented Leary's fractured, fragmented, fractal take on things.
http://www.interverse.com/~leary/

NB: For up to the minute advice, check out local magazines:

Internet.au (**http://www.ia.com.au**)

Internet Australasia (**http://www.interaus.net**) and

The Australian Net Guide (**http://netguide.aust.com**)

From England, *.net* magazine (**http://www.futurenet.co.uk**) publishes quarterly site directories that are pretty good value too, if you can find them in a local newsagency. From the US, *Internet Underground* (**http://www.underground-online.com**) keeps track of some pretty cool stuff. Happy drifting.

Acknowledgements

Sections of this book have reared their ugly heads, in various disguises, in the *Sydney Morning Herald*. They have appeared in the Driftnet columns in the Computers section and elsewhere. Some have also made it into the *Age*, in the computer section's Sitings column. Another version of the Australian politics piece appeared in the May 1996 issue of *Rolling Stone* magazine. And a few little bits were part of a speech I gave to the Democrats National Conference in January 1996.

This book would not have been possible without the help of: all the site operators who answered my email; Sophie Cunningham, who oversaw the whole project and lived through lots of badgering phone calls; Jo Jarrah, who managed the editing and production; John Alexander, who decided the *Sydney Morning Herald* ought to pay me to tool about on the Net; Tony Sarno, who understood what I meant when I told him that I wanted to write about what was *out there*; Julie Robotham and Sue Lowe, who graciously let me push in; Fiona Inglis and Matt Condon, who offered quiet encouragement; and Helen Greenwood, the cyber widow, who provided support and nourishment, and got out of the house as often as she could.